Praise for the hardback edition

T0311120

Why Women Mean Business

Why Women Mean Business

Avivah Wittenberg-Cox
and
Alison Maitland

A John Wiley & Sons, Ltd., Publication

CONTENTS

Foreword by Niall FitzGerald KBE   ix

Acknowledgements   xi

About the authors   xvii

Chapter One: Womenomics   1

Chapter Two: Most of the talent   35

Chapter Three: Much of the market   79

Chapter Four: Becoming "bilingual", what companies can do   109

Chapter Five: Seven steps to successful implementation   149

Chapter Six: Culture counts, what countries can do   193

Chapter Seven: Figuring out females   235

Chapter Eight: Tomorrow's talent trends ... today, "women friendly" means "people friendly"   281

Contents

Chapter Nine: Conclusion, from better business to a
better world?   311

References and Further Reading   327
Index   341

FOREWORD

The issue of women in business is one that has preoccupied me for many years. Alison and Avivah's book is a timely contribution to the increasingly vocal debate about the economic importance of women. It is refreshing to read their comprehensive analysis of gender as a business issue, not a women's issue.

I strongly believe that women leaders are critical for business, and not only because they are 50% of available talent! Women have different ways of achieving results, and leadership qualities that are becoming more important as our organizations become less hierarchical and more loosely organized around matrix structures.

There is a feminine approach to leadership, which is not of course confined to women. It is about being intuitive as well as rational. It is about multi-tasking and being sensitive to people's needs and emotions, as well as relationship building and generous listening.

To transform organizations, drive change, challenge conventions, leaders need to inspire people and that is only possible if you connect emotionally with your followers; that you show self awareness and openness; integrity and authenticity.

Women have an inherent advantage in the softer aspects of leadership. These are also the areas where business is changing most rapidly. I feel that women are in a unique position today, and over the next few years, to make a step change in filling leadership roles.

I also believe it is increasingly important that women should stop feeling they have to be like men to succeed like men. This is going in the wrong direction. My advice is: do not seek to develop male strengths, just when female strengths may be in the ascent. Remain yourselves and encourage new patterns of male behaviour. We can't make the future happen unless women help the men adjust. All our leaders, female and male, need to be skilled and confident in drawing on all aspects of their persona to be effective leaders.

The near destruction of the world's largest financial Institutions is forcing renewed questioning of Boardroom behaviour. I have no doubt that Boards which have the benefit of greater diversity will deliver a more balanced and sustainable corporate performance.

Niall FitzGerald KBE, Deputy Chairman, Thomson Reuters

ACKNOWLEDGEMENTS

This book grew out of our parallel work on women and leadership in the business world over the past decade. In our respective professions as a consultant and a journalist, we have advised on or written about the huge changes that are taking place in the labour force and in the way people work, and spent much time examining why these changes have not been reflected in the executive suite and the boardroom.

Among the many people we have worked with and consulted for the book, we have encountered a combination of frustration at women's lack of progress into leadership and of eagerness for new solutions. Both have reinforced our belief that there is an urgent need for a fresh perspective.

We are grateful to the business people and professionals we spoke to, both on and off the record, for giving us their time and their views. In particular, we would like to thank:

Jim Andrews at Schlumberger; Pia Bohlen of xByte; Frank Brown and Herminia Ibarra at INSEAD; Sarah Butler at Booz

Allen Hamilton; Fiona Cannon at LloydsTSB; Nuria Chinchilla at IESE; Sarah Churchman and Ed Smith at PwC; Sam Collins at Aspire Coaching & Development; Kevin Daly and Laura Liswood at Goldman Sachs; Caroline Detalle at Bain & Co.; Liann Eden and Dena McCallum at Eden McCallum; the staff of the former Equal Opportunities Commission in Britain; Kristin Engvig, founder & CEO of the WIN Conference; Kate Grussing of Sapphire Partners; Alec Guettel, Troy Smeal and Wayne Henderson, pioneers of new ways to work; Jody Heymann at the Project on Global Working Families; Austin Hogan at AIB Group; Richard Jones at HSBC; Christine Lagarde for her support over the years; Ilene Lang and Susan Nierenberg at Catalyst; Gemma Lines and Amanda Chick at Cass Business School; Renée Mauborgne, co-author of *Blue Ocean Strategy*; Margaret Milan, Marie-Claude Peyrache and Mirella Visser, some of the key motors behind the success of the European Professional Women's Network; the directors and managers at the OECD; Rhodora Palomar-Fresnedi at Unilever; Heikki Poutiainen at Abloy; Davia Temin and her team at Temin and Company; Sandrine Tézé-Limal; Susan Vinnicombe and Val Singh at the International Centre for Women Business Leaders at Cranfield School of Management; Wanda Wallace at Leadership Forum; and Aude Zieseniss de Thuin and her team at the Women's Forum for the Economy and Society.

We would like to acknowledge the business leaders who have shared their personal observations and stories: Helen

Alexander, former CEO of The Economist Group; Peter Bakker of TNT; Vivienne Cox of BP; Sam DiPiazza of PricewaterhouseCoopers; Andrew Gould of Schlumberger; Lars-Peter Harbing of Johnson & Johnson; Barbara Thomas Judge of the UK Atomic Energy Authority; Anne Lauvergeon of Areva; Marie-Christine Levet of T-Online; Anne Mulcahy of Xerox; and Olivier Marchal of Bain & Co.

We would also like to thank:

- The CEOs who joined us at the "Men's Corner" that Avivah created and ran with Bain & Co. at the 2007 and 2008 Women's Forum in Deauville: Carlos Ghosn of Renault and Nissan, Michel Landel of Sodexo, Frank Brown of INSEAD, Jean-Paul Tricoire of Schneider Electric, Gerald Lema of Baxter International and the others who enthusiastically responded to the first presentations about this book.
- The CEOs and other leaders who joined us in subsequent panels and debates in cities and countries around the globe and who have been instrumental in raising awareness of the business importance of the gender issue. They include Piyush Gupta of Citibank South East Asia Pacific and Gary Tiernan of Standard Chartered who joined us in Singapore, Sakie Fukushima of Korn Ferry, Yoshimi Nakajima of American Express in Tokyo, Sultan Al Jajji and Fatima Al Jaber in Abu Dhabi, Nikolaus van der Pas of the European Commission in Brussels and Dean

Thomas Cooley of the Stern School of Business in New York.

- All those who made these events possible. We have had tremendous support from PwC, with a very special mention for Cleo Thompson, in hosting book launches in London, Toronto and New York, from INSEAD in Singapore and Abu Dhabi, from Paul Adamson and Simon Wilson at The Centre in Brussels, from Elin Hurvenes and Hilde Myrberg in Oslo, from Mary Van Der Boon in Amsterdam, from Kate Grussing in London, as well as Caroline Miller for many events in Geneva. We were lucky to have superb moderators including Stefan Stern and Chrystia Freeland of the Financial Times and Christina Pantin of Reuters.

We don't have room on this page to include all the names of the many people, men and women, members of associations as well as members of boardrooms, who helped organize and participated in events that have so greatly contributed to enhancing the impact of our ideas. We do have room for them in our thoughts, and our gratitude is deep and ongoing. We look forward to combining our efforts with you in the years to come.

We have had invaluable advice and affectionate support from our families, colleagues and friends including Pascale Depre, JoAnne Freeman, Margaret Heffernan, Judith Hunt, Janne Lambert, Margaret Milan, Peta Payne, Helene Ratte, Ros Scott,

Stephen Scott, and Joanne Thomas Yaccato. This whole project would never have launched without Jennifer Flock's help with the initial push.

Grateful thoughts go to all the people who have shared their experiences, views and ideas with us over the past decade, too numerous to mention, including the thousands of women members of the European Professional Women's Network that Avivah founded in 1996, the women in the corporate women's networks we've had the pleasure of being involved in, and all the executives who have debated and evolved with us during hundreds of workshops, seminars and conferences on gender in many countries and companies.

Our special thanks go to:

Roger Beale, for his wonderful cartoons
Niall FitzGerald, for writing the foreword
Andrew Lamb, for his genius with a camera
Colin Maitland, for his expert editing advice
The team at John Wiley & Co for all their support

The authors first met in 2000, when Alison interviewed Avivah for a *Financial Times* article headlined "Not enough time to be superwoman". We finally found the time. Our collaboration on the book began after a conversation at the Women's Forum (the "female Davos") in Deauville in October 2006. It has been a stimulating and entertaining cross-Channel partnership, Avivah in France, Alison in Britain. In our book, we note the enthusiasm with which young women are embracing the internet. We have long believed that technology is a girl's best friend. This book is indebted to Skype, instant messaging and the economies of triple play technologies, which greatly eased the process both on the first edition and this new paperback edition.

The project has been hard work and immensely fulfilling. Some authors retreat to solitary beach huts or rural hideaways to complete their books. On reflection, we're glad we did not have this option. The bustle of family and work lives has helped to keep things in perspective during the most intense periods of writing and editing.

We have sought to be as accurate as possible, checking and re-checking our facts. We are grateful to our many interlocutors for their patience and support in all our conversations.

Avivah Wittenberg-Cox
Alison Maitland

June 2009

ABOUT THE AUTHORS

Avivah Wittenberg-Cox is CEO of 20-First, a leading gender consultancy, and a global expert on how businesses can manage difference more effectively. She is also the founder and honorary president of the European Professional Women's Network, and a certified executive coach. Elle Magazine recognised her as one of the top 40 women leading change. She lives in France with her husband and gender balanced children (a son and a daughter).

Alison Maitland is an independent journalist and commentator. She spent 20 years with the Financial Times, including eight years as Management Writer. She has been writing about women and business for over a decade. She is also a regular conference speaker and moderator on issues relating to women, leadership and corporate responsibility. Alison is a Senior Visiting Fellow at Cass Business School. She lives in the UK with her husband and two daughters.

Chapter One

WOMENOMICS

"Forget China, India and the internet: economic growth is driven by women"

The Economist

The 20th century saw the rise of women. The 21st century will witness the economic, political and social consequences. Few developments have had such far-reaching effects on the lives of every man, woman and child today than the rapid change in the status and role of women. Over the past 30 years, and for the first time in history, women have been working alongside men in the same jobs and the same companies, with the same levels of education, the same qualifications, and comparable ambitions. Today, they represent most of the talent pool and much of the market. They have unprecedented economic influence. In America, for example, women make 80% of consumer purchasing decisions.

Women's mass arrival into the world of work in the 20th century is emerging as an economic revolution with enormous consequences. In developed countries, women are becoming central to labour market solutions to the combined challenges of an ageing workforce, falling birth rates and skill shortages. In the developing world, women's economic participation is increasingly seen as the key to lasting, long-term development.

We embarked on the first edition of this book in very different economic circumstances from today. The exuberance and confidence of the bubble years have been smashed by a financial crisis the likes of which the world has not seen for 80 years. A recovery will follow, but the outlook remains deeply uncertain and the economic damage is likely to cause prolonged suffering for many.

From the perspective of this man-made global recession, our updated paperback edition is more relevant than ever. The crisis has led to a re-evaluation of the leadership, rules and regulations governing so many of our institutions, in particular those upon which the world relies for financial stability and security. It has cast a painful light on the male domination of the corporate sector in general, and the banking sector in particular. It has revealed much that was rotten in the system, and demonstrated that "business as usual" has changed forever.

The need for countries and companies to make best use of women's potential in addressing the challenges of the 21st century is even more urgent today. It is only through the leadership of women *and* men, working as partners, that we can build a saner, safer and more sustainable model of capitalism.

International attention to the economic importance of women has been rising sharply in the past few years. The position of women is now recognised as a measure of health, maturity and economic viability. The World Economic Forum, organiser of the influential Davos conference, publishes an annual Global Gender Gap Report, ranking countries according to women's access to education and healthcare, and their participation in the economy and the political process.

The Organisation for Economic Cooperation and Development (OECD) has declared that "gender equality strengthens long-term economic development". In 2007, it set up a gender website to focus on "the implications of [gender] inequalities for economic development and what can be done to develop policies for parity". In a similar vein, the World Bank launched a Gender Action Plan in 2007.

Goldman Sachs, the leading investment bank, is one of those using the term "womenomics" to express the force that women represent as guarantors of growth. It points to the huge implications that closing the gap between male and female employment rates could have for the global economy, giving a powerful boost to GDP in Europe, the US and Japan.

Reducing gender inequality could play a key role in addressing the twin problems of population ageing and pension sustainability. Crucially, Goldman notes, female employment and fertility *both* tend to be higher in countries where it is relatively easy for women to work *and* have children (Daly, 2007).

Not surprisingly, governments are looking anxiously for solutions to the persistent undervaluing of women's skills. Vladimír Špidla, the European Commissioner for Employment, Social Affairs and Equal Opportunities, says the economic crisis has made it even more vital to close the gender pay gap and redress the serious under-representation of women in economic decision-making and European politics. "In today's economic climate, equality between women and men is more important than ever," he says. "Only by reaping the potential of all our talents can we face up to the crisis." (New Europe, 2009)

Women have filled 6 million of the 8 million jobs created in the European Union since 2000, and 59% of university graduates are female. "Women are driving job growth in Europe and helping us reach our economic targets," Špidla says. "But they still face too many barriers to realising their full potential."

Angela Merkel, the German chancellor, has also pointed to women's low representation in top jobs, arguing that this must be corrected to help Europe become the world's most dynamic economy. In the UK, a government-appointed commission on women and work has reported that the country could gain £23bn – or 2% of gross domestic product (GDP) – by better harnessing women's skills. (Women and Work Commission, 2006).

The economic downturn is changing the composition of the workforce in some countries, perhaps speeding processes that were already underway. The New York Times reported that women were likely to become a majority of the US workforce for the first time in 2009 because about 80% of the layoffs to date had fallen on men, notably in manufacturing and construction. (Rampell, 2009). Similarly, the destruction of blue-collar jobs in Australia meant that, in the first quarter of 2009, there were more women in full- and part-time jobs than men in full-time jobs (Megalogenis, 2009).

Women's employment is more concentrated in areas like education and health care, which are less vulnerable to economic ups and downs. However, these are traditionally lower paid professions, and women generally are far more likely than men to work part-time. Many families are now relying on one income instead of two, and a lower one at that. Over the longer term, this may change as more men enter these female-dominated professions in search of stable employment, putting upward pressure on wages.

Why Women Mean Business takes these powerful economic arguments to the heart of the corporate world. We analyse the opportunities open to companies which really understand what motivates women in the workplace and the marketplace. We explain the impact of national cultures on women's participation in the labour force. We show how corporate policies that make women welcome will help business respond to the challenge of an ageing workforce and the demands of the next generation of knowledge workers. We examine why many of the current approaches to gender have not worked and why we need a new perspective: one that sees women not as a problem but as a solution – and that treats them not as a mythical minority but as full partners in leadership. With the new perspective, we offer companies and managers a step-by-step guide on how to integrate women successfully into their recovery and growth strategies.

Gender is a business issue, not a "women's issue". The under-use of women's talent has an impact on the bottom line. Taking action to address this will require sustained courage and conviction from today's corporate leadership. This is an opportunity that must be seized. It is time for CEOs to get serious about sex.

The strategic side of the gender divide

Like countries, companies have forceful demographic and economic motives for making gender a top priority. The **first motive** is their need for skilled and talented people.

Even in recession, business knows that the best talent is scarce and is worried about how to find more of it or to hold onto what it has. Employers are still reporting shortages of key skills, and they know demand for such skills will increase over the longer term. They could start by doing far more to optimise an important part of the talent they already have – the female part.

Girls are now outperforming boys in many subjects and at almost every level of education. Women already account for a majority of university graduates in Europe, the US, and other OECD countries. This majority across the developed world is projected to rise from 57% in 2005 to 63% in 2025, according to the OECD. The OECD average figure hides wide variations, and women are expected to account for more than 70% of graduates by 2020 in seven countries: Sweden, Iceland, New Zealand, Hungary, the UK, Italy and the Netherlands (OECD, Higher Education to 2030). (Vincent-Lancrin, 2008).

Against the background of these profound shifts in the composition of the talent pool, we have seen two very different reactions from business to the topic of gender during the economic crisis. On the one side are companies that are using this turbulent time to think ahead and innovate in preparation for the post-recovery world in which they expect to have a competitive advantage. Most of these companies have already made enough progress to recognise the benefits of greater gender balance. They have discovered that women can be active agents of change and bring something qualitatively different to the table, along with improved performance to the bottom line. These companies have been using the difficult economic context to promote and position women to lead change. There may be unprecedented opportunities here for women to make their voices heard, amid increased tolerance for new ideas and contrarian views. We offer some examples of such companies later in this chapter.

On the other side are companies that have reacted defensively to the crisis, focusing on cutting costs and reducing "headcount" as much as possible. There is a retreat to approaches that have worked in the past, and a tendency to "hunker down", protect trusted employees and hope the storms abate. This strategy has a high cost for women, as well as for a lot of men, as they tend not to be part of the establishment team and are treated as "nice to have" but not essential. Tolerance for new ideas, for difference of any kind, and for innovative proposals is not high.

Many companies have a long way to go in recognising women's potential. Some have not even counted how many women they have. Others have made great strides in increasing their recruitment of women, but have not adapted their internal systems and cultures to ensure that these recruits make the most of their abilities over the course of their careers.

The low representation of women in senior leadership is a scandalous missed opportunity. It could weigh heavily on companies as they seek to survive the crisis and to thrive again. A recent report by DDI, the international talent management consultancy, found that women in companies around the world continue to be held back by hidden obstacles on the route to promotion. "Particularly in today's sagging global economy, helping women move up the organization ladder could well be one of the best survival strategies that an organization could undertake," say authors Ann Howard and Richard S. Wellins. "Isn't it time organizations stopped blocking the development and progress of the kind of talent that could fortify the executive suite?" (Development Dimensions International, Inc, 2009)

The **second motive** for business to make gender a top priority is the importance of getting the right leadership team. Companies operating in a multicultural, heterogeneous and unpredictable world are beginning to acknowledge that changes in the make-up of their top teams may be a good idea. Executive committees and corporate boards composed of white men between the ages of 50 and 65 – often of the same nationality, sometimes with the same educational background – may not be best equipped to deal with so much cultural diversity and complexity. Can they really be promoting the best talent, if 80% or more of those they are promoting to the top are men?

Progressive business leaders have begun to speak out about why it is vital to redress the gender imbalance now. In an

unprecedented open letter at the height of the financial and economic crisis, 17 chairmen and chief executives of well-known companies, including Anglo American, BP, Cadbury and Tesco, called for more women to be appointed to senior positions. They said that extraordinary times required innovative solutions and that it was more necessary than ever to deploy the best talent. "Business leaders have spoken out on the need for action on climate change and poverty," they wrote to *The Daily Telegraph*. "It is time to do the same on gender." (*The Daily Telegraph*, 2008)

The meltdown in the financial sector triggered much media speculation about whether things would have been better if there had been women in charge. Rarely has women's invisibility at the top been so apparent. Remember the line-up of male leaders of Wall Street's toppled giants, and the suited bank chiefs called to account for their actions before Britain's fearsome House of Commons Treasury Committee? "This mess was made by men," ran the headline in Britain's *Observer* newspaper. "Now let the women have their say." *The Washington Post* headlined its article: "In banking crisis, guys get the blame – more women needed in top jobs, critics say".

In Iceland, women were indeed brought in to clear up the mess after the economy was devastated by the collapse of an unstable banking edifice built by the country's go-getting, young, male business elite. Elín Sigfúsdóttir and Birna

Einarsdóttir were appointed chief executives of the newly nationalised Landsbanki and Glitnir banks. Within months, Iceland also had a new government led by a woman, with an equal number of men and women for the first time in the country's history.

Halla Tomasdóttir, an Icelandic fund manager who had predicted the economic disaster, was quoted by the *Daily Mail* as saying there had been an extreme imbalance in the business world. "While male values are about risk-taking, short-term gain and a focus on the individual, female values tend towards risk-awareness, the long term and team goals. What is needed for a successful future is a better balance of the two and a greater focus on long-term sustainability." (MailOnline, 2009)

We would caution against people misinterpreting "risk-aware" as "risk-averse". There is evidence, both quantitative and qualitative, that women in business are willing to take big personal risks: launching new ventures, making major career changes, or taking on difficult and high-profile assignments. At the same time, research suggests that gender balance is not only good for innovation and performance but can also have a protective effect on a company during a downturn.

One recent study, by Leeds University Business School, found that having at least one female director on the board cut a company's chances of going into liquidation by about 20%. Having two or three female directors further reduced the risk of bankruptcy, but the advantage eased once the board reached gender parity. Nick Wilson, professor of credit management at the business school, based his findings on 17,000 UK companies that became insolvent in 2008. He suggests diversity of opinion is an advantage that women bring to the board. Other possible explanations are that they resist high debt while being better at cash-flow management, and that they are better, on average, at people management. (*The Times*, 2009)

French research links the presence of more women in management with greater share price resistance during falling markets. Professor Michel Ferrary of Ceram Business School looked at companies listed on the French CAC 40 and found that the more women there were in a company's management, the less the share price fell in 2008. The only large French company to record a share price gain during that year was Hermès, whose management is 55% women – the second largest representation among French blue chips. In general, companies with a management of at least 38% women suffered less than the CAC 40 benchmark index.

These recent studies complement and reinforce a wealth of evidence that gender balance is good for economic growth and wellbeing, as well as for the business bottom line:

- A US study of the *Fortune* 500 in 2004 found that companies with the highest proportion of women in their senior teams significantly outperformed those with the lowest proportion on both return on equity and total shareholder return (Catalyst, 2004). This correlation between greater gender mix and better performance was strongly backed up in a subsequent study of *Fortune* 500 boards of directors in 2007 (Catalyst, 2007) and by McKinsey research (McKinsey & Company, 2007) into companies in Europe, America and Asia in the same year.

- The "correlation between high-level female executives and business success has been consistent and revealing," according to researchers at Pepperdine University in California, who studied Fortune 500 companies and the Fortune 100 Most Desirable MBA Employers, which is based on votes by women. The companies that employed a higher percentage of women executives – and also the companies which appealed to women – performed better than other companies. One possible explanation the researchers put forward is that the higher performing companies attracted the brightest executives, drawn from the best of both sexes, who are then "available to continue making smart, and profitable, decisions." (Adler and Conlin, 2009)

- A large US study, Girl Power, found a strong link between female participation in senior management and better financial performance in companies that are good at innovation, for which collaboration and creativity may be particularly important. The researchers, who looked at data on the largest 1,500 public US companies from 1992 to 2006, found "evidence for a female management style that enhances performance by facilitating teamwork and innovation". Since not all companies have women in senior positions, the ability "to identify, attract, and develop female managerial talent may be a source of competitive advantage," they say. (Dezsö and Ross, 2008).

The **third motive** for companies is that women represent more than half the marketplace. After decades in the workforce, women now pack a punch in their pocketbooks: purchasing power. As noted above, research in the US shows that women are making 80% of consumer purchasing decisions, covering everything from cars and computers to IT and insurance.

A spate of recent books on female consumers attests that selling to these "new" women is not the same as selling to men. The status and roles of women have changed dramatically in a few short decades. Keeping up with this multifaceted and heterogeneous population is no small feat. Their expectations and motivations require innovation in customer relationships.

Responsive companies are adapting their consumer research and product development to take this reality into account.

An all-female team at Volvo designed a concept car based on in-depth research into women's motoring needs and desires. Dove, the Unilever personal care brand, broke new ground in depicting women of different shapes, colours and sizes in its advertising, recognising that there is no longer such a thing (if there ever was) as a single "woman's segment" of the market. The first-mover advantages of understanding women can be great. As Volvo put it: "Meeting women's expectations makes us exceed the expectations of men" (Widell Christiansen, 2004).

American Express now employs a 70% female sales force in Japan, according to Yoshimi Nakajima, Vice President, Consumer Card Marketing. "The traditional housewife controls everything here, and all the money," she says. "Men get an allowance and must ask their wife for larger items. We used to target our cards only to men, and the ads spoke to successful men. We have a new concept that targets women, that has proved very successful" (Speaking at author book presentation in Tokyo, March 2009).

The investment opportunities have been highlighted by Goldman Sachs, which created a "Women 30" basket of shares of companies benefiting from growing female consumer clout. These stocks performed better than global equities over the 10 years to 2007.

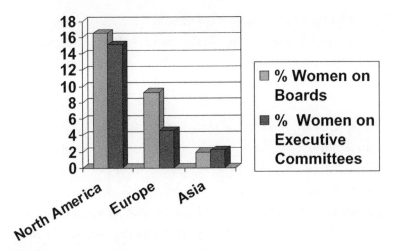

Women in Leadership Worldwide[1]

Valuing difference: becoming "gender-bilingual"

"Women bring something different to business, and you need to leverage both genders. It's a substantive business issue. It is not about being kind to women. It is about ensuring the success of our business in the future."

Piyush Gupta, CEO, South East Asia Pacific, Citibank

Women have moved from a role centred on home and hearth to being joint, and sometimes principal, breadwinners in a

---

[1]Source: The presence of women in executive committees and on boards of directors in the world's top 300 companies, Ricol, Lasteyrie & Associés, 2006

remarkably short time. Companies and their managers – and the business schools that train them – have struggled to keep pace with these changes and are now trying to catch up.

As progressive leaders are recognising, the corporate systems and cultures developed over more than two centuries of industrialisation and post-industrialisation are no longer suited to today's workforce or tomorrow's challenges. Companies were largely designed by men with spouses who took care of life. As a result, they perpetuate the attitudes, career cycles and motivations that characterised half the population, half a century ago.

Many employers have long believed that the best way to integrate women is to treat everyone in the same way. This approach was reinforced over decades by equal opportunities legislation, and by women themselves demanding equal treatment. The only problem was that in pursuing fairness and equality, companies resolutely ignored differences between women and the male employees on whom they had previously relied. They dealt with the arrival of women en masse by requiring them to fit in – and to adapt to male career models and leadership styles.

Corporate cultures were not deliberately designed to exclude women from power. They were simply left largely untouched as crowds of women swept through the door. Now, women have moved from marginal to mainstream. Companies are learning that they need to change how they market to women. They also need to change how they manage them.

Employers who want to capitalise on their investment in women will seek to create cultures that value and appreciate gender differences. This will give women permission to achieve power on their own terms, using their own language, with their own style.

Businesses have invested vast sums in learning the languages and cultures of emerging powerhouses such as Brazil, Russia, India and China. Now it is time to invest in learning the language and culture of a large section of their own employees – women. Companies and managers, both men and women, will reap the benefits of "womenomics" by learning to become "gender-bilingual". Understanding gender differences will enable them to manage mixed teams more effectively and to respond more relevantly to a growing share of their customer base.

Corporate initiatives on gender usually start by focusing on women as employees, rather than women as customers. These "diversity" initiatives can actually reinforce stereotypes by over-emphasising parenting and work-life balance issues and framing them primarily as a "women's problem" that has to be managed.

Aimed at creating more gender-balanced management and leadership teams, these approaches are based on the presumption that women are the ones who need helping, in order to be more competent at (male) corporate norms of behaviour. They launch women's events and networks, and provide women with training, coaching and a variety of other support mechanisms.

These measures can be a helpful *start* in empowering women. Many still struggle with issues common to the out-of-power: lack of confidence, stereotyping, exclusion from informal networks. The companies that provide the services and products they buy are mostly run by men. Women don't yet know what it is like to have their needs fully understood and catered to. There is an immense "blue ocean" (Chan Kim and Mauborgne, 2005) of opportunity in tapping into what are still only latent, unexpressed and probably unrecognised desires.

Yet companies that limit their gender initiatives to networking or development programmes for women miss the bigger picture. This kind of "fix-the-women" approach focuses its efforts on the wrong segment of the population. Women don't need "fixing". Most of the attention and money given to this would be better spent on fixing the systemic issue of outmoded corporate attitudes and processes.

When women hear this, the effect is hugely liberating. Paula Holt is one of hundreds of women who have responded enthusiastically to this book. "As someone who spent years being told to work on 'impact', it was fantastic to read that the way forward is not to 'fix' the women with assertiveness-training, but to fix the company by making sure it values both female and male attributes," she says. "It was amazingly reassuring to hear that generally women are motivated by 'making a difference' … and that other people find it 'just so tiring trying to be yourself'."

"Recently a male peer asked me: 'Why do you persist in being different when you know it will hinder your career progression in the firm?' I 'persist in being different' because I am different, because that difference is precisely where I add value, because I get more satisfaction from making a difference than I do from being rewarded for the difference I make. Obviously I would like to be rewarded too, but I couldn't ever be happy conforming to the mould and adding no value just to be rewarded."

One of the challenges is that gender is routinely positioned within diversity programmes. Diversity is too often about making minorities comfortable with a dominant norm. As long as women are considered one minority among many to be managed, the issue will not be resolved. Women's growing economic importance requires turning the analysis upside down and pointing out to those currently in power what their dominance is costing business.

As a business issue, it must be addressed at the level of the board and the executive committee, not in a diversity ghetto. Senior management must make, and sell, the business case before setting targets. Like any strategic initiative, gender needs a budget, not just teams of female volunteers. It involves making changes *before* claiming the high ground, and allowing dissent to be aired openly and addressed. The challenge is to create workplaces more welcoming to both sexes – and thereby to reap the full benefits of their complementary perspectives.

Innovative approaches

A number of companies or business leaders have taken innovative measures in recent years to drive the "gender agenda". What is common to the cases below is that they focus on gender as a business issue, and have targeted male leaders as the critical players in the push for greater gender balance. This small but seismic shift in focus is, as we wrote in the first edition of this book, the key to successful implementation of gender initiatives.

Alcoa: 80-20 recruitment rule

Rudi Huber, European President of Alcoa, the aluminium company, operates a 50-50 rule by which managers have to make sure half of their new graduate hires are women or from minority groups. When he previously ran the company's Global Business Services division, he introduced an 80-20 rule in favour of women and minorities. Over the last five years, that division maintained an average ratio of 60% females and minorities and 40% white males at the interview stage. By the time they received a job offer or were hired, the ratio had shifted to 70% women and minorities and 30% white males. Alcoa finds it harder to attract recruits to other parts of the business such as rolling aluminium and manufacturing, where the locations are often remote and the work can be hot and dirty. However, managers still have to adhere to a 50-50 rule. From mid-management upwards, their incentive pay is partly linked to achieving these goals, in order to ensure there is no slackening-off in the efforts.

ICICI: going "gender neutral"

Kundapur Vaman Kamath, long-serving former chief executive of ICICI Bank in India, built an organisation based on equal opportunities and "gender neutrality". Women account for just under 30% of the 35,000 employees in the group and 25% of its senior managers, healthy ratios for Asia. In May 2009, Chanda D. Kochhar, joint managing director and chief financial officer, took over as CEO, becoming the third woman to run an Indian domestic bank.

"When we recruit, we do that with true merit in mind and … if there are any challenges, we take steps to overcome them," says Kamath. "Around 1996–97, I remember that

Chanda Kochhar told us that she needed to take time off to look after her baby. And when she came back, she did so hitting the road running and has kept running thereafter.

"Meritocracy to me is a tool to achieve gender neutrality and equal opportunity ... otherwise you would have ended up evaluating only half the population in the company and not getting the benefit of the other half. Instead, you now have a 100% strong organisation. You then truly have a much better organisation because you have had a much wider selection process" (Interview on 20-first.com website, 2009).

Nestlé: involving men

Nestlé has taken a proactive approach to gender balance since the first edition of this book. Paul Bulcke, the new CEO, has made it a key priority for the Swiss-based global nutrition and health company. "Our future success is not secure without it," he says (See full interview in Chapter 5).

The company has taken very different measures from many US-based multinationals. Rather than launching a "diversity" initiative, it has specifically focused on gender balance, driven from the top. Gender awareness workshops have been run for the entire top leadership team, and then for each executive board member with the people directly reporting to them.

Their input and reactions have defined the company's approach and the roll-out of the programme. The emphasis has been on involving men, who represent the majority of the company's leadership, in the process, and ensuring that they lead the change. That has avoided the backlash that is common in companies that launch "women's" initiatives. The approach has proved popular with male as well as female leaders, who have discovered a shared agreement on the strategic and business reasons for the company to prioritise the issue and have become enthusiastic champions of change.

The leadership team at headquarters in Vevey and the management committee for some key markets have participated in all-day sessions to define a global action plan. A first woman, Patraea Heynike, a 30-year company veteran, has been appointed to the executive board, joining one of the world's most culturally diverse management teams. A host of measures for leaders have been put into place at the suggestion of the senior managers directly targeted. Their involvement and commitment have created a strong and positive momentum for the change initiative.

Nissan: driving change in Japan

Nissan Motor Company is pioneering gender diversity in its sales and management teams in a country with exceptionally low numbers of women in management. Two-thirds of car purchasing decisions in Japan are made or influenced by women, and Carlos Ghosn, CEO of Nissan and Renault, realised it made business sense to increase the low numbers of women employees.

Between 2004 and 2008, the percentage of women in the sales force rose from 4% to 6% and the percentage of women in management increased from 1.6% to 5.0%. This may seem low by American and European standards, says Miyuki Takahashi, general manager of the Diversity Development Office (DDO), but in Japan, the average proportion of women managers in manufacturing is 1.9%, and in the auto industry just 0.6%.

Toshiyuki Shiga, chief operating officer, chairs the diversity steering committee, demonstrating top-level commitment. Other members are executive vice presidents from all the functions. Diversity training is mandatory for managers and is particularly aimed at making male managers more effective in hiring and developing women.

PricewaterhouseCoopers: global agenda

Sam DiPiazza, as chief executive of PricewaterhouseCoopers, set up a global Gender Advisory Council in 2006 to address recruitment and retention of women in the firm and the shortage of women in its leadership ranks. Although women make up half its recruits, only 15% of its partners are female, and he was determined more should be done.

The Council, which won the first Opportunity Now global award in the UK in 2009 for its innovative work, brings together the CEO and 14 senior male and female leaders from strategically significant countries, including Australia, China, France, India, South Africa and the US. This has helped successful initiatives in one country to be shared and replicated in others (Opportunity Now Awards, 2009).

The Council's work, under programme office leader Cleo Thompson, began by gathering data on the status of women in PwC in 24 countries. It produced country-specific recommendations about the use of targets, and how to manage culture change and sustain progress. DiPiazza frequently talked about the issue of gender, both in internal and external communications. Things are changing. The firm now has two women on its global leadership team, and the share of women in the 2008 promotions to partnership was 29%.

Declining demographics is not destiny

If countries and companies are to achieve a breakthrough in gender-balanced leadership, private sector initiatives must be supported by public policy, as we explain in Chapter 6. The increased attention being paid to the role women play in boosting economic growth comes against a background of falling birth rates and ageing populations in much of the developed world.

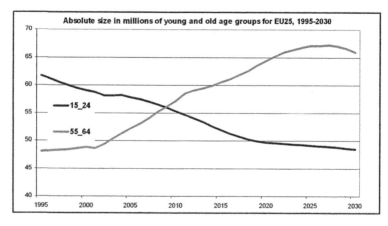

Size of youngest and oldest working age groups[2]

The OECD has warned that "the decline in birth rates that has characterised the past few decades is unlikely to be reversed in the near future." Adding to the concern, an article in the *International Herald Tribune* said: "There is significant risk that if Europe cannot figure out how to get its citizens to reproduce, the EU will be unable to evolve into a unified economic community, and will instead end up fighting for people." (Rosenthal, 2006). The media have been mesmerised by the birth rate figures, predicting that if the trend continues, entire countries may see their populations halve by 2050.

Yet declining birth rates do not have to be our demographic destiny. As the *Financial Times's* US managing editor,

---

[2]Source: Eurostat; 2004 onwards: 2004 Demographic Projections

Chrystia Freeland, pointed out, some of the developed countries with the highest birth rates, such as the US and Sweden, have far higher levels of women in paid employment than those such as Japan and Italy, where birth rates are lower, too (Freeland, 2006). The OECD, *The Economist*, and Goldman Sachs have also pointed out the correlation between women working and bearing children.

Countries, like companies, can address the demographic and talent crises by adapting to the changing realities of women's and men's lives. Governments can update logistical systems based on the 20th-century notion of full-time mothers at home. The few countries which created societies based on the concept that both parents work – notably the former communist states of eastern Europe – actually went backwards on gender balance on their journey to "freedom". For women in these countries, discovering what really happens on the other side of the Wall has been a bittersweet journey characterised by a dramatic drop in birth rates.

Policies and programmes need to respond better to women and their modern motivations. Recognising that today most children have two working parents, rather than just the mother implicit in much policy-making, is an important first step. The assumption that families are not having babies because they cannot afford to stay home to take care of them is a misinterpretation of the falling fertility statistics. In the 21st century, if forced to choose between working and having a family, women are opting for work (given record high divorce rates, it can be financial folly not to). Birth rates will rise when governments and the private sector understand and support the reality of dual-income working parents. Instead of forcing people into outdated choices, they should facilitate a modern-day conciliation between work and family.

The progress on modernising gender approaches is clearest in countries and companies which recognise that "women's" issues are crucial political and economic subjects, ones requiring public sector solutions as well as private sector ones. To date, around the globe, the two have rarely acted in tandem. The US has favoured private sector *pushes*, with individual companies developing and promoting their employees internally. The UK has looked to a combination of the two. Europe and Asia have relied more on public sector *pulls*.

As "womenomics" becomes more powerful, these approaches are becoming more integrated. The next decade is likely to see the birth of combined public and private sector efforts to have the best of both worlds – allowing women both to make babies and become bosses, like the title of the series of OECD reports on the subject (OECD).

21st-century forces: weather, women, web

For most of the last century, the issue of women was promoted mostly by women. More generally, women's debate on gender has largely been a conversation among women. A review of the literature reveals a litany of books by women for women about women. From the lightning rod of Betty Friedan's *The Feminine Mystique* or Simone de Beauvoir's *The Second Sex* to the more recent "women are better" books like Sally Helgesen's *The Female Advantage* and Helen Fisher's *The First Sex*, it has been an important and empowering discussion.

Very little, however, has been written about the economic and political influence of women for an audience which includes the men currently in power. Women's growing purchasing power has recently been described through the angle of "women as consumers" in a flurry of books that incite companies to target this market better. But there is more to women than their bank accounts.

This book offers the bigger picture on gender. It does not take the view that women are better than men. A host of recent publications has announced the obsolescence of men and/or the superiority of women. This "them versus us" approach is as much cannon fodder for continuing gender wars as it is for religious and political ones.

The time has come for fresh thinking, less attached to "glass ceilings" and "opposite-sex-as-opponent" starting points. Women, and the professional issues they raise, are related to many other impending changes in the way we work. "Figuring out" females will help organisations understand and respond to these developments – from the evolving expectations and roles of men, to the flexibility and adaptations needed by an ageing workforce and demanded by the generation now entering the workforce. Countries and companies that are women-friendly will be better placed to benefit from these demographic and social trends.

Our goal is an approach to gender that includes both halves of the human race. Our aim is a new kind of "bilingual" leadership, one that maximises the abilities and potential of both men and women by recognising the competitive advantages of our complementary skills and natures.

We propose a reframing of the gender debate, taking it out of the various boxes into which it has been awkwardly pushed for the past decades – whether as a "women's issue", a dimension of diversity, or an equal opportunity argument. All of these categorisations underestimate both the impact of women on the world, and the opportunity in better harnessing their potential.

Economic concerns and religious and political conflicts understandably dominate most of the current airwaves and column-inches and command the attention of governments and business leaders. But we also need collectively to look ahead and understand the emerging forces shaping the 21st century. Women are one of these, along with global warming and the internet. We call them the three Ws:

- W*eather* – the mass acceptance of the need for environmental sustainability that is changing the way we think about the Earth and our relation to it.
- W*omen* – the massive contribution women can make to future economic growth and leadership.
- W*eb* – the extraordinary transformation of the way we live, work and communicate through new technology.

These are three huge and irreversible movements that came into view in the 20th century, but will reach their full impact in coming decades. The first presents a terrible challenge, but also an opportunity to build a more sustainable future for our planet. The other two offer enormous opportunities, first and foremost, but also present risks if we misuse them or underestimate their significance. Will we recognise them all for what they are?

While this book focuses on gender, progressive forces are often inter-linked. These are some of our century's greatest developments. Let us weigh them well, and address them together.

Chapter Two

MOST OF THE TALENT

"Of our 8,000 partners worldwide, 15% are women. We are white males – that's where we come from. Our objective is not 50/50. It's the best people. But that is closer to 50/50 than it is to 85/15"

Samuel DiPiazza, Jr, CEO, PricewaterhouseCoopers
(DiPiazza, 2006)

A French industrial company decided to examine its poor record on recruiting and retaining women. It invited all its human resources directors from around the world to a seminar. They were handed a two-page list of job openings, taken from their internal jobs website, and asked to check it for gender bias. The 16 men and six women scanned the pages and shook their heads. They could see nothing that would offend.

Of the 20 jobs listed, all but one began by describing the ideal candidate as: "He will be ...". The exception was what brought the point home. It was for a secretarial post and began with the words: "She will be ...". The HR experts were doubly shocked: they found it hard to believe the ads had been written that way, and were dismayed that not one of them had even noticed, despite longstanding legislation in the European Union outlawing sex discrimination. The shock galvanised the company into action. It set itself a target to recruit 40% women (author's case study).

Talent wars

Sometimes, a rude awakening is required for companies to start taking serious action on gender. Their motive for looking at the issue in the first place is usually self-interest, rather than a desire to achieve gender parity for its own sake. Today, most companies have some sort of policy on gender or are thinking of having one, driven by the need to be seen as "equal" or "diverse", or not to be missing out on the talent.

As the vast baby boom generation begins to retire (60-plus years after the men came home to their wives from WWII), the talent wars which the McKinsey consultants started writing about in the late 1990s are still with us, even in bad economic times. In some industries – like defence, oil and gas, IT and healthcare – skills shortages have already caused serious problems.

Competition for valuable skills and experience remains intense. Before the downturn, 75% of senior human resources managers around the world said that attracting and retaining talent was their top priority, while 62% were concerned about talent shortages in their companies (*The Economist*, 2006). Even in the economically grim months of late 2008, the biggest concerns of organizations around the world included recruiting and retaining key employees, according to a Hay Group survey. "While employees fear losing their jobs, organizations fear the loss of top talent and critical skills," it said (Hay Group Global Employee Pay and Staffing Survey, 2008).

Despite these concerns, much of the business world seems to have difficulty recognising that one of the most sweeping and effective solutions is right there, staring it in the face: making better use of women's potential. Although we would not necessarily equate the female sex with all the attributes of a pachyderm, the situation is akin to that of the "elephant in the room", the big truth that people prefer to ignore. *The Economist* dedicated a special survey to the subject of talent in its 7 October 2006 issue. Curiously, women were not mentioned as a solution.

The challenge is often presented primarily as one of matching mobile capital with a mobile workforce. Yet making the most of female brainpower represents an opportunity to maximise growth without the social upheavals, real or imagined, that nations fear will accompany the mass migration of people. Doing so will benefit economies, companies and the boards which run them.

As research by Goldman Sachs points out, gender equality in the labour force could boost gross domestic product by as much as 9% in the US, 13% in the Eurozone and 16% in Japan (Daly, 2007). Goldman's Kevin Daly says that Scandinavia's experience suggests such an outcome is achievable, "given the right government policies and a wide cultural acceptance of equal female employment".

Closing the gap between male and female labour participation would help address the urgent problem of pension sustainability, Daly notes. Increasing employment among people of working age would reduce the dependency ratio, the ratio of retired people to workers. Old-age dependency is most worrying in countries such as Japan and Italy, which have ageing populations, low female employment and low fertility rates.

Female brainpower

Women now make up a majority (57%) of university graduates across OECD countries (Vincent-Lancrin, 2008). Countries and companies which enable women to reach their full potential at work will reap the rewards of girls' educational attainment. Among the general population of 25- to 34-year-olds, a third of women, on average, have tertiary education, compared with 28% of men (OECD, 2006). In Europe, women now earn 59% of university diplomas (EU, 2007) and 61% of PhD degrees (EU, 2006). In the US in

2002–03, women also outdid men, gaining 58% of all bachelor's degrees and 59% of all master's degrees. In higher academic qualifications, they ran a close second, earning 47% of doctorates in all fields, and 48% of "first professional" degrees, which cover practices such as dentistry, medicine and law (US Dept of Education, 2005).

Research shows girls doing better than boys in many subjects and at almost every academic level. Is this because girls are smarter all of a sudden, or have school curricula and a predominantly female teaching profession adapted education to the way girls learn, perhaps to the detriment of boys?

It is an important question. A *Financial Times* writer reflected the concern over boys' relative performance at school. "I am worried that if my sons have to share classrooms with high-achieving girls at 13 and 14, their self-confidence may suffer and they may take a longer time to learn who they are, what they are good at and what they want to do" (MacGregor, 2006). The article examined the argument that girls do better in single-sex schools, while boys benefit from the "civilising" influence of girls in co-education. Society certainly needs to address the underperformance of boys at school. But it also makes sense for business to get better at wooing, keeping and promoting more of these outperforming young women.

Given their educational achievements and their entry into many companies in numbers equal with men, it seems only common sense to enable women to share leadership and power. Yet many companies and boards still seem to be unprepared for the tide, or else to be awaiting proof that it is good for business, before they address the issue seriously.

The evidence suggests that having more women at the top is, in fact, good for the bottom line. In a groundbreaking piece of research, Catalyst, the US think-tank, examined the link between women leaders and the performance of the *Fortune* 500 companies. It found that the group of companies with the highest average representation of women in their top management teams significantly outperformed those with the lowest average representation. Return on equity was 35.1% higher, while the total return to shareholders was 34% better (Catalyst, 2004). Catalyst followed this with research in 2007 looking at Fortune 500 boards of directors, finding that companies with the highest representation of women directors were more profitable and more efficient on average than those with the lowest (Catalyst, 2007). The out-performance was even greater where there were three or more women on the board, suggesting the significance of having a "critical mass", rather than a token woman. Companies with three or more female directors had 83% greater return on equity, on average, than those with the lowest representation of women, 73% better return on sales, and 112% higher return on invested capital.

Similarly, a 2007 McKinsey study found that companies in Europe, America and Asia with 30% or more women in their senior management team achieved higher average scores for "organizational excellence" (things like leadership, account-ability, innovation, work environment and external orienta-tion) than those with no women. McKinsey, together with Amazone Euro Fund, also found that European companies with the greatest gender diversity in top management out-performed their sector average in terms of return on equity, share price growth and operating result (McKinsey & Company, 2007). Whether these studies mean that women's presence can directly boost financial performance or that more open and better-run companies tend to attract more women to the top, the arguments in favour of greater gender balance are hard to ignore. No wonder fund managers such as the Geneva-based Amazone Euro Fund have decided to put money into shares of companies demonstrating a strong gender mix in senior management (AMM Finance announce-ment, 2007).

Research from the Conference Board of Canada and from Cranfield School of Management in the UK offers further weight to the business case for top-level gender balance. Having more than one female director seems to be linked to better corporate governance, more activity and more independence on the part of the board, according to the Canadian study (The Conference Board of Canada, 2002). Cranfield's International Centre for Women Business Leaders found that FTSE 100 companies which adhere most closely to guidelines on good corporate governance are far more likely to have women directors than those that do not (*The Female FTSE*, 2004). The research centre, which has tracked UK board composition since 1999, has also found that companies with women directors tend to do better at bringing more women on board (*The Female FTSE*, 2003). In a 2008 study, Catalyst additionally found that the more women board directors a company has, the more women it will have in the future in its senior management, particularly in operational roles (Catalyst, Advancing Women Leaders, 2008).

Under-used talent

So what is the problem? A decade or so ago, it was thought that once the educational playing field levelled out and equal opportunities legislation had achieved its effect, women would naturally take their rightful place in the world of work. It might take a little time, but patience would prove that parity at all levels, including the very top, was achievable – even inevitable. Many women also accepted this argument, diligently put their heads down and got on with work.

It is now clear this expectation was wrong. Although women have entered the workforce en masse, they remain largely excluded from certain economic sectors – and from the senior ranks of companies. They are concentrated in areas such as healthcare, education and hospitality, often work part-time and earn less than men. Inequality tends to be greatest in the private sector. In the UK, for instance, official data show a gender pay gap for full-time workers of 22.5% in the private sector, compared with 13.3% in the public sector. Even Nordic countries, which have made so much progress on gender balance in the political and public sphere, cannot boast similar accomplishments in the private sector.

Women's representation is particularly low in certain areas crucial to economic growth and competitiveness, such as scientific research and development. A UNESCO study showed that just 27% of researchers worldwide were female. In Europe, women account for only 32% of state laboratory employees and 18% of private laboratory staff, according to the European Commission. "Women are too often ignored and discriminated against in the scientific arena," said UNESCO, in a joint statement with L'Oréal, the cosmetics group, expressing concern about the situation (L'Oréal-Unesco, 2007).

The link between women's under-representation and gaps in important skills is not lost on policy-makers. As Meg Munn, then the UK's deputy minister for women and equality, put it: "Skills shortages in the UK are matched to the areas where we have difficulty recruiting women" (Munn,

2007). Male-dominated sectors with shortages of workers include engineering, construction, information technology and skilled trades such as plumbing. In the UK, 70% of women with science, engineering or technology qualifications are not working in these professions.

Women are also largely missing from the leadership ranks in the corporate world. The private sector, more than any other, is failing to capitalise on the talents of half the workforce. The vast majority of women remains stuck in middle management or below, while boards and executive teams are still resolutely male-dominated. Even in America, where women represent nearly 40% of the managerial workforce (Catalyst, 2005), their progress into positions of real power has been excruciatingly slow. A US study shows that as recently as 2000 – a quarter of a century after women started moving into management – almost half of America's 1000 largest companies had not a single female in their top executive layer (Helfat et al., 2006).

Managers mull over the statistics, extrapolate their regression analyses, shake their rational heads and ponder what to do. One large French multinational calculated that, on current career trends, if they recruited only women and no men for the next 20 years, they would still have just 20% in senior management. If they stuck to their current level of recruiting 40% women, in 20 years they would have ... 8% in senior management.

The role of business schools

One big barrier to a better gender balance in senior corporate management is that top business schools have, for decades, had far fewer women students (typically 30% of the total) than either law or medical schools, which have been near parity.

The constantly cited reason for the lack of women on MBAs is that the programme requires participants to have several years' work experience and this puts them in their late 20s when they apply, a point at which they are likely to face strong personal demands, such as starting a family. Whatever one thinks of the qualities or lack thereof of the MBA degree, it is an important badge of talent for many big corporations around the globe. This apparently small requirement for prior work experience has limited the number of women moving into senior management careers. The deans of these schools acknowledged this issue years ago. But they were, in retrospect, in no hurry to do much about it.

There have been some attempts at change. A flurry of North American deans and professors has been promoting the gender agenda in Europe's business schools. The former dean of London Business School, Laura Tyson, said before her arrival in January 2002 that her appointment could help to boost the low numbers of female students (*Business Week* online, 2001). The number of women students has edged up from 22% at the turn of the century to 25% in 2009. The female faculty at LBS has made greater strides, reaching 23% in 2009 from a paltry 7% in 2002 (Financial Times MBA 2009 Rankings).

At INSEAD, another American, Dean J. Frank Brown, is pushing gender up the priority list. The school increased its female MBA students from 18% in 2004 to 29% in 2009, though its female faculty was a woeful 11%. (Financial Times MBA 2009 Rankings) It launched its first women-only Executive Programme (run by Cuban-born American Professor Herminia Ibarra) in 2006, after IMD in Lausanne led the way with Canadian Martha Maznevski doing the same the previous year. The growing attention that business schools are affording women is in part driven by rankings that highlight gender imbalance and in part by comments in the media like that of one City of London bank recruiter that "the holy grail is a woman with an MBA" (Bradshaw, 2007).

Only one of the top 50 business schools, as ranked by the Financial Times, has more than 40% women MBA students, and that is New York University Stern School with 41%. A number of American schools have finally decided to change their entrance requirements. As of 2006, they were tempering their appetite for prior experience because of the competition from other graduate degrees, like law, which accept students with no professional experience. This meant they were lowering the average age of entry, and even allowing some students to come in directly from undergraduate degrees. This will probably have a big impact on the number of women who choose to do business degrees and could boost their participation to levels similar to those in law and medical schools. In a report on the changes, the *Financial Times* quoted Thomas Caleel, director of admissions at Wharton, saying: "We've come to understand that it's a much different life choice for a woman to get her MBA at age 23 versus 28" (Knight, 2006).

There have been other moves, too, to increase visibility on gender. LBS launched a Centre for Women in Business in late 2006, in partnership with Lehman Brothers, to research into areas such as women's contribution to innovation, the impact of gender in teams, and the career aspirations and business school experiences of MBA students. However, the collapse of Lehman in 2008 left it without corporate funding to continue.

Tapping into the pool

So far, this chapter has highlighted the disparity between women's educational out-performance and the under-use of their qualifications, skills and experience in a corporate world crying out for talent. Correcting this disparity, for the benefit of individual businesses and the wider economy, means doing a better job of managing women. It is not enough simply to recruit more women, as many companies have learned at considerable cost. Once they have recruited them, they still need to work out how to keep them and how to promote them into power. Otherwise their recruitment efforts risk being expensively wasted.

Each of these areas – recruitment, retention and promotion – requires specific adaptation to the reality of 21st century talent. Together, they require a solid understanding of the issues women face at each phase of their careers. The next section offers an initial guide to how companies can make these adjustments through a better appreciation of the "other half" of the talent. Our recommendations for creating a corporate strategy on gender are set out in detail in Chapters Four and Five.

Recruiting: attracting women

Companies with few women often say that they would love to have more, but that they "just can't find any". They explain that women are simply not attracted to their company or their sector. This chicken-and-egg argument is no longer particularly credible. Women have moved into every occupation not originally designed for them. From the military to the moon, from oil fields to political minefields, women have proved that nothing is too big, too bad or too ugly. (The highest representation of women in parliament is in Rwanda: women represented 56% of the lower house in 2009, against just 20% in the UK and 17% in the US (Inter-Parliamentary Union, 2009).)

Where a first generation of women was willing to play pioneer in relatively unfriendly contexts, the current generation is more discerning. Today's woman has more choice and is better informed, both as an employee and as a consumer. There are more data on companies' efforts on gender, and women are becoming less shy about asking a few basic questions, like "How many women are there on your board? And on your executive committee?" If the answer, at the beginning of the 21st century, is "none" or even "one", the company will have trouble convincing women of its equal opportunity credentials.

Peter Brabeck-Letmathe, global head of Nestlé, the world's biggest food group, unintentionally illustrated the distance that many companies still have to travel. He was giving a keynote address in 2006 to a high-level international conference of more than 900 women (Brabeck-Letmathe, 2006). He opened by suavely announcing how delighted he was to be there, and how automatically he had accepted the invitation, as women were the very heart and soul of his customer base.

The first question after his eloquent and well-written speech was: "How many women are on your executive committee?" He replied that there were none. No woman had yet gained enough international experience to be promoted to this level. He then added that he was against quotas. He even expressed surprise at the question, saying that he had not expected such powerful women to be so defensive. The audience booed in displeasure – both at the statistics and at his mis-understanding of the issue being raised. His speech had underlined how women represented the quasi-totality of his company's customers and how important it was to build trust with customers and other stakeholders.

Whether it was this event, or a succession of such stories, Mr. Brabeck-Letmathe, even though he was close to retire-ment, decided the time had come for Nestlé to come to terms with these new issues. He became determined to transfer his learning into the company – that women were evolving, that Nestlé's consumer base had new expectations and demands and that the company's talent pool would need to reflect and serve these changes. He got to work to change the huge, global company he led, and handed on to his successor, Paul Bulcke, a careful legacy to do the same. See the case study on Nestlé on page 180 in Chapter 5.

How attractive are companies to women? Reviewing recruit-ment ads is a quick and effective way of checking whether companies understand how women think and feel. Many companies still communicate a tough, masculine image. The question is whether this is done consciously to warn women off, or unconsciously because it has not occurred to anyone and because the male creative director at their ad agency happens to like it (the majority of ad agency creative direc-tors are men, according to *Inside Her Pretty Little Head*, a book by two women advertising industry directors).

Even in companies that have become more sensitive to the kind of linguistic faux pas in recruitment ads that we described at the start of this chapter, other forms of unintended bias persist. There are positive, effective ways to deal with them.

One company was concerned about the lack of women applying for jobs. The problem was particularly acute in Europe, where only about 5% of applications came from women. It assumed that its technical, sales-oriented business simply did not appeal to them. Its recruitment ad featured a yuppie man with dark suit and briefcase, and the text copy vaunted the need for dynamism, aggression and competitiveness. This is pretty standard stuff in the business world. The company redesigned the ad. Instead of using a stock photo of an unidentified man, it featured senior women from its own ranks instead. The text focused on very different messages with a different vocabulary about enthusiasm, innovation and audacity. The application rate from women jumped to 40%, simply with a change of visuals and vocabulary. The advert which proved so attractive to women was also found to be more effective in recruiting the type of men the company was looking for (Author case study).

Companies often say that they do not hire more women because their recruitment agencies do not provide them with enough female candidates. They conclude that "there are no women." In some companies, this tale is told at all levels, from sales staff to boardroom directors. But recruitment agencies suffer from exactly the same sort of unconscious biases as many internal company recruiters and their ads often carry subliminal forms of discouragement. A few progressive companies have taken to training their agencies to make them more "gender-bilingual".

Tips on recruiting women

- Do not assume your sector is "not attractive" to women.
- Audit current recruitment statistics by gender.
- Check how attractive your company image is to women.
- Review recruiting ads and announcements for unconscious bias.
- Do the same with the recruitment agencies you use.
- Develop gender-inclusive recruitment communications.
- Have enough women in leadership to be credible to female recruits.

Retaining: the leaking pipeline

Companies are trying to fill the "pipeline" of women by opening the recruitment tap. This essential step will be of limited use if they do not simultaneously plug the management pipes out of which women are leaking further along in their careers.

Many companies have been hiring women for a long time, some with greater success than others. What most of them have not worked out is how to use their talents effectively.

From the moment women walk through the door, their careers and aspirations are not understood or managed in a "gender-adapted" way. To develop the structural metaphor, it is not a mythical "ceiling" that needs to be dismantled. The renovation work required is more substantial. The whole edifice needs to be checked for what could be called "gender asbestos": the values, systems and processes designed for a different era, which can cause permanent but hidden damage to women's chances. The costs of not modernising the managerial edifice, in terms of a poor return on investment in recruitment and training, are huge.

Although companies are used to analysing workforce turn-over, they are not used to analysing it by gender. Few companies have made in-depth comparative studies of when and why men and women leave. Those which have done so know that women do not generally quit to stay at home, although this is still a common assumption. Of course some do, especially if they have high-earning partners, but many leave for a more attractive workplace, for greater control over their lives, or for the renewed meaning and motivation offered by alternative careers like entrepreneurship.

More and more highly educated managers are making such choices. They are described in detail in Herminia Ibarra's excellent book, *Working Identity*, which discusses the process of reinvention people go through as they step out of one career and experiment with radically new things. The transitions she describes apply just as much to men as to women. Indeed, policies making the workplace more attractive to women are likely to help retain men who also want a different model of work and leadership, as we explain in Chapter Eight.

Men and women have different career life-cycles, however. Women tend to leave at different stages, and with different consequences, from men. A major study carried out in the US revealed that 37% of high-achieving women took time out of their career. All but 7% of these women wanted to return to work. Yet finding their way back onto the career ladder proved harder than they anticipated. Only 74% managed to rejoin the workforce and only 40% returned to full-time jobs, according to the survey of 3000 women and men published by *Harvard Business Review* and the Center for Work-Life Policy in New York (Hewlett and Buck Luce, 2005).

What were their reasons for taking time out? While childcare and elderly care were cited by many of the women in different economic sectors, the dominant trigger for those in business, banking and finance jobs was that they did not find their career satisfying or enjoyable. Only 5% of all the women who took breaks – and *none* of the women from business and finance – wanted to go back to their previous employers, according to the study, "Off-ramps and on-ramps".

To date, there has been no equivalent pan-European research into this phenomenon. However, national and sector-specific studies are building up a striking picture of professional women moving out of corporate jobs to achieve greater control over their lives and work. They show that the most complicated decade for them is their 30s.

A survey of the top 300 companies in France found that, of the people who left them, women were five times more likely than men to go in their early 30s. The research, published by IPSOS and an association of alumnae of the country's *grandes écoles* (GEF), showed these women left their jobs not to stay at home, but to find employment where they could better manage their lives. Men were more likely to leave in their 40s (Grandes Ecoles au Féminin, 2005).

Childbearing is usually the first visible fork in the career path for women, coinciding as it does with the time when those on the fast track are moving into their first management positions. But it is by no means the only obstacle preventing women from reaching senior leadership, as we explain later in this chapter and in Chapter Seven.

In some countries and in some cases, the childbearing issues that tend to dominate the 30s can emerge in the early 40s, especially if women start families later. In the UK, a recent study of one highly skilled profession – chartered surveying – found that women were leaving in large numbers after the age of 40. As with the French findings above, many were quitting for other jobs such as teaching or administration, which allow them better to balance their careers with family life. Louis Armstrong, chief executive of the Royal Institution of Chartered Surveyors, commented: "If well-educated, experienced women surveyors are working below their potential in other industries and sectors because they have not been able to make surveying fit with family life, we need to re-examine the best ways to help them back to work."

This widespread picture, evident across many countries and many sectors, represents a serious brain drain for all types of organisation. But it is a particular challenge for the private sector. Research by the Equal Opportunities Commission (EOC) in Britain, for example, shows that 20% of full-time female managers in the private sector left the workforce in the year after giving birth, more than twice the 9% figure in the public sector (Equal Opportunities Commission, 2007).

The under-use of women's skills seems to be worsening in some countries. In the UK, despite the growing numbers of women graduates in the workforce, only 45% occupied higher paid jobs in 2007 – down from 65% a decade earlier. In the US, a study of three classes of Harvard Business School MBA women revealed that only 38% of those with children worked full time (Hirschman, 2007). What is the point of investing in education if we do not enable the beneficiaries to make full use of their skills?

Career progression into higher paid jobs is similar for women and men until the age of 30, EOC research in Britain shows. But after that age, the proportion of men in these jobs increases steadily until their 40s and 50s, while the proportion of women declines. See figure overleaf: Different Career Cycles.

"Client-driven" cultures

High-status professional service firms covering law, consulting and accountancy face some of the biggest retention

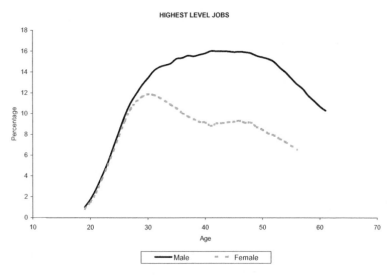

HIGHEST LEVEL JOBS

Different Career Cycles: % men and women in high-level jobs in UK[1]

problems. These firms pride themselves on recruiting the very brightest graduates, among which is usually a sizeable crop of women, and then funnelling them through an "up or out" system. The fees charged by these firms are high enough for clients to expect 24/7 service (often despite the client's own internal efforts to introduce some form of work-life balance for employees).

---

[1]Source: "Poor Returns: winners and losers in the job market", P. Jones and A. Dickerson, Equal Opportunities Commission, Britain, 2007

The culture in these firms reflects a round-the-clock and round-the-world work ethos. They have struggled to keep women through their 30s, and struggle even harder to promote them to partner level. Despite having potentially one of the most flexible forms of knowledge work in the world, many of these firms resist questioning whether theirs is the best way to serve their clients, and appear reluctant to adapt their model to integrate women's needs and life-cycles.

They believe they are being rigorously objective in treating men and women in exactly the same way – which they do. That is the problem. They are unaware of the bias inherent in assuming everyone is the same when everything about their culture and promotion tracks is based on a traditional, linear, single-income male career model. Since men and women are equal and the same in their eyes, the only difference that women appear to bring to the table is less time, less availability to travel and therefore less "commitment". A majority of the male partners who run these kinds of firms have wives who do not work, while most of the women who work for them have husbands who do.

However, even these fast-paced firms are feeling the pinch of changing employee motivations. A younger generation is often less willing to put its professional life on a pinnacle of total devotion. So, in markets like London, some professional services firms have been toying with the idea of marketing "preferable lifestyle" offerings – once they have crafted them.

Deloitte, the professional services firm, was early to recognise it had a problem and to set about dealing with it. Well over a decade ago, it realised it was haemorrhaging women. Early in the 1990s, it organised two-day workshops for every management professional – 5000 people in all at a cost of some $8 m – to focus on gender issues. These events were "a turning point, a pivotal event in the life of the firm ... ultimately, they converted a critical mass of Deloitte's leaders," wrote Deloitte Consulting CEO Douglas McCracken in a *Harvard Business Review* article entitled "Winning the talent war for women" (McCracken, 2000). "The message was out: don't make assumptions about what women do or don't want. Ask them."

Case Study: Retention at PwC

When Sarah Churchman started working on diversity at PricewaterhouseCoopers UK in 2001, the firm was losing a lot of women from middle management grades. That trend has been reversed, but women are still not getting through to senior levels, says Churchman, UK director of diversity. When she presented the position to partners in early 2007, "they realised what was getting in the way was not obvious. As they said: 'There's something about our culture.'"

This is reflected in a lack of role models at the top of the organisation. "In the last few years, of the students we have recruited, less than half are white men. But at the very top of the organisation, of the 800 or so partners, 90% are male and 98% are white. The top is not in any way like the bottom. That will pose problems. People tend to leave not because of family or childcare issues. They leave because they look up and don't see anyone like them" (interview with author, 2007).

The shortage of women at the top is a big challenge for PwC globally. Women make up half its workforce but account for only 15% of its partners. As PwC's website puts it: "Although great progress has been made to help women climb the corporate ladder, we know we need to do more." (Price-waterhouseCoopers website, 2009). The firm's Gender Advisory Council, sponsored by the CEO, has been addressing the issue internally since 2006, raising awareness of the business case and recommending specific initiatives. "As men we have a vested interest in closing the gender gap on both a business and a personal level," said CEO Sam DiPiazza. "The gender issue is a business issue. It's about your bottom line, and the benefits to an organization are huge" (Pricewater-houseCoopers, Closing the gender gap, 2008).

Companies need to recognise that the solution to the retention challenge requires a deeper questioning of their culture than most have bargained for. While women may sometimes be pulled out of corporate jobs by personal aspirations and family commitments, more often it is the many cumulative factors inside companies themselves which force them out (see Close Up text below).

While it can be relatively quick and easy to show improvements in recruitment, retention requires greater adaptation. Companies usually approach it as one would a minor leak in a basement bathroom – not realising that the entire house needs new pipes.

Tips on retaining women

- Recognise the leaking pipeline in the first place.
- Evaluate its size and cost.
- Analyse when and why it occurs, and if the reasons differ by gender.
- Recognise that male and female career paths may be different, and non-linear.
- Acknowledge the systemic issues at the source of the problem.
- Implement the changes needed to plug the leak permanently.

Close Up: What alienates women

What is it that women find alienating about corporate culture? Although periodic lawsuits demonstrate that overt hostility and discrimination sadly persist, it is more often to do with the subtle, undermining effect of cumulative "micro-inequities" – messages or signals that unconsciously convey a bias or misunderstanding.

It may be things like having a senior manager who seems unable to distinguish his female colleagues from one another or recall what each of them does. So he feels free to call for secretarial help from whichever woman happens to be passing – much to their astonishment and irritation. Or he patronisingly takes over her ideas at meetings and – speaking rather more loudly than she does – presents them as his own.

Or it may be to do with communication styles. At Unilever, the dominant culture was reflected in the way people expressed themselves, as Niall FitzGerald, former co-chairman, explained in an interview with the *Financial Times*. "It's a very male, aggressive culture ... the language people fall into using is sometimes unacceptable" (Maitland, 2003).

Wanda Wallace, chief executive of Leadership Forum, a consultancy operating in the US and Europe, sought to find out what led senior women to quit, and how those who decided to stay felt about their situation. She interviewed 53 women in posts that were no more than four levels down from chief executive. The women worked for international organisations in the UK, Germany and the US. She also talked to 11 women who had left similarly senior jobs.

Twenty-nine of the 53 in post had thought about leaving, or were considering doing so. Their reasons were varied:

politics, a change in organisational structure, not getting a sought-after promotion, not learning anything new, and not having enough fun.

Over the course of their careers, she found, the following things had an impact on their effectiveness as senior leaders: lack of broad networks and of the kind of relationships they felt their male colleagues enjoyed; lack of operational experience; inadequate informal feedback, and over-reliance on a single boss. Since her original study in 2003, most of the women have left their organisations.

Of the 11 women in the study who had already quit their jobs, only two said the decision was due to family responsibilities. Some were fed up with the politics. Other reasons included: feeling undervalued; not winning the promotion they wanted; a change of boss; and just not enjoying the job any longer. Some, however, left because they felt there were other things to accomplish and they had achieved more in their careers than they had expected to (Maitland, 2003, 2005).

Former investment banker Kate Grussing is founder and managing director of Sapphire Partners, a London firm matching experienced professionals, many of whom want to work flexibly, with companies seeking interim or project managers or non-executive directors. Most of its 1000-strong "talent pool" are women and 90% have worked for large organisations. They are typically in their early 40s, and not all have families.

The women's reasons for leaving big companies are pretty consistent, says Grussing. "They want to do something where they feel they have more control, and they want to have more impact personally. Sometimes it's because of a family crisis: an ill child, a divorce, or a parent dying. Sometimes it's because their company was restructuring and it felt like it was not going to be a fun place to be for a while. For about a third of the women, it's when they get to their second or third maternity leave and everything becomes less do-able or more frustrating. They've tried the 'flexible' option, for example a four-day week, and it's not working for them. They're not taken seriously. Their pay is cut, but they're doing the same job. They are looking for fulfilment and a way to integrate their life and their work" (Interview with author, 2009).

In 2009, Sapphire Partners carried out a survey to assess how women were being impacted by the downturn, following media interest and anecdotal reports that they were suffering more than men. Over 400 senior professionals responded to the survey, most of them female. The overall findings suggested women had not been affected more than men. However, women who were in financial services, working flexibly or in lower paid jobs were perceived to have taken more of a hit. (There is a silver lining, Sapphire Partners, 2009) "There remains a material gulf between the corporate diversity slogans and the reality facing women professionals, whether or not they are working flexibly," Grussing says.

Promoting: return on investment

Like PwC above, many companies recruit men and women into management in nearly equal numbers. But almost from the first level up, a gender split begins to appear, with the number of women dropping off steadily and the number of men rising to fill the senior executive ranks almost entirely.

A typical graph on female representation at different management levels in a multinational company looks something like the figure overleaf: Promotion Trends.

The result is that there are very few women at the top. The US can claim that 15% of its board directors are women, Europe less than 10% and Asia only about 2%. While these figures are generally low, the number of women on executive committees – where operational decisions are taken – is even lower. The US is at 16%, but the European figure is just 4%, while Asia is in the starting blocks with 2% (Ricol et al., 2006).

Nor are these numbers moving much. The European Professional Women's Network's BoardWomen Monitor found that Europe's top 300 companies had increased female participation on their boards from 8% on average in 2004 to 9.7% in 2008. Only the boardrooms of Norway, now with over 40% women directors, remotely reflect the working population, an achievement that resulted from enforced quotas. It is

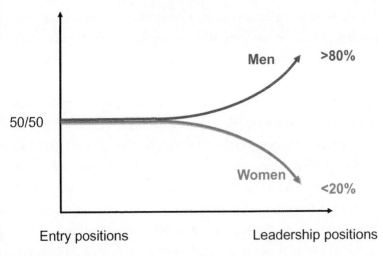

Most of the Talent

Men >80%

50/50

Women <20%

Entry positions   Leadership positions

Promotion Trends

wrong to assume that women will rise like the proverbial cream to the top of the company, while pursuing business as usual.

Companies have tried to boost the number of women they recruit, retain and promote with "gender diversity" programmes. These have generally not achieved the desired result. As *The Economist* put it: "'Diversity programmes' are as common as diversity on the board is rare" (*The Economist*, 2005). Many programmes send women off for assertiveness training, or to join women's networks, to try to teach them to behave more like men. In most companies, there is not yet anything that resembles an effective strategy.

There is growing impatience, among both women and companies, at this persistently slow progress in senior ranks. The style and composition of the leadership team is a visible and increasingly measured indicator for stakeholders of all kinds, including shareholders. The media, non-profit bodies and women's associations all now focus on the gender gap at the top as a quick way to gauge the success of diversity efforts. Rating agencies do not like boards and executive committees which are entirely composed of white, middle-aged men from similar backgrounds. European rating agency Vigeo claims that "diversity, if neglected, constitutes a risk factor both at a strategic and operational level. However, managing diversity can strengthen a company's global performance" (Vigeo website).

Even the men in the boardroom sometimes admit to getting a little bored. As one senior French executive remarked: "Better gender balance works because it makes women less bitchy and men less foolish" (the French original is even better: "la mixité marche parce que ça rend les femmes moins chiantes et les hommes moins cons").

There are as many good female managers as male. Indeed, several recent studies have shown women scoring higher than their male colleagues on a majority of managerial or leadership skills. However, a big problem is that women are disproportionately channelled into staff roles rather than the operational roles that are the main highway to the top.

Fewer than 10% of female managers in the US are in "line jobs" with profit-and-loss responsibility, according to figures from the National Association of Female Executives (NAFE) (Newswise, 2006). This limits the next generation of women leaders to certain functional roles (legal, communications or human resources, for example). These expert roles are important. However, occupying them can drastically limit the scope for moving into the top positions of corporate power. On executive teams, there is only room for one HR, communications or finance person, while the majority of the team are people with profit-and-loss experience. One option for companies is to give greater weight to functional experience when considering candidates for the executive team and board. Another is for them to do more, and earlier, to encourage women to assume operational roles.

Women are often unaware, early in their careers, of the importance of operational experience. They may lack the networks which provide informal guidance about the right choices to make. The first promotions into significant operational jobs often coincide with the period when women are starting families. So their ignorance, and companies' lack of communication about the consequences of early choices, hugely contribute to what senior managers consider one of the major things holding women back: a lack of experience of jobs with direct profit-and-loss responsibility.

Many women remain wedded to the idea that "it will be different for me", that they will succeed on exceptional performance alone, that they will shine through. When that does not happen, they are often bitterly disappointed. "Because women now hold managerial positions at most American companies, women's advancement remains a problem that many don't recognise as one," says NAFE President Dr Betty Spence. "In organisations where women are truly succeeding – where we find women running divisions and country operations – they have implemented tough measures, like having the board review succession planning and compensation for gender equity, and holding managers accountable with their own advancement and pay …" (Newswise, 2006).

Building better boards

We highlighted at the start of this chapter the evidence that power-sharing between men and women is good for the bottom line. Gender balance can also change the nature of boardroom dynamics.

Marie-Christine Lombard, head of TNT Express, was the first woman on the board of TNT, the Dutch-based international delivery group. The year after her arrival, Peter Bakker, the chief executive, commented on the impact she was having. "The egos have left the room," he said. Other male company bosses cited in Peninah Thomson and Jacey Graham's revealing book, *A Woman's Place is in the Boardroom*, say women "are better lateral thinkers", "more sensitive to people-related issues", "more idealistic" and "bring calmness and objectivity" (Thomson and Graham, 2005).

Some of these qualities were also on view when Angela Merkel, the German Chancellor, took the helm of the European Union for the rotating presidency. A laudatory article in France's *Le Monde* newspaper acknowledged her unusual ability to bridge national disagreements on issues such as climate change. "Member countries were profoundly divided on the nuclear question and on the share of renewable energy in the overall mix. It took all Mrs Merkel's tenacity and savoir-faire to rally the hesitant and convince the reluctant. ... The Chancellor's approach is based on listening, prudence and firmness. Without declarations or spectacular gestures, Mrs Merkel makes her way" (Ferenczi, 2007).

On boards, gender diversity appears to strengthen good corporate governance and lead to more gender diversity. Research from the Conference Board in Canada stated that "far from focusing on traditionally 'soft' areas, boards with more women surpass all-male boards in their attention to audit and risk oversight and control" (Stephenson, 2004). Carol Stephenson from Canada's Ivey School of Business added that "gender diversity on the board and senior management team helps organisations to attract and retain valuable female talent."

In its *Female FTSE Report 2006*, Cranfield University noted the gap between those companies with growing numbers of

women in senior management and on their boards and those with none. In 2008, Lloyds TSB ranked top for the proportion of women on its executive committee (over 44%). Five companies had more than 40% female committee members and just three others had more than the critical mass of 30% (Female FTSE Report 2008: A decade of delay).

A female director told the Cranfield researchers that having more than one woman on the board "balances behaviour and widens off-agenda discussions to cover more than football and golf." Another commented: "I enjoy working with other female directors, often because they have more highly developed emotional intelligence" (*The Female FTSE*, 2006).

Tokenism, on the other hand, can mean years of stagnation. Having a single woman on a board is neither much fun, nor very effective in ensuring that the difference women can make is actually realised. "Two or more give mutual psychological support and start to change the culture and behaviour," says Sir Rob Margetts, chairman of Legal & General, a UK financial services company (Maitland, A. 2007, "Top women tip the scales", *Financial Times*, 10 October).

Legislating solutions – the controversial quota

A Scandinavian country with a population of just 4.6 million has taken a more radical (and highly controversial) approach. Norway's politicians, half of whom are women, decided early this century that it was time for the private sector to feminise its leadership in the way the government had. So they agreed a target of 40% women on the boards of all publicly quoted companies. It was a polite invitation – delivered with a stick. If the target were not reached voluntarily, it would become law.

In 2005, as voluntary progress had not been satisfactory, it was voted into law, with the quotas to be met by 2008. Between 2004 and 2006, Norway managed to raise the representation of women on its largest company boards from

22% to 29%. In 2007, realising the deadline was for real, companies scrambled to meet the quota, and in 2009 the figure was over 40%. The idea is spreading, in diluted form. The Spanish government is putting pressure on boards to give 40% of seats to women. France tried, but rejected, a law to have 20% female representation on boards. Whatever companies feel about quotas, they should include them in their scenario planning.

In the US and Canada, a concerted focus on the issue of women and leadership by women's associations and think tanks has achieved at least a token female presence. All of the top 100 companies in the US now have at least one woman on their board and executive committees, while nearly a third have gone beyond the lone woman phase. In Europe, 82 of the top 100 companies have at least one woman on the governing body but only five have more than the one. In Asia, however, only 34% has even a single female representative (Ricol et al., 2006).

At the international Women's Forum conference in Deauville, in northern France, in 2006, there was a wide-ranging debate on the relevance and efficacy of quotas as a way forward. The audience was polled at the beginning and the end of the debate. At the start, 40% were unconvinced by the system. At the end, 90% voted for quotas, at least temporarily, to redress some of the imbalances working against women.

This seems a fair summary of the debate. Most men and women are against quotas. But faced with decades of slow progress, some turn reluctantly to the option of shock treatment. There are those, like Cherie Blair (Blair, 2005), who think quotas are only applicable to governments, whose core business is representation. The private sector, she insists (and most business leaders with her) is "more about skills and competence" and should be left to choose the appropriateness of its leaders.

The debate is highly dependent on culture. Countries comfortable with a greater degree of government intervention are more likely to experiment with gender quotas. They are therefore likely to be first to discover the benefits or drawbacks of dramatically increasing the presence of women at senior levels in the private sector. Both Norway and Sweden regularly head global rankings both for economic performance and quality of life. Will they soon show similar improvements to private sector performance?

Signs of awareness are growing. Take a look at some recent annual reports. There used always to be attractive photos of the executive committee and board. Lately, these photos seem to be regarded as a liability. Although most companies have failed to diversify their leadership teams significantly, they have progressed to the point where they are uncomfortable with the uniformity of the image they project. So the traditional photos of the boards are now harder to find. It is easier, though, to banish the pictures than to achieve greater diversity at the top.

Tips on promoting women

- Find out at what level or grade the percentages of women in your organisation start to drop sharply.
- Analyse the reasons why.
- Define tomorrow's ideal leadership profile for your organisation and review performance evaluation systems to ensure that they deliver this.
- Define targets for women in leadership programmes, in pools of high-potential employees, and on succession planning lists.
- Ensure that shortlists for senior jobs include women.
- Make managers accountable for promoting women.
- Measure progress by division, country, department and manager to identify blockages and encourage progress.

The most progressive companies are realising that women represent a critical, and still largely untapped, source of talent for current and future generations of leadership. Demographics and skill shortages are starting to worry other companies to the point where they are compelled to take gender more seriously.

The next chapter explores the other major reason why women mean business. Women are not only the majority of the talent pool. They also comprise most of the market for many companies. A handful of forward-thinking corporations, mostly in America, have understood the enormous potential that lies in better understanding and addressing the ocean of opportunity in selling to women. It is time for the rest of the world to catch up.

Chapter Three

MUCH OF THE MARKET

"The average American woman will earn more money than the average man within 20 years. Women make up 57% of undergraduates and 59% of graduate students. There is a perfect correlation between education and income. As a result, the balance of power at home has shifted and will shift further. We are seeing women 'control' and 'direct' family discretionary spend. 'She' decides when the family is going to eat out, when they will order the new kitchen or bath, go on vacation, buy a new car. It is the first steps in the creation of a matriarchal society where the female uses economic and social power. This trend is most pronounced in the US. But the UK, Scandinavia and France are not far behind. There is evidence that Germany and China may also follow this trend eventually."

Michael J Silverstein, Senior Vice President, The Boston Consulting Group[1]

---

[1]Interview with author, 17 April 2007

Women's mass presence in higher education and the world of work means an equally massive increase in their disposable incomes. The more women work, and the more senior they become, the more income they earn and the more they buy, both as individual consumers and as purchasing agents for their companies.

"Women in the US today make 80% of all consumer purchasing decisions and the majority of corporate purchasing agents and managers are women. Women entrepreneurs account for 70% of new business start-ups," says Marti Barletta in her book *Marketing to Women* (Barletta, 2006). American women add up to the biggest national economy in the world, presenting an opportunity that is "bigger than the internet", declares Tom Peters, in his foreword to the book (Peters, 2006).

Across the rest of the developed world, too, women are buying more of everything, from cars and computers to mortgages and insurance. Companies that understand this adapt their consumer research, product development and customer relationship strategies to take the new reality into account. This gives them the upper hand in the market now and in the future, because this is a consumer trend that is set to grow and grow. In the business-to-business market, women's rise into management is making some of them key purchasing decision-makers across the spectrum of goods and services. A better understanding of women, in their multiplicity of decision-making roles, must be a crucial goal for any business wanting to compete for this market.

Purchasing power – beyond parity

In North America, a host of books with evocative titles has been published in the past five years describing the market opportunities presented by women. From Joanne Thomas Yaccato's *The 80% Minority* and Johnson and Learned's *Don't Think Pink* to Fara Warner's *The Power of the Purse* and Barletta's *Marketing to Women,* they are ramming home the message to corporate America that the future is female. A recent British addition to this growing library is *Inside Her Pretty Little Head,* by Jane Cunningham and Philippa Roberts. Continental Europe has not yet turned its attention to the phenomenon in this way. Yet the analysis of women's purchasing power is equally applicable to many parts of Europe and Asia.

Women's growing economic influence has led financial institutions like Goldman Sachs to pinpoint investment opportunities in stocks that are benefiting from this trend. The investment bank's "Women 30" basket has outperformed global equities over the past decade and it is predicting similar trends in the next decade. As Goldman's Kevin Daly says: "The relative rise in female affluence is also likely to result in a shift in consumption patterns; a shift that is likely to be most notable as female incomes exceed the level

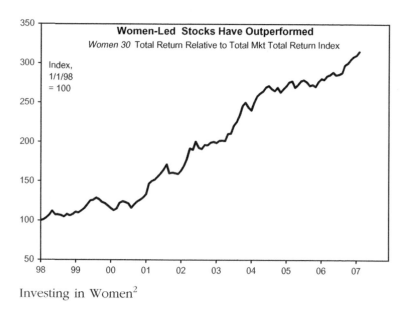

Investing in Women[2]

required to acquire essential goods and services, and rise to the point where a significant proportion of income can be spent on discretionary goods. Such a shift is likely to boost both the consumption of goods and services marketed exclusively to women (such as luxury women's clothing and accessories) and also the consumption of products that are not gender-specific" (Daly, 2007).

In Japan, where women's participation in the labour force is behind other developed countries but rising, young female consumers represent an interesting population for the global

---

[2]Source: Datastream, Goldman Sachs Equity Strategy Calculations

marketing industry, Goldman Sachs notes in another report (Goldman Sachs, 2005). The average disposable income of single women under 34 reached 86% of that of their male counterparts in 2004. Their spending is increasingly going on services, rather than more predictable goods such as clothes and watches.

At the other end of the age range from young salaried women, there is a growing contingent of elderly ladies in affluent countries who outlive their spouses and have plenty of cash. Life expectancy of both women and men has risen sharply in OECD countries in the past 40 years and is forecast to continue to do so – although there are large variations across the group. On average, women now aged 65 have more than 19 years of life ahead of them, and men 16 years (OECD, 2005). Across the OECD, the average number of years that women can expect to spend in retirement jumped from less than 14 in 1970 to nearly 23 in 2004, while for men it rose from 11 to 18 (OECD, 2006).

"In developed countries," says Tom Kowaleski, an ex-Vice President at General Motors, "older consumers outspend the young in nearly every department, but business has been slow to adapt to this growing market." Across a range of categories, "mature consumers have a 40%+ market share, while in the US over-50s account for nearly half of total consumer spending (Kowaleski, 2006)." Most of those over-50s, we would add, are women.

Female finances

The financial services industry faces clear opportunities here. For many private banks, a substantial portion of their

---

Female life expectancy at birth in selected OECD countries (in years) in 1960 and in 2003/05

	1960	*2003/05*
Japan	70	86
Mexico	59	78
Spain	72	84
Turkey	50	74
US	73	80

Female life expectancy at age 65 in selected OECD countries (in years) in 1960 and in 2003/05

	1960	*2003/05*
Japan	14	23
Mexico	15	19
Spain	15	21
Turkey	12	15
US	16	20

Female Life Expectancy[3]

---

[3]Source: *OECD Health Data 2006*

wealthiest clients is now composed of women, both young and old. In a report entitled "Targeting Women in Private Banking", Datamonitor says that women in the US will control a mind-boggling $22 trillion by 2010. Women's wealth is increasing in many other parts of the world too (Datamonitor, 2007).

In the UK, women are expected to own 60% of all personal wealth by 2025. There are now more female than male millionaires aged between 18 and 44. There are also more female than male millionaires over 65 (Carter, 2006).

A majority of women is generating its wealth independently, largely from earnings and business ownership, but also from personal investments. A global survey by Barclays Wealth and The Economist Intelligence Unit found that these sources of affluence have all become more significant than wealth through marriage, inheritance or divorce (Barclays, 2007).

The survey also revealed that women are more cautious than men when it comes to investing in "the riskier end of the financial spectrum", areas such as private equity, derivatives or hedge funds. "Financial institutions need to appreciate that men and women's motivations can be different, and that a one size fits all approach to managing this influential audience may not work," according to Amy Nauiokas, managing director and head of brokerage at Barclays Wealth.

Datamonitor says that US private and investment banks are leading the field with innovative methods of attracting wealthy women. Citigroup Private Bank has launched a service targeted specifically at women, while other banks are beginning to provide women's website resources or networking events.

Many UK banks have yet to make a move in this area. While many private banks and wealth management divisions say they recognise the market significance of the wealthy woman, only a few appear to have taken direct action, says Lauren McAughtry, financial services analyst at Datamonitor and author of the report. Many banks are missing opportunities because they are not thinking strategically about the issue, due to a lack of specific budgets to research the female market.

A "champagne and chocolate approach" will not work, warns McAughtry. "Women are looking for more from their private bank than a spa discount and a pink website. The ability to add value hinges instead upon truly understanding their needs – day to day and long term – and providing relationship managers who can relate and speak their language."

There is also a financial advice gap in relation to the wealthy female population. "We need more women advisers to attract more affluent women. Only about 10% of independent financial advisers in the UK are women, and there's been very little growth in the past 25 years," says Fiona Price, a pioneer of independent financial advisory services for women. She set up her business, Fiona Price & Partners, in 1988 and sold it in 2004.

Price makes a link between female talent and the female market, arguing that the same culture needed to nurture women in the corporate workplace is needed to nurture women as financial clients. "In the financial world, there's an ageing male population, which is going to be retiring in the next 10 to 15 years, with very little chance of replacements being found. The career [of financial adviser] is suitable to women's attributes and lifestyle, but nobody is trying to bring them through. It's one of the last male bastions, highly driven by targets and quick results. Women don't tend to respond to the carrot-stick approach. The environment encourages women to think they're failing because they don't produce the results quickly enough. But women tend to be better qualified than the average man because they don't like to sit there and bluff it. They are long-termers and, if they are allowed to develop more slowly and [are] encouraged, they are often top producers."

In her experience, women financial advisers tend to look at their clients holistically, rather than focusing immediately on selling them a product. "It's about developing a life-long relationship with people. It's also about talking in plain

Female Factoids

Women contribute 40% of the developed world's GDP

US
Women make:

- 83% of all consumer purchases including:
- 94% of home furnishings;
- 91% of new homes;
- 80% of Do-It-Yourself purchases;
- 60% of new cars;
- 89% of new bank accounts;
- 80% of healthcare.
- The number of women earning $100,000 or more has tripled in the last decade.
- Women will acquire over 90% of the growth in private wealth between now and 2010.

UK

- 80% of consumer goods decisions involve women.
- 75% of over the counter drugs are bought by women.
- 80% of healthcare decisions are taken by women.
- 66% of computer purchases are the responsibility of women.
- A third of new businesses in the UK are started by women.
- Women make up 63% of online shoppers who buy more than once a week.
- Women will be richer than men by 2025 and will own 60% (up from the current 48%) of the UK's personal wealth.
- There are more women millionaires aged 18 to 44 than men, and more over 65.

Source: Cunningham and Roberts, 2006

English and creating a space for women to ask what they think are silly questions, which are usually very shrewd questions. It shouldn't be necessary to have a woman adviser see a woman client because financial advice is unisex. But as long as it remains so male-dominated and patronising, there is a communication barrier" (Interview with author, May 2007).

Other sectors also still have some way to go to understand women's burgeoning consumer power. In the technology field, the opportunities offered by female buyers – and the risks of ignoring them – are underlined by Gartner, a leading international technology research and consulting firm. "Women influence or control 80% of consumer spending decisions; men design 90% of IT products and services," says a recent Gartner study. "If men only are designing IT, it's a 'going out of business' sale. Diversity is *not* the issue; survival is."

Women and men take different approaches to their IT purchasing decisions. "Women tend to look at convenience and productivity, while men tend to look at features. Business and IT organizations need new approaches to satisfy the growing consumer base of independent women – and doing otherwise is simply foolish (Morello et al., 2006)."

A UK survey by Saatchi & Saatchi, the advertising agency, calculated that consumer electronics manufacturers and retailers missed out on £600 m in 2007 by "failing to connect" with female customers. It found that nearly one in three women did not consider technology advertising relevant to them. Only 9% felt it was important that gadgets looked feminine. "This is supported by qualitative feedback from opinion leaders and consumers who feel 'patronised' and 'offended' by the abundance of pink products available at the expense of the sleek and beautifully designed and packaged products they want to see," said Saatchi (Saatchi & Saatchi, 2007).

Best Buy, the North American electronics retailer, has recognised the rise of female purchasing power. We "used to be a boy store, built by boys, for boys, but four to five years ago, there was a dramatic flip," according to Julie Gilbert, a vice-president with the company. That change occurred with the rise of must-have products like digital cameras, MP3 players, cell phones and other mobile devices, and products like flat-screen televisions which have become fashionable accessories for the home. "Women are outspending men in our industry $55 bn to $41 bn," she said. "Not only that, they are actually influencing 90% of the purchases. It is a new day in consumer electronics" (Meece, 2006).

Simultaneously, women are becoming increasingly important users of the internet. In the UK, the single biggest group of web users is women aged 18 to 34, according to a 2007 analysis by Nielsen/NetRatings. "The internet is no longer dominated by young male adults," according to Alex Bur-master, the company's European internet analyst. "The results, showing young adult women now account for 27% more of total UK computer time than their male counterparts, indicates how the internet landscape is shifting; a shift which is sure to send shockwaves through the entire online industry" (Nielsen, 2007).

Overall, there are almost as many female as male web users in the UK. So women, especially the 18–34s, should be big targets for online advertising. But many companies have yet to seize the opportunity. As the *Financial Times* pointed out, household goods, style and retail companies that have traditionally advertised heavily to women through television and magazines are still allocating only a relatively small part of their spending to the web (*Financial Times*, 2007).

Sex and segmentation

The first thing for companies to do is to recognise that women today represent a myriad of different market segments. We sympathise with the marketing people. "Figuring out" females is not easy. The status of women has changed so dramatically over the past 30 years that it is hard for anyone, even sometimes women themselves, to work out "what women want". There is no longer a single "women's segment" of the overall consumer market, if indeed there ever was.

However, it helps to keep in mind that each of the recent generations of women has been born and raised in dramatically different contexts. This is also true of men, of course. But for women, opportunities and expectations have been dramatically unleashed over the span of three generations. Looking at generational cohorts in the educated, salaried population gives an idea of the expanse of women's experiences and the need to fine-tune market research and analysis.

Young women – born and bred to be equal. These women have been raised with expectations of equality and ambition that are unprecedented. They don't expect any barriers on their paths and find the whole issue of gender distinctly historical. They have grown up taking opportunity for granted and expecting a world adapted to their needs. They buy houses, cars and investment plans on their own. They work, many of them marry later and delay having children, and many also have significant disposable income – although the economic downturn has been a rude awakening for a whole generation that has never experienced recession before.

In-betweens – in the thick of things. These women are the "second-generation immigrants" who have followed their pioneer mothers en masse into the world of work. They are juggling many roles and identities on their own, or with the increasingly willing support of their partners. They want their accomplishments recognised and their needs met efficiently.

They are frequently time-pressed, caught between many conflicting demands, not least those of young adult children and aged parents. They are used to managing anything and everyone – at work and at home – but they often feel the jagged edges of the corners they have to cut in order to fit everything in.

Mature women – the first "young-old" generation. These are the women who changed the rules for the generations who followed. They struggled and worked hard, and those who got ahead are now enjoying the fruits of their revolution. Today's affluent retired population in the developed world holds much of the world's assets – although falling markets have recently put many retirement plans on hold – and is active and involved far longer than its predecessors were. The 60-year-old woman working out at the gym looks 45. Such women don't want to hear about their age, they want to manage it, as they have everything else. Women entering this category have more time and money than almost anyone else ... as well as increasing life expectancy.

Each of these segments, and the many sub-segments they cover (single/married/divorced, employee/manager/business owner, parent/non-parent, minority ethnic/white, and so on) offer significant and still untapped market opportunities. Many of these segments are largely invisible in contemporary advertising.

But some companies have started to tap into the "60 is the new 40" idea. One much-remarked and much-rewarded example is Unilever's advertising campaign for its Dove personal care brand. Running counter to conventional wisdom that women only respond to idealised images of young, rake-thin models, this campaign created a new range of products for women over 50, using "real" women, of different shapes, sizes and colours.

The campaign trumpeted its intention to change attitudes about ageing "from anti and defiance to affirmative and celebratory". The brand did a survey of women aged 50 to 64 around the world and found that an overwhelming 91% felt it was time society changed its views about women and ageing. 87% said they were too young to be "old" (Unilever, 2007).

Likewise, Marks & Spencer in the UK has run highly successful advertising campaigns for its women's wear using Twiggy, the 1960s fashion icon now in late middle age, alongside younger models, cleverly appealing to the full age range of customers while reinforcing mature women's beliefs that they can still be sexy and beautiful.

To many women, such campaigns are a breath of fresh air in a visual desert that resisted reality for too long. Fara Warner, a journalist with the *Wall Street Journal*, describes her shocked pleasure at seeing an ad from the diamond company DeBeers that read: "The left hand rocks the cradle. The right hand rules the world." "In those two simple sentences I saw a view of women I had not seen before in advertising. Here was a company ... that had the guts to openly talk about what women were still struggling to understand and embrace," she enthuses (Warner, 2006).

The vast majority of campaigns, as well as the products associated with them, still feature women in far more limited roles, or force them to choose among one-dimensional depictions ("young-and-on-the-make", "mum-at-home" or "scary power-suit") rather than recognising and celebrating the many roles and relationships that women enjoy today.

Huge opportunities exist for companies to be innovative in addressing and servicing women as they are now, at every age and stage. Modern women represent a vast "blue ocean" (Chan Kim and Mauborgne, 2005) of largely unexplored opportunity, both as a source of talent and as a new market space. Discovering and exploiting the latter depends, at least in part, on being able to manage and promote the former. It is easier to understand women customers if you have a few of them in your leadership team.

As Cunningham and Roberts have put it, "there is a strong link between the characteristics of an organization (how masculine or feminine it is) and its ability to develop relevant marketing to the female audience. Respect for feminine differences, and therefore respect for female customers and employees, is essential to success" (Cunningham and Roberts, 2006).

The many faces of marketing to women

There are many ways of including women and gender in corporate sales and marketing strategies. Companies often start with highly focused "pink" pushes. The most progressive approach, and the most sustainable in our view, is one that moves beyond "special treatment" to embracing both genders with a rainbow of different tastes and preferences.

Below is a quick overview of existing approaches to marketing to women:

- **Shut-your-eyes:** this approach ignores the proportion of women among customers or end-users and any specific requirements they may have.
- **Marginalise:** this markets to a one-dimensional definition of "female".
- **Specialise:** this targets an exclusively female segment in a very focused way.
- **Prioritise:** this approach involves reviewing core sales and marketing processes to ensure that they include both women and men, in all their variety.

We present each of these in more detail below.

Shut-your-eyes

It is now fairly common knowledge that the majority of car-buying decisions are made or heavily influenced by women. Yet most car marketing and sales techniques are still so unadapted to women that in the US specialised websites have sprung up to specifically address women's purchasing and maintenance queries (see www.askpatty.com).

How many car companies actually cater to the reality of women as key buyers? How many car salespeople are women, and how much have sales forces been sensitised to the different priorities that research demonstrates women have in buying cars in the first place? There seems to be enormous competitive advantage in better responding to a majority of the market. That only 10% of Japanese car salespeople are female when most Japanese women car buyers would like to have saleswomen in the showrooms may be explained by the cultural context. But the same difficulties persist in the US despite decades of "marketing to women" debates. That companies are unaware, unwilling or unable to adapt to market realities leads one to believe that they may not be quite such rational players as they think they are.

Case Study: Mini Magic

One of the authors [of this book] recently bought a car. She is deeply partial to design and wanted a small, city car. She was hesitating between an attractive new, lime-green Citroën and a bright red Mini, both of which she had thoroughly researched online. A trip to the respective showrooms facilitated the decision in a comically stereotypical way. Both car dealerships had only sales*men*. In the Citroën dealer, the salesman was ill at ease and asked questions that felt like a test of the author's homework. She said she didn't want any special options, just a basic car with a radio and air conditioning. Those were options, he responded. Then he frowningly asked how she would pay for the car and looked very suspicious when she said it was a company car and that she was the boss. "I'll need papers," he said. She left, disgusted. At the Mini dealer, the reception was different. A congenial salesman came over straight away, explained how Minis were selling like hot cakes and said he quite understood why because they are incredibly cute. He talked design and manoeuvrability and said the radio and air conditioning were basic components included in the base price (making it cheaper than the Citroën). She bought the Mini on the spot. When it was delivered, the same salesman went over every detail of how to turn on the motor and how the signals worked, yet avoided condescension. Then he opened the trunk with a flourish and produced a bouquet of flowers. Needless to say, she is an avid fan.

Marginalise

This is where companies know that their market is female but are still marketing to, and developing products and services for, stereotypes of what women used to be.

A large American white goods company which makes everything from washing machines to dishwashers, microwaves and tumble dryers, is run in Europe by a couple of hundred men – there is just one woman on the executive committee. In an interview, the R&D director, a gentleman of a certain age, insisted enthusiastically that his job "contributed to the liberation of women". Asked whether his company could better contribute to women's liberation by deploying its advertising to convince men to start doing some laundry, he stared in blank surprise. The interview took place in

21st-century Italy. The company's end-users are mostly women. But the management's idea of what contemporary women need and want appears to be locked in a historical deep freezer. Since there are almost no women in the senior management team, it is hard for them to update their approach (Interview with author).

Even companies marketing almost exclusively to women, like cosmetics or luxury goods brands, often seem to be marketing to an image that does not quite resonate with a contemporary working woman's perception of reality. L'Oréal's decades-old tag line, "because I'm worth it", (recently transmogrified into "you're worth it") dates back to a time when women thought they weren't, and needed encouragement. A more contemporary reading of today's generation is that they no longer need to be convinced to spend on themselves, and might appreciate slightly more inspiring evaluations of their current worth.

Specialise

Here, companies develop highly targeted products or marketing campaigns which focus on a purely women's segment, but are not "mainstreamed" across the company. This is often the first step companies take when discovering that women are a market – or as Cunningham and Roberts suggest in their book, when they are trying to distinguish from an otherwise highly male-dominated market segment or product line. It is the equivalent of the women-focused initiatives launched by companies internally on the talent side of the equation. It lets companies test whether there is really a women's market, what it might look like and how it might be different.

Such approaches can be hugely successful or backfire badly. It seems to depend a lot on the cultural context, and the sensitivity and authenticity with which they are launched. They are best received ... where women themselves are not. So targeting women with "girls' toys" appears to work best in countries where women are not given access to real power. This kind of approach needs to be handled with care to avoid condescension – but they can be wildly popular if women discover, often for the first time, products developed for them. In specific product areas, women may also enjoy reversing stereotypically "female" icons and reclaiming them with a very different sub-text.

Resona Holdings, one of Goldman Sachs' basket of "womenomics" stocks in Japan, (a country notorious for its barriers to women in business), launched an investment product targeted at women, with the name "Love Me!" The launch came after surveys of potential female investors, carried out by the company's female employees, showed that women were less tolerant of risk than men and wanted a regular fixed return from their funds. Perks for investors included beauty and hot spring treatments and financial courses (Goldman Sachs, 2005).

In countries where women have made much greater strides in the workplace, such as the UK, the "girls' toys" approach is still sometimes used in advertising – though in a rather more tongue-in-cheek way. Take the direct mailing campaign (run in combination with television advertising) of Sheilas' Wheels, the women's car insurance subsidiary of Halifax and Bank of Scotland Group. The envelope features three pouting glamour girls in pink sequin dresses, perched inside a pink sports car, with the tag line "Something for the ladies". The letter inside offers extra cover against handbag theft, "non-patronising garages" and even a counselling service, in addition to some hard-hitting statistics on how much safer women drivers are.

The mobile phone market is an interesting example of where "pink" approaches have been tried around the world. Electronics has for so long been dominated by grey products for geeks that the new "pink" campaigns have blown in on a wind of design innovation and fun. So, for example, in Japan, a host of pink and pretty products has proved hugely popular with women – and therefore lucrative.

Few mobile phone companies have not developed a specific "women's" phone. Motorola has its "pink" phone, Alcatel teamed up with *Elle* magazine to launch the GlamPhone, and Siemens developed a handset for women designed by an all-female team, complete with a screen that, at the touch of a button, turns into a mirror, and an advertising tag line that says "some phones are from Mars, this one's from Venus." It's the kind of thing that presses all the right buttons for the "young women" segment described above.

Prioritise

The most alert companies research women's needs and expectations and use this to rethink their entire business and marketing approach for their core customers – both male and female.

Volvo tried this when it used an all-woman team to design a "concept car" aimed at women. Many of its features and new approaches were integrated into the company's other models because, as they found in their research, "if you meet the expectations of women, you exceed the expectations of men" (Widell Christiansen, 2004).

Another innovative take on this notion of what we could call "gender-relevant" approaches is the series of award-winning ads developed by Johnson & Johnson (and visible on their website homepage). The series, entitled *Having a Baby Changes Everything*, features beautifully filmed black and white ads depicting the shift in lifestyle that parents face after the birth of a baby. The revolution in the warm, touching series lies in the fact that the ads feature fathers and mothers equally. This simple switch both speaks to men in their new roles and reaffirms women in their efforts not to be the only parent given recognition in most contemporary advertising. It's brilliant, effective, and inclusive.

Even in traditionally more male-dominated sectors, big shifts linked to gender are just waiting to happen. Apple revolutionised both the computer and the MP3 player fields with its well-known design innovations. What has perhaps gained less attention is how female-friendly it has been – and how much both men and women appreciate this. All the characteristics of female-friendly brands are present – attention to design, both in product development and marketing communications, well-thought-out simplicity of use without any deviation into technology for technology's sake, extreme attention to detail and packaging. Part of the revolution that Apple wrought was to bring colour and design into a dark, techie world. Other technology companies still have not caught up, although they have tried to add colour to their computer boxes. These superficial efforts to target women serve only to show there is much more to gender-inclusive electronics than pretty outer things.

Do-it-yourself used to be a male pastime. But DIY stores around the world, from Home Depot in North America to Bricorama in France, have learned that women are a big growth market. In France, the feminine half of the population seems to have taken to home improvement with gusto. One study shows 80% of French women have picked up their hammers in what has become an industry worth some €19 billion. "Influenced by the growing share of female clients, materials have become easier to handle and tools have been simplified," (Amalou, 2006) for the benefit of all, one can only assume. Sales tactics have also evolved, with many of these stores integrating training presentations in their stores based on research showing that women appreciate educational approaches rather than a hard sell.

Taking gender into account in a holistic way can be relevant to even the heaviest industrial sectors. When BP started analysing customer research by gender in the 1990s, it discovered that women felt uncomfortable and even unsafe using petrol stations. They did not like having to leave children sitting in the car to go and pay for their petrol in a distant and shut away shop. So BP innovated by creating payment islands out near the pump or automated card payment systems. This kind of change, initially suggested by women, ends up benefiting all users – women, men and the children in the car (Interview with author, November 2006).

Broad, inclusive approaches don't need to be gender *neutral*. They need to be gender-*bilingual*. That means expertly and seamlessly adapting to the needs and latent expectations of men and women in everything from market research and segmentation to product development, advertising and customer relationship management.

Bilingual companies know how to use humour, irony and realism as powerful tools in the race to keep up with women.

They assume that their audience is as smart as their ad. Nike broke new ground with images of powerful, athletic women of all shapes and sizes accompanied by a voice-over extolling typical "ideals" of beauty (blonde, long legs, 24-inch waists). The punch line concludes with a sudden shift – from looking at the last of the list of female attributes to spoofing the entire approach … "An ass … is what you are if you believe all that crap." A Kellogg's ad for Special K cereal gently pokes fun at women's obsession with their appearance. It features men agonising about how various parts of their body look, making every viewer realise how far from the average man's preoccupations they are. These ads speak to women "knowingly", as from one woman to another. They are still as rare as they are refreshing.

So women are both a huge source of talent *and* a huge new market space. Discovering and exploiting the latter will probably depend – at least in part – on being able appropriately to manage and promote the former. It is easier to understand women customers if you have some of them in your leadership team. In the next chapter, we look at what companies can do to start addressing the gaping gender gap at the top.

Tips for tapping into the female market

- Start by analysing what share of your existing market are women and how that share has been evolving.

- Know which generations of women you are targeting and what their expectations are.
- Audit your consumer research approaches for unconscious gender bias (who defines the research, runs the focus groups, writes the questions?).
- Find out if there are women in your product development, design, innovation and communications teams. Who runs these departments?
- Check the approach you take to marketing to women and make it a conscious choice and strategy, while also understanding the consequences:
  — Shut Your Eyes – ignore women;
  — Marginalise – market to women of yesteryear;
  — Specialise – think pink;
  — Prioritise – market bilingually across genders.

Chapter Four

BECOMING "BILINGUAL"

What Companies Can Do

"Figuring out the gender issue isn't an option. It is do or die."

Lars-Peter Harbing (President, Europe, Endo-Surgery, Johnson & Johnson)

To lay the groundwork for becoming bilingual in gender, it is first necessary to understand why many of the efforts expended to date have not delivered the expected results. We evaluate traditional approaches to gender and some of their drawbacks, analyse where most companies start, and propose a framework to handle the issue more successfully.

A fresh look at traditional approaches to gender

As we have shown in the preceding chapters, there are powerful forces, both in the labour market and in the consumer market, driving companies to take women seriously. For some businesses, however, it requires a seismic shift in thinking to understand that women are less a liability than a giant opportunity.

This is partly because the issue of gender has for so long been associated with compliance. The business world started down the road more than 30 years ago, following directions on a map based on legal and ethical principles. Policies that emerged first in America were founded on the laws of the land – and the discrimination lawsuits that women started to bring. In the US, the Equal Pay Act dates back to 1963, while equal pay legislation was enacted in the UK in 1970, followed five years later by the Sex Discrimination Act.

It was an admirable cause: to keep everyone equal (and thereby to escape hefty payouts). The vocabulary that evolved reflects this laudable aim – equal opportunities, non-discrimination, pay parity – as well as the numerous barriers to achieving it – glass ceilings or, more recently, sticky floors and glass cliffs.

In this legalistic framework, women have been depicted primarily as victims, men as oppressors, and companies as the scene of the crime. It began with pretty basic human rights. In one of the earliest sex discrimination cases, taken by Ida Phillips against Martin Marietta Corporation, the US

Supreme Court ruled in 1971 that an employer could not refuse to hire women with pre-school children while hiring men with pre-school children.

In the UK in 1977, Belinda Price won the first indirect sex discrimination case, against the Civil Service. She had been told she was ineligible for an executive officer job at 35 because there was an age limit of 28, a rule which the tribunal found affected more women than men, since women took time out to have children. Today, women make up half the Civil Service workforce, and a quarter of senior jobs (Equal Opportunities Commission, 2005).

Since those days, the discrimination and harassment lawsuits have kept coming. Class action suits became common in employment disputes in the US, and the financial fallout was potentially huge. For example, in 1992, State Farm Insurance Company in Illinois settled a sex discrimination class action for $157 m.

Lawsuits on Wall Street have attracted huge publicity. One example was Morgan Stanley's $54m settlement of a class action sex discrimination suit involving 340 female workers in 2004. The women claimed they were denied equal pay and opportunities for promotion – discrimination the bank denied, although it agreed to work with the US Equal Employment Opportunity Commission for three years to improve working conditions.

In 2007, the bank agreed to pay at least \$46m to settle another class action lawsuit brought by existing and former women brokers who claimed they suffered discrimination in the way they were trained, promoted and paid. Reporting on the settlement, the *New York Times* pointed out that the case contained no accusations of the offensive use of strip clubs or crude antics, "but sought to tackle a subtler, if arguably systemic, form of discrimination that has long troubled Wall Street". As part of the settlement, the firm said it would overhaul its system for distributing new accounts among brokers, a system which the women argued favoured the men who dominated the business (Anderson, 2007).

Early in the same year came the biggest US employment lawsuit to date. A federal appeals court panel gave the go-ahead to a sex discrimination class action against Wal-Mart, the country's largest private employer, involving about 1.6m existing and former women workers. The *Financial Times* reported that the panel ruling could make large corporations more vulnerable to costly mass actions. Wal-Mart said it would appeal to reverse the ruling (Waldmeir, 2007).

To ensure equality of treatment, and minimise the risks of lawsuits such as these, managers across the corporate world were put on parole and taught to treat everyone exactly the same. So most of them did. They complied with the letter of the law. They treated everyone equally and the same. Over the decades, many managers became deeply and personally committed to the equality principle and convinced that the more they treated everyone the same, the fairer and more objective their management style was.

This approach had an unintended side effect, however. The more companies treated women equally and the same (and the more women militated for this equal treatment), the more the differences which women brought to the workplace were brushed aside. In this climate, women were encouraged to behave as much like men as possible and hide or ignore the strengths of difference.

This "sameness" is highlighted in some prominent research. Catalyst, the leading gender think tank in North America, now expanding into Europe, highlights empirical research demonstrating that men and women lead in very similar ways (Catalyst, 2005, 2006). This is perhaps not such a surprising finding, since the women referred to might well not have reached top positions had they done otherwise.

Equal and different

We think it is still too early to conclude that women's leadership styles are the same as men's, however. Women in corporate leadership roles are still a small minority, and many who managed to get there either had to adapt their style on the way up or were naturally inclined to (and recognised for) a relatively masculine style.

We suspect that women's leadership styles, if allowed to be authentic, may actually be rather different from men's. We have already highlighted evidence that mixed senior teams are good for business, which suggests women do bring something else to the table. There is a body of research (*The Female Brain*, by Louann Brizendine, *The Essential Difference*, by Simon Baron-Cohen, *Leadership: a Masculine Past, but a Feminine Future*, by Beverly Alimo-Metcalfe, *Talking from 9 to 5: Women and Men at Work*, by Deborah Tannen) describing how men and women are different in a host of fascinating ways. Why would differences in communication styles, biological rhythms, hormones, and brain functioning (to mention only a few) stop just short of leadership styles? More importantly, why would we want them to?

The "sameness" trend was ironically most true in the first companies to try to support the advancement of women – mostly large American multinationals. As a result, both men and women complain about some of those in the first wave of pioneering women who accepted the rules of the game and adapted their lives and management styles to succeed. They have attracted muttered labels as diversely corrosive as "pseudo-men" or "bitches" (Heffernan, 2004). Long-held social norms are at play here – and women are caught in the middle. Aggressiveness, still condoned in male bosses, is seen as unfemininely strident when deployed by women. Yet companies collude with this behaviour by organising assertiveness training for their female executives.

The resulting hybrid seems to please no one, not even some of the individuals themselves. Dame Jocelyn Bell Burnell is a distinguished Northern Irish astrophysicist who discovered pulsars (pulsating stars) while researching her PhD in radio astronomy, but had to struggle for recognition in the face of resistance at home and at work. In 1974, the Nobel prize was awarded to Antony Hewish, her thesis adviser, and Martin Ryle, a fellow radio-astronomer, but she was passed over. At a recent conference on female leadership, she summarised in striking terms the price that pioneering women in all fields have to pay. "What did the few women that there are at the top of those fields, what do those women have to do to get there and what did getting there do to them?" she asked. "Or put more crudely: Am I still a woman? Am I a little man? A she-male? A virago? An Amazon? There are a hell of a lot of words to describe women like me" (Bell Burnell, 2007).

Now, after 30 years of claims that we are all the same, the tide is shifting. There is a growing acceptance that women and men can be equal and *different*, and that what adds value is the optimisation of these differences, not their suppression.

Several recent reports have underlined this new approach, suggesting that men and women have different and complementary strengths. McKinsey, in a large-scale research survey of over a thousand managers from a wide range of companies, found that differences exist in the frequency with which men and women use different leadership behaviours (McKinsey & Company, 2008). The report concludes that "these leadership behaviours – in short supply in today's corporations – will be critical in meeting the expected challenges companies will face over the coming years." The table below summarises their findings:

Frequency of use of major leadership behaviours

Women use more	Men use more	Both genders use equally often
• People development • Expectations and rewards • Role model • Inspiration • Participative decision making	• Individualistic decision making • Control and corrective action	• Intellectual stimulation • Efficient communication

Herminia Ibarra and Otilia Obodaru from INSEAD found that women were seen by their colleagues to outperform men on seven out of 10 leadership competencies, listed below (Ibarra and Obodaru, 2009):

• Energizing
• Designing and aligning
• Rewarding and feedback
• Team building
• Outside orientation
• Tenacity
• Emotional intelligence

In addition, women were rated by their male and female subordinates (and female peers) to outperform men on "Envisioning".

A new tune is overwriting the old in the diversity song-book – one of competitive advantage rather than victim-hood. After a half-century of revolution in the roles and influence of women and men in society, CEOs are realis-ing the potential profit in taking sex seriously. But many fragments of the old tune remain obstinately stuck in the head.

Diversity dilemmas

One of the obstacles to this coming of age is the tension between gender and diversity. The corporate application of the diversity principle is the management of minorities. The origin of the movement is a US-led drive to avoid lawsuits and better reflect evolving social trends. Diversity – as it is currently spreading round the globe, led by a powerful group of American corporations – involves a wide array of complex differences: ethnic minorities, sexual orientations, religious beliefs, cultural diversity ... and gender.

One can't help wondering if the unquestioned inclusion of "women's issues" under the diversity umbrella is not simply a tidy (and effective) way of ensuring that women are still treated as a minority. It boils down to a numbers game. To manage a minority, companies take the view that it is important to hear their views, adapt a bit, and welcome them, in representative doses, to the table.

Accepting a numerically equal partner into leadership is a different ballgame. The difference between managing diversity and managing women is like the difference between IBM's funding a start-up and merging with Microsoft. The underlying issue is fundamental: *who changes?* Women are half the population, a majority of university graduates, even a majority of employees in many companies, and they make the majority of purchasing decisions.

Women operating in male-dominated corporate cultures certainly share some of the experiences felt by minorities in society (see Chapter Seven). But including gender within diversity programmes positions it incorrectly – almost dooming companies to fail in their efforts. It also hugely underestimates the potential gains that better management of half the population could make.

Integrating women fully into organisational leadership will require serious cultural change. This is spelled out, step by step, in the section on page 129 headed "A new approach to gender". Positioning women as one of half a dozen subsets of an HR-driven diversity programme is unlikely to carry the conviction necessary to achieve this.

Most managers feel much more comfortable with "diversity" than they do with gender. Many prefer to associate gender with something – anything – else. This may help explain why diversity has snowballed into an over-wieldy and vague concept, embracing everything – yet changing little. As *The Economist* reported: "So-called diversity programmes are as common as diversity on the board is rare" (*The Economist,* 2005).

Each of these groups of employees has important, and very different, issues in the workplace that need to be addressed. There are dangers in bundling them all up in one "diversity" package. One danger is that these very different, and legiti- mate, concerns are treated as one big *problem* of "minorities to be managed" and are therefore marginalised. The second is that it encourages a tick-list mentality, along the lines of "We've 'done' women, now we're moving on to ethnic minorities". The third, and most serious when it comes to the subject of this book, is that it obscures the strategic importance of women to companies, both as a market and a source of current and future talent.

Case Study: Undermining Gender

A high-tech company was launching a diversity programme in Europe. It had identified its key, business-driven, diversity challenge as women – it didn't have enough of them in its management teams or pipeline to the board and knew that its market was becoming increasingly female. It hired a woman from an operational role to run the programme. The executive committee sponsor in Europe was an ardent advocate of people with disabilities. He asked his consultant on disability to sit on the diversity steering committee. Then the company's US headquarters weighed in with its priorities for the year, focusing on sexual orientation. So the diversity policy that was launched in Europe covered women, disability, and gays and lesbians, losing sight of the original business imperative of adapting to female customers' requirements.

It is time to stop treating gender as a minority issue. In the next section, we explain how to address managers' unease over the issue head on, and how corporate leaders can become more familiar with a subject that has such huge implications for the future of business.

Recognise that "best" is biased

Building on the diversity discourse, managers in most organisations today are convinced that they are resolutely egalitarian – even when they haven't a single woman on their executive committee or in the leadership pipeline. They pride themselves on the objectivity of their systems. Their leitmotiv is that they reward and promote everyone based on competence, irrespective of gender. The subtext is that women are just not quite up to the task.

Women often set their bar of competence higher than men do. Internal company research at Hewlett Packard demonstrated that women apply for open job positions if they think they respond to 100% of the criteria listed, while men respond as soon as they feel they cover 60% of the requirements, according to Cara Antoine, a general manager at the company in Europe. Worse though, she noted, is that hiring managers do the same. They recruit women if they respond to 100% of the criteria, but they are ready to recruit men as long as they respond to 60% (and women recruiters are tougher on women candidates than men are) (Antoine, 2005).

At a recent seminar for the OECD, run by one of the authors, a top manager summarised the point. "It's not affirmative action *per se* that we are discussing. It's the need for a generalised acknowledgement among us that the female candidate we have ranked Number Two may actually be, in terms of our future needs and strategy, Number One. In fact, the woman who is ranked Number Three may also actually be Number One. It is time we recognise our biases and update our thinking about what Number One actually needs to look and sound like" (OECD, 2007).

These findings correspond with Catalyst's studies showing that stereotyped views of male and female leadership qualities hold women back. "Men are still largely seen as the leaders by default," it says. "Women are often perceived as going against the norms of leadership or those of femininity.

Caught between impossible choices, those who try to conform to traditional – i.e., masculine – leadership behaviors are damned if they do, doomed if they don't" (Catalyst, 2007). (See also interview with Ilene Lang, president of Catalyst, below.)

Samuel DiPiazza Jr, Global Chief Executive Officer of PricewaterhouseCoopers, knew that it would take work and focus to move beyond the 15% level of women the firm counts among its 8000 partners worldwide. But he still labelled this necessity a form of affirmative action. "Without some form of positive discrimination," he said, "we will not make progress" (DiPiazza, 2006). We would beg to differ. We do not recommend positive discrimination. Part of waking up to gender involves undoing the positive discrimination that currently exists – in favour of men.

Companies and managers will make more progress in attracting and keeping women if they recognise that performance, competence and leadership are concepts heavily biased towards the prevailing norm, which for the most part remains overwhelmingly male.

Close Up: Why the slow progress to the top in the US?

America has led the diversity drive for years. Why has it failed to get more women into corporate leadership? A census by Catalyst in 2006 found that the progress of women into top corporate jobs in the *Fortune* 500 had actually slowed over the previous three years. If it continues at this rate, the study showed it could take 47 years before women achieve parity with men in corporate officer roles (Catalyst, 2006).

Ilene Lang, president of the non-profit research and advisory organisation, explains what she thinks are the persistent barriers. "Catalyst has been working on this for 45 years. For the first 27 years, our focus was on helping to get women into the workforce and helping mothers to re-enter. It was the movement for careers. Women wanted advancement. In the mid-80s, we shifted to saying: 'This is not just about individual women. Women are running up against a glass ceiling. We have to do something about the workplace.'"

Lang likens it to peeling an onion. "You address the obvious problems and it turns out these are just symptoms of deeper problems. Originally, everyone thought this was about being a mother and work-life challenges and that if you put in a daycare centre it would solve the problem. We've learned that that is useful but not enough. Career development was a real challenge. Now it's corporate culture and social culture that's a real challenge."

Women's networks have been useful in overcoming their lack of access to informal old boys' networks, she says. "They've helped women dig into leadership opportunities and get visibility around the business." But, according to

Catalyst research, gender-based stereotyping persists in the social and cultural norms of the workplace environment.

Catalyst has done a lot of research into this. "Regardless of the culture, women are *perceived* as being supportive and nurturing, which is not *perceived* as leader-like; it's lady-like," says Lang. "As we've investigated gender-based stereotyping both in the US and Europe, we've noted that, in many cases, whatever the leadership qualities the culture values most, men see women as not being effective. This is not conscious, but it is pervasive. It pervades performance management systems and creates a double standard that individuals aren't aware of. In doing so, it affects how women are evaluated and advanced – or not advanced – to senior leadership.

"Companies don't want to have a double standard. They want a meritocracy. They look to the leadership of tomorrow and say that the talent has to come from women as well. But if you're only looking to the traditional old boys' club, then you are missing out on an untapped and growing pool of talent. The leadership is, then, going to become more and more estranged from the reality of who your workforce is."

What does she think about the plateau in progress in the US? "We're disappointed about the numbers. The expectation, of course, is that there's going to be progress every year. The trailblazers – the first women – are getting to retirement age and we're seeing perhaps a leveling off of the next generation taking their place."

Catalyst recently embarked on researching an important new area. "We've observed that in the companies in which progress is being made, there are key men involved," Lang says. "We're trying to figure out how you can get more men involved in leading this transition. It's not just a women's problem, it's a leadership and a business imperative. Men are a key part of that."

Getting men to lead the charge

Catalyst's first report from this new orientation has a promising title: Engaging Men in Gender Initiatives (Catalyst, 2009). It asks why so many gender programmes have missed the mark. "One reason is that too many gender initiatives focus solely on changing women," it says, adding that "in their exclusive focus on women, rather than engaging men, many companies have unwittingly alienated them."

The report then falls into the all too-common habit of concentrating on obstacles. Catalyst has spent years examining the bias and barriers blocking women's advancement, and now it is focusing on the bias and barriers to men's involvement. Its research reveals that the main barriers to men's involvement in gender initiatives are apathy (74%), fear (74%) and real and perceived ignorance (51%). It contains interesting evidence of the struggles that individual men have faced in challenging masculine norms inside their organisations. However, we would argue that the real problem is that until now no one has gone out and demonstrated the business reasons why men should take a leading role on gender, nor invited them to do so.

The report focuses on men as "champions" and "supporters" of gender initiatives – rather in the way that men are helpers and supporters of women when they change a diaper. This misses the real issue. Gender is a strategic business matter. Any CEO worthy of his (or her) seat should be aware that women are now the majority of the educated talent pool in the developed world, and the majority of the market. Leaders need to be accountable to their shareholders for their ability to create gender balance in their companies right to the top, a now-proven link to greater profitability.

It's time, not to get men's "support", but to make leaders accountable. Companies have become increasingly good at hiding the gender reality of their leadership teams. Check out any corporate website: the photos went first, now the first names of leaders are on their way out too.

We should not simply move from decades of ineffective fix-the-women strategies to timidly asking men for some help. Women need to adapt their own attitudes and vocabulary. When addressing gender, companies should be recognising opportunity, sustainability, and profitability. In our experience, men are often more willing change agents on gender than their female colleagues. So let us make them more than allies. Let us invite them to lead the charge on gender, and then judge their performance.

Surprising sectors

Interestingly, some of the sectors and companies most successful to date in promoting women are not the most obvious candidates. *Fortune*'s 2008 listing of top international women was led by Cynthia Carroll, the head of mining company Anglo American, Gail Kelly, hired to re-invent Westpac, the leading Australian bank, and Linda Cook, until recently head of Gas & Power at Shell. *The Female FTSE 100 Index* (*The Female FTSE*, 2008) produced by Cranfield School of Management finds that male-dominated sectors like oil and gas, mining and electricity have more senior executive women than sectors like retail, which have a preponderance of female employees. In the US, the few big corporations run by women include Xerox, PepsiCo, and Archer Daniels Midland, the agricultural processor.

How do some of these more traditionally male industries allow women to succeed? Because companies in these sectors have often had to work very hard to attract women at all, which makes them try even harder to hold onto them and promote them, says Jacey Graham, a diversity consultant and co-author of *A Woman's Place is in the Boardroom*. "In other sectors, there's often a feeling that the cream will rise to the top, but then it doesn't because of cultural barriers" (Maitland, 2006).

So what do the best companies do when they want to correct the gender balance? They start to become "bilingual", first by recognising that the existing situation may not be as unbiased as everyone thought, and then by adapting leadership language and behaviour to 21st century talent and market realities.

A new approach to gender

Before navigating across unfamiliar territory, it helps to plot your starting point on the map. While many companies are convinced of their egalitarian gender credentials, a little scratching below the surface often reveals a more complicated reality.

Understand the starting point

We have run audits of attitudes towards gender diversity in companies across Europe, asking male and female managers about their perspectives in order to evaluate the existing internal "climate" in organisations. In almost every case, attitudes among managers can be split into three segments, with women managers usually evenly divided between the first two. The three groups are as follows:

The Progressive: a third of managers are progressive, often sensitised to the issues because of personal convictions, their own dual-career families or their daughters' emerging ambitions. These executives are the natural champions of gender balancing. The male ones point to the benefits that mixed teams offer and cite positive experiences of female colleagues and bosses. In fact, the progressive men are often far more direct and uncompromising in their support of women than women can allow themselves to be: if men do it, it will be seen as selfless or altruistic, while women are handicapped by the risk of a perceived self-interest. Women managers who fall into this group tend to have supportive spouses who have worked to balance dual careers. They believe that the advancement of women in their firms is likely to improve the culture for all employees. They are comfortable citing the "different" skills or approaches that women bring to the table and can usually explain why having more women will be good for business. These are the key change agents of any gender initiative. It is crucial to be able to identify and involve them.

The Patient: a third are neutral, convinced that time will solve everything, that women are already well on their way, that things are changing at a satisfying pace and that no specific actions are required. This group is the "swing vote". They are the people who need to be convinced so that they may develop into progressives. They point to the number of women in management and say that there are some who make it, so things must be fair and accessible. They fear that pushing the issue of gender will create resistance or a backlash. They don't usually see any pressing business reasons for having more women, and insist that competence and performance are duly rewarded in their organisation.

The Plodding: a third are clearly reticent, rejecting the goal as well as the means. There are still many men (the levels vary by country) who are hostile to women at work for a variety of reasons. Not least is the fact that their own spouses have sometimes given up careers to support theirs. Backing women's advancement, some will admit to feeling, would be committing the equivalent of marital treason. Or else they are convinced that women are just not relevant to the realities they face professionally. They look around and point to the growing number of women in their ranks – far more than there were before, and more than enough. These managers (mostly male) are deeply unconvinced that women will bring anything significant or new to the table. They believe that if there are few women in their organisations, it is because of women themselves and they are quick to cite women's lack of commitment and ambition, their family priorities or the dearth of women with relevant degrees.

They argue that their sector, industry or company is simply not attractive to women or that family life allows only one career parent.

It is easy to imagine that deep-seated antagonism to women at work disappeared years ago. So thought Joan Bakewell, the eminent writer and television personality who was once herself described as "the thinking man's crumpet". Then she overheard a recent conversation between four elegantly dressed businessmen in a first-class train carriage. "Talking of women colleagues, their conversation ranged over their 'buxom' attributes, whether 'wearing short skirts was asking for it' and speculated that one of the women was 'a bit past it'," she wrote in the *Independent* newspaper. They behaved like "masters of the universe", she said. "No wonder there are not more women in the top boardrooms of industry and commerce" (Bakewell, 2006).

The three-part segmentation of opinion described above also exists at the executive committee level. Once the CEO has launched a gender initiative, no one is likely to object openly. But the "plodders" will block progress in their areas.

Overcoming resistance and getting the swing voters to become convinced and convincing proponents of change requires strong leadership and awareness. It means that men and women will have to become far more fluent in each other's languages. This involves understanding how we differ in order to appreciate those differences and manage them constructively.

"Gender-bilingual" leaders are easy to identify. They know that there are two important issues to keep in mind when opening a mutually positive dialogue with women: they personalise the conversation, and they watch their metaphors.

Personalise the conversation

Bilingual leaders understand that most women don't compartmentalise their lives into personal and professional. They tend to mix it all up and are curious about – and comfortable with – the human being behind the professional. The traditional corporate norm of never speaking about anything personal at work is a particular weight on women, who are more comfortable multi-tasking among their many roles but often feel constrained in a male corporate culture to keep their personal lives under wraps. So leaders in the know usually make a point of talking about themselves first, in a very personal way, in order to build the trust and credibility to be listened to.

Carlos Ghosn, the Brazilian-born Franco-Lebanese head of Renault and Nissan, knows this. Speaking at the Women's Forum in Deauville on diversity, he explains how he personally understands that "being a black sheep is always hard". His childhood was one long experience of being "different", he tells an empathetic audience, as he moved from his native Brazil to Lebanon, then to France and the US. "Working together towards a single goal is good – unless being together means negating one's own identity. If you are all the same, you don't ask yourself many questions about who you are or why you're there. But you mostly learn from those who are different" (Ghosn, 2006).

The "bottom line" on the gender issue for him is that "I have three daughters and one son. It is intolerable to me to think that one day my daughters will not be able to do what they want because they are women. Absolutely intolerable. And what is valid for the people I love is valid for the society I live in. CEOs have to play a role, particularly women CEOs. You have to prove that you can be at the top and women need a lot of examples." At this point, he has the audience eating out of his hand.

Niall FitzGerald, the Irish-born chairman of Reuters and former head of Unilever, said in a *Financial Times* interview that his attitudes to the gender issue had been heavily influenced by his daughters: the first, a "feisty" journalist, a young professional woman who successfully challenged his views, the second, still a pre-schooler, with whom he wanted to share precious time in the mornings and evenings (Maitland, 2003).

Eric Daniels, an American of Chinese and German parentage, is chief executive of Lloyds TSB, the UK banking group. He has made a point of recruiting women into senior management. When discussing the importance of having a good balance of women and men at all levels, he often refers to his sister Diana, who was one of the first three women to get into Harvard Law School. She rose to be chief legal counsel for the *Washington Post* and was, for many years, a lone woman in middle and senior management. Through her experience, he understands what it feels like.

These personal vignettes might seem out of place at the average business gathering, but are typical of the way women communicate among themselves. For men who wish to speak across genders, they act like a magic door opener, a password unlocking a mix of surprise, relief, appreciation and trust. And it's cheap, requiring nothing more than emotional intelligence and a readiness to reveal vulnerability. In a more masculine metaphor, it could be referred to as a laying-down of arms.

Manage the metaphors – the power of vocabulary and vision

This leads to another major issue of bilingualism. It's not only what you say, but how you say it that counts. Vocabulary is one of the interesting differences between genders, as Deborah Tannen, author and linguistics professor, has explored at length (Tannen, 2001).

There is one particular element of language that affects the business world, and men's concept of it. Business is rife with the messages and metaphors of military conquest. Didier Lombard, Chairman and CEO of France Télécom, gave a demonstration at a conference. Speaking about innovation, one could feel him fully engaged and mobilised by a fierce struggle in a highly competitive global industry. His language was unconsciously sprinkled with images of "charging up the packs" to be "ready for battle" and get "experience of war". He is obviously personally motivated and stimulated by the fight he faces and feels that rattling linguistic sabres helps to motivate the troops.

But as the troops include more and more women, the vocabulary needs to evolve. Michèle Alliot-Marie, France's first female Minister of Defence, (subsequently appointed Interior Minister under the Sarkozy presidency) has understood this. She did not speak of war, but of peace. While defence minister, she explained she was shifting the communication and recruitment campaigns of the professional army she managed to underline that its mission today is less about waging war than about keeping the peace around the globe. In this way, she said, the army was attracting a growing pool of women (Alliot-Marie, 2006).

Just as women need to understand prevalent modes of male communication, so men need to become familiar with women's communication styles. "Ambition", "politics" and "power" are uncomfortable words for many women, who prefer to deny their ambitious or political tendencies rather than come across as "bossy" or "pushy". Merrill Lynch ran a programme for women to improve their political skills and found that they resisted the chosen terminology. Sue Henley, head of diversity in Europe, explained: "Women didn't want to do politics. We changed the word 'politics' to 'profile' and that was fine" (Maitland, 2006).

Women can be unconsciously – or consciously – marked down in companies for using hesitant or deferential speech in preference to commanding, or "powerful", language. Hedging an idea with the words "I'm not sure if this would work, but ..." or prefacing a request for a job to be done with "Sorry, but perhaps you could ..." can be interpreted as a lack of confidence or assertiveness.

Such assumptions need to be challenged. Commanding speech that excludes the listener's opinion – "I need you to do this now", "Make it 1 o'clock" – is out of place in modern organisations claiming to be collegiate and inclusive. Communicating this way is also quite possibly less effective at conferring status than the speaker believes. In teams of people heavily dependent on one another to complete a task, research has found that those who use more tentative speech styles actually command greater status (Fragale, 2006). Moreover, many cultures of the world do not subscribe to Anglo-American leadership communication styles.

Perhaps not surprisingly, women tend to be more attuned to these differences in communication styles than men. At a mixed workshop on gender differences, a male middle manager from IBM, whether out of political correctness or conviction, denied that women and men communicate in different ways. At the same event, a senior woman from Ford remarked: "I've spent 25 years in the car industry making sure men feel comfortable with me, rather than the other way around."

The building blocks of bilingualism

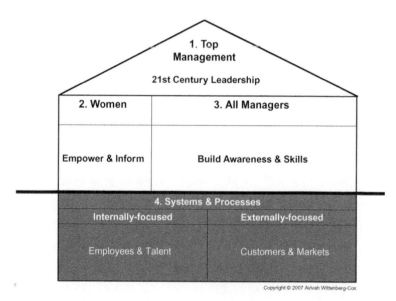

Copyright © 2007 Avivah Wittenberg-Cox

The four building blocks of bilingualism

There are four essential elements to implementing gender-bilingualism in organisations. There is no hard rule about which is put in place first. This depends on the organisation and its strategy, objectives and priorities concerning gender. However, each element is necessary to tap into the full potential of women – as stakeholders, customers, employees and leaders.

Most companies launching gender initiatives over-emphasise one of the four elements: they invest most of the resources in "fix-the-women" strategies. They create women's events and networks, provide women with training and coaching and a variety of other "support" mechanisms. These measures can be a helpful step in empowering women. However, many such approaches are based, deliberately or not, on encouraging women to behave more like men. Rather than eradicate bias, these approaches unwittingly reinforce them.

One American multinational organised a day-long conference for its women's network. It had run several workshops, one of them focused on "powerful communications". The workshop started with a video of a speech given by the company's very tough male CEO. For an hour, the workshop facilitator proceeded to analyse his strengths and encourage the women in the room to emulate them.

This "fix-the-women" mentality focuses its efforts on the wrong segment of the population. Women don't need "fixing". Most of the energy and investment would be better spent on the other elements presented below.

1 "Getting it": top management commitment

As in any strategic change initiative, top management needs to be convinced of the business reasons for more gender balance in its leadership teams. This is particularly true of gender diversity since it is a subject which elicits strong reactions and resistance. If the senior leadership team is not convinced and ready to show the way (which includes promoting women to the executive committee), it is almost impossible to convince managers that this is an organisational priority.

This phase includes leaders building the business case, persuading the leadership team to rally behind it and repeating the message about its strategic importance. It means speaking, regularly and routinely about the issue, setting objectives and leading by example. This is an essential – and preferably first – step.

2 Management bilingualism: proactively managing difference

This is the core of any gender initiative. It represents the majority of the effort and budget that should be spent. This is when change will happen – or not. It is where many gender initiatives fail to bear fruit. If successful, however, it can transform the cultures of organisations, making them more responsive to both men and women – in other words, more human.

This phase prepares all managers (male and female) to be effective, inclusive managers of men and women. It trains them to be fluent in the differences between genders and helps to adapt management styles appropriately. It involves awareness-building workshops, training, individual or group coaching, mentoring and reverse mentoring programmes.

The underlying objectives here are to:

- demonstrate the strategic business case for better gender balance;
- allow men and women to recognise and accept differences between genders and see those as opportunities;
- adapt management and leadership styles to become more inclusive of women, both as employees and customers;
- offer pragmatic examples of *how* to do this;
- use both intellectual approaches, and more emotionally-driven experiential methods.

3   Empowering women: the knowledge and networks to succeed

As we shall examine in Chapter Seven, women are often not fully familiar with the "codes" of organisational politics, culture and rules of the male corporate game. With less access to the informal networks where much of this crucial information is exchanged, parallel systems need, for a time, to be created.

There are a variety of options here, and companies have experimented with many of them – women's networks, tailored training, mentoring systems, individual or group coaching. Whatever the vehicle chosen, the ingredients are:

- making the corporate rules of career progression and promotion more transparent and explicit, particularly through the crucial 30s decade;
- getting senior executives – male and female – to pass on experience and facilitate introductions;
- establishing and extending professional networks internally and externally;
- empowering women by building their confidence, political competence and professionalism in a gender-tailored way;
- *not* expecting women's networks to solve the issue of gender imbalance on their own.

4   Banning bias: identifying and eliminating systemic bias from corporate systems and processes

Progressive companies carefully scan existing processes and systems in a hunt for unconscious biases that may affect women's careers or experience as customers. There are two dimensions to these efforts, one that focuses on employees internally, the other on the market.

Internally, it means looking at career management systems and data on promotions, and asking the following questions:

- **Recruitment** – Are recruitment campaigns effective at attracting women or do managers claim that they would love to hire more women but "just can't find any"? Where are jobs advertised, and what images are used to convey the corporate culture? Many companies find that they have actively to brief and even train their HR and recruitment agencies to eliminate bias at the interview stage.
- **Pay** – Is there bias in the pay system? Do women stay longer in certain pay bands than men? Do employees only get increases if they ask for them? Auditing compensation practices and trends is an ideal way to uncover hidden discrimination.
- **High-potential identification** – Does the company have a structured programme to identify high-potential people, with a defined age for participants? If this age is capped (typically the age range of these programmes is 28 to 35), it unwittingly discriminates against child-bearing women. Progressive companies are raising the upper limit to 40 or 45 or, like some Scandinavian companies, removing it altogether.

- **Succession Planning and Promotion** – Is there a target for mixed succession planning lists? If there are consistently no women on these lists, this may be an indication of other biases at play. Is there a grade or ranking level at which the percentage of women precipitously drops off? This "glass ceiling" is usually bias at play.

- **Performance Evaluation** – Performance evaluations are often more subjective than managers would like to think, and more self-fulfilling. They tend to reproduce a dominant norm of leader aligned with each organisation's culture and may not correspond to the style with which many women are comfortable. Training managers to understand differences between genders usually helps them look a little more closely at whom they are promoting and why.

- **Flexible working** – Is this aimed primarily at women? Are the top jobs at the company excluded? Are men encouraged to be role models for flexible working of all kinds? These programmes are still often treated as an "employee benefit" aimed at women with children. This casts them into a ghetto associated with low commitment. Yet flexibility and control are increasingly sought by employees of all kinds and can confer a competitive advantage on companies that encourage them (see Chapter Eight). UK research shows that regular working from home using a computer and phone ("teleworking") is actually most common among highly skilled, senior-ranking men. Flexibility needs to be rethought, taken out of the "gender" arena, and made a priority tool for attracting and retaining all kinds of employees, both male and female, in response to changing social attitudes.

Externally, banning bias involves looking at all the ways in which companies analyse and respond to their customers and stakeholders.

- **Market research** – Is market research conducted and then analysed by gender? When BP first analysed some customer research by gender, it discovered a decade ago that women felt unsafe paying for petrol far away from their cars (and children). That led the company to innovate by introducing payment islands next to the pump and drive-by cashiers.
- **Product development** – Are products developed to respond to the needs and expectations of male and female customers? Volvo developed a "concept car" designed by a team of women specifically for women. Many of its features were integrated into the company's wider product range.
- **Marketing and product communication** – Are the company's image and external communications attractive to both male and female customers? Leading DIY stores like Home Depot or Leroy Merlin have gone through an enormous transformation of their stores in recent years,

for example creating in-store training and education, a potent sales tactic for the growing number of female renovators and craftspeople.

- **Customer service** – Is customer service tailored to women's needs? Some banks are beginning to understand that more and more "high net worth" clients are female – and to ensure that, if they want to, they can have access to another woman to talk to about money and investment.

The next chapter examines some of the key success factors in launching a gender initiative.

In conclusion, the essential step to becoming bilingual is recognising that a different language exists in the first place – and that it is now spoken by an economically powerful majority. It is no longer useful – and will soon be harmful – to insist (consciously or not) that women adapt to the existing norms and rules of the game. Companies wanting to harness this revolutionary economic force need to understand that the days of women's adapting to the work world are drawing to an end. Tomorrow's female money and talent will go to the companies adapted to their needs, styles and motivations. This will require leadership, conviction and language skills. Getting the best out of women – as customers, employees or shareholders – requires managers and organisations to be genuinely gender-bilingual. Are you?

Traditional and bilingual approaches

Traditional Approaches	Bilingual Approaches
• Include gender in umbrella diversity approaches • Treat everyone equally and the same. • Assume fairness of performance assumptions and existence of meritocracy. • Approach gender through a "compliance" lens.	• Position gender as a strategic priority. • Audit and understand the existing reality of attitudes on gender – and their impact. • Analyse where your company currently stands on each of the four building blocks described above. • Adapt leadership language to signal an understanding of "difference".

Chapter Five

SEVEN STEPS TO SUCCESSFUL IMPLEMENTATION

"We've created a real momentum, especially with those of our clients who are very interested in the gender balance issue themselves ... We're even starting to be seen as a benchmark. It's a significant competitive advantage for us. We win contracts thanks to our efforts."[1]

Michel Landel, Chief Executive Officer, Sodexo

Key success factors

Becoming bilingual begins with a shift in perspective. It depends on recognising that responsibility for better gender balance lies with all managers, not just with women. It focuses its efforts on teaching the current majority to become bilingual, fluent in the language and culture of both men and women. Only once all managers understand that the methods

---

[1]Author interview for the 20-first.com website, March 2009

and messages used to recruit, manage and evaluate men do not necessarily work for women will women's talents stand a chance of being accurately recognised and optimised.

Gender initiatives are far from simple. Companies often underestimate the reactions they elicit – both from men and women. To add a layer of complexity, attitudes to gender and the respective roles of men and women differ sharply from country to country and from region to region, as we explain in Chapter Six.

The way a gender initiative is launched is the key to its success. Getting it wrong can stir up resentment and hamper the very objectives it was meant to achieve, sometimes for years. Getting it right requires a sound understanding of what the issues are about – and what they are not about.

Below, we outline seven steps to launching an effective gender strategy, one that is inclusive of both men and women. We make liberal reference here to the management "spin" put on Malcolm Gladwell's book *The Tipping Point* (Gladwell, 2000) by W. Chan Kim and Renée Mauborgne in their *Harvard Business Review* article, "Tipping Point Leadership" (Chan Kim and Mauborgne, 2003).

The steps are as follows:

1. Awaken your leadership team.
2. Define the business case.

3. Let people express resistance.
4. Make it a *business* issue, not a *women's* issue.
5. Make changes before making noise.
6. Don't mix up the messages.
7. Give it a budget, not just volunteers.

Each of these steps is described in detail below.

1 Awaken your leadership team

The signal for change frequently comes from the CEO. Often he (or, more rarely, she) is new to the company, and brings with him a culture of gender balance from previous employers, or he is newly awakened to the issue and would like his firm to awaken with him. The CEO tells his executive committee to fix the problem. Then the executive committee appoints someone to take responsibility for the topic, and everyone else goes about business as usual.

Break through the cognitive hurdle:

> "To make a compelling case for change, don't just point at the numbers and demand better ones. Your abstract message won't stick. Instead, make key managers experience your organisation's problems."
>
> Chan Kim and Mauborgne, 2003

The first step of an effective gender initiative is to convince senior management that gender is a business issue. For many senior executives around the world, this subject is far off their radar screens. They have not necessarily been sensitised to the dramatic changes described in the earlier chapters of this book. Many of them make the following assumptions:

- Gender is not an issue.
- Men and women are equal and the same.
- The business world is rational and performance-driven.
- The cream of managerial talent rises automatically to the top.

While all readily acknowledge the importance of national and cultural diversity for their globalising businesses, few are aware of the impending impact of gender. Raising their awareness of women's evolving roles as employees, customers and shareholders (the latter also increasingly important given the rise in asset ownership described in Chapter Three) is an essential first step. This awareness is particularly effective if it can be done experientially as well as intellectually.

Case Study: Hands-on Experience

One large Canadian DIY company, described in Joanne Thomas Yaccato's book *The 80% Minority,* sent its entire executive committee into one of its stores, equipped with imitation babies in baby-carriers on their fronts, purses in hand and the store's huge and unwieldy shopping carts to push around. In the store, the vice-president of operations was bumped into by a keen young staffer who came rushing round a corner not paying attention and clipped the front end of the executive's cart. The "baby" on the executive's chest was crushed in the accident. The whole national market was re-equipped with smaller and lighter shopping carts the following month.

Case Study: Role reversal

Another technique is getting male executives to address all-women groups, something that many even highly experienced men find disconcerting. An executive committee member of one of France's largest companies was invited to speak at the monthly lunch of the European Professional Women's Network in Paris, (one of Europe's largest, founded by Avivah Wittenberg-Cox). Faced with 50 friendly female faces, he discovered his hands shaking and sweat pouring down his face. He had the grace and the courage to laugh openly at himself, while wiping the sweat from his brow. He acknowledged that experiencing for the first time in his life what many senior women face every day was unexpectedly uncomfortable.

These are tipping point experiences that sensitise men to the issues women still face, and make them more open to addressing them. Or, as diversity expert Jacey Graham, who initiated the FTSE 100 Cross-Company Mentoring Programme with Peninah Thomson, frames it, such experiences engage both the heart and the head, and it is the combination that moves people to action.

Close Up: Learning through reciprocal mentoring

Some companies establish reciprocal or "reverse" mentoring schemes, in which senior executives are paired up with younger high-potential women in their firms or in other companies. Under the joint leadership of Niall FitzGerald and Antony Burgmans, Unilever's male executive team acknowledged they had to challenge their own thinking if things were going to change for women in the consumer goods multinational. Each of them mentored, and was mentored by, senior women in the company who helped to open their eyes to some of the obstacles in their way. Focus groups with managers helped reveal that women felt excluded by the dominant culture.

"What will change the nature of the conversation will be when senior men talk about it honestly," says Rhodora Palomar-Fresnedi, who set up the reciprocal mentoring scheme as Global Head of Diversity. "One of the things I find is that it's really one-on-one work with the men. It has to be personal, like when they find that their daughters face these issues at work. Unless they can relate to it, nothing's going to happen. FitzGerald and Burgmans both 'got it'." The Unilever board has since become much more diverse and currently includes three women – Hixonia Nyasulu, one of South Africa's leading businesswomen, Louise Fresco, a

Dutch professor of international development and sustainability, and Ann Fudge, former chair and CEO of Young & Rubicam Brands. The representation of women in Unilever's top two levels of global management rose from 14% in 2002 to 25% in 2009, she adds (interviews with author, 2007, 2009).

There are also several recent examples of mentoring approaches established across companies, specifically addressing the issue of bringing more women onto corporate boards. The Confederation of Norwegian Business and Industry (NHO) launched the Female Future initiative in 2003 to identify qualified women – what it calls "pearl diving" – and prepare them for board roles through networking and tailor-made mentoring.

Under the UK's FTSE 100 Cross-Company Mentoring Programme, mentioned above and publicly launched in 2004, chief executives or chairmen mentor senior women from other companies. An initiative modelled on the UK programme was launched in France in 2007 under the name BoardWomen Partners. The primary purpose of these schemes is for the women to gain advice from, and access to, well-networked senior business leaders. A side effect is that top men begin to see the gender issues, first-hand, from a woman's perspective. Alison Wheaton, one of the women who has been on the UK programme, would like to see more female leaders as mentors, but takes a pragmatic view. "We're going to have to be mentored by men until more women are in these positions," she says (Maitland, 2006).

2 Define the business case

The next step is to spend time discussing the issue within the executive committee, whose overloaded agendas need to make it enough of a priority to include it. The senior team needs to be able to voice their concerns and their scepticism. The CEO has to sell the idea to the team in a way that will allow them to sell it onwards to their own teams. Taking time to craft a convincing, company-specific business case for gender diversity within the executive committee is a crucial step. Why and how is gender a business issue for the company? What is the existing reality in the organisation – how good is the company's current image and relationship with women customers and employees? What are the opportunities for growth in harnessing the talents or purchasing power of women? If top managers do not craft a strategic case for change, they are unlikely to address it effectively – or convince their colleagues to do so.

This phase involves getting executive committee members to debate their analysis and definition of the business case. These sessions can present the research and data on gender at work and in the market and the challenges described earlier in this book, benchmark how other companies in the same country and sector are responding, and analyse the existing situation in the organisation (through internal and customer audits). The aim is to align the top management team on *why* a gender initiative is necessary and win agreement on *how* to address it. These meetings are also helpful in identifying potential champions and supporters for the journey ahead.

Case Study: Opening eyes

One such session at a large European industrial group helped to reveal to the highly committed CEO that there were different levels of awareness within the executive team and little agreement about the importance of the subject or how to evaluate the potential impact on the company.

During the ensuing debate, the group learned key facts about gender, realised that some of their main competitors were aggressively positioning themselves to attract female talent, evaluated each individual's awareness of and openness to the issue, and learned from an audit that their female employees were stuck firmly underneath a clearly situated glass ceiling which they had previously been convinced did not exist.

Many also realised that the subject of gender was a much bigger topic than they suspected – and that resolving it would have ramifications well beyond the limited HR initiatives tabled up until then. They decided that it was important enough to build awareness of the topic across the company, and rolled out similar sessions for all their top managers as a preparatory phase of a proactive strategy to deal with it.

This is not usually how gender initiatives are launched. More often than not, companies start by taking a more numerically-driven approach, without recognising the rather complex social and emotional issues underlying gender. Often, once the CEO decides to move on gender, a typical next step is to settle on a numerical target. This number currently ranges somewhere between 25% and 40% of women in management, and at least one woman on the board and the executive committee. For professional services firms, where the level of women partners is currently in the low teens (despite recruitment figures that are often at parity), the target is more likely to be around 20% or 25%.

The argument put forward is often that the target statistic for women in senior management should *at least* reflect the percentage of women graduates in the recruitment pool (for engineering-oriented industrial firms this is often argued to be around 20%) or the percentage of women recruited into the firm at graduate level (a wide range depending on sectors and industries and the perceived attractiveness of the company to women).

The consequence of setting targets is that (most) people try to meet them. After an analysis of the existing gender statistics, some benchmarking of the competition, and a determined plan to get the numbers right, targets are set, deadlines assigned and managers are told to make it happen. Scratch a bit beneath the surface, however, and you find that many of the executive committee members are unconvinced of the strategic case for such pushes. Many mutter under their breath that "quotas" and positive discrimination will affect competence (positive discrimination in favour of the current dominant group is rarely mentioned). Even those intellectually willing to give it a try are often far from understanding what the issue is all about, how to fix it or how to sell it to their own teams.

So managers gamely start promoting any woman they can find, occasionally knowing that she may not quite be ready for the job, and if she fails this is taken as proof that women just aren't made for these kinds of positions. After a year or so of this, as one company manager commented, they have "shot all their bullets" and there is no one left to promote. Then they point their fingers at recruitment and the empty pipeline and wait for things to happen ... next decade.

3 Let people express resistance

In every gender initiative, on every executive committee, and in every group of managers there exist the segmentations of opinion we described in Chapter Four: the progressive, the patient and the plodding. Recognising this reality is not as straightforward as it seems.

Most CEOs launching such initiatives are personally convinced of the importance of the gender issue. But they often assume that their team does not need convincing, that all are equally open and receptive to the idea of proactively promoting women into management. It is difficult for progressive men to see that they are not (yet) necessarily representative of their gender. They are sure that setting targets will be sufficient to fix the numbers and the problem will then disappear. This approach usually ends up with a frustrated CEO asking two years later why the numbers aren't moving.

It is better to address dissidence and disagreement head on (as any change management expert will tell you). Typically, this type of work involves surveying the attitudes of the executive committee and a representative sampling of managers – men and women – across the company before designing remedies or setting targets. It is essential to get an idea of the culture and context in which you are working. Getting an external consultant to interview people on this subject can avoid much of the political correctness that surrounds the issue. Most people are delighted to vent their true feelings to an outsider, allowing them to identify the natural champions and the potential nay-sayers – as well as their arguments. Open and wide-ranging discussions with an expert also serve as an effective first step in raising the awareness of the people being interviewed.

These reactions can then be anonymously aired back to the executive committee and debated. A few group exercises can clearly position, in public, where people stand on the subject. This allows everyone to realise – including the CEO – that the issue is far from being unanimously accepted. Those who are not convinced will not be effective implementers. They may, in fact, be powerful underminers. It is better to know who they are early on, hear their objections and answer them convincingly. Nay-sayers, once convinced, can become some of the strongest proponents of change.

In one large multinational company, a full day was spent working on the business case for gender with a group of HR managers. At the end of the day, a quick round table discussion demonstrated that the largely female group of managers were defensive and uncomfortable with the whole topic and unconvinced of the company's business case. Rather than taking their reluctance on board, in order to respond more persuasively, the head of human resources stood up and metaphorically stamped his foot. He angrily commented that they were not there to ask about why the company was focusing on gender, but to implement the CEO's decisions. This company can be sure to have alienated the very group on which it largely depends to embrace and roll out the policy. Recovering from this 10-minute error may take years.

The most ineffective scenario is simply to set a policy and assume that everyone will subscribe to it wholeheartedly. In the area of gender, in a management world still shaped by male norms, this is naïve and disingenuous. It takes time, persuasion and persistence to align people on controversial policies that touch them deeply, both professionally and personally.

Case Study: Clearing the air

It took some subtle work by an external "change" consultant to tackle the thoroughly macho culture at a company's media-buying division. Swearing, heavy drinking, lewd jokes and sexist comments were so ingrained in the way people worked that some of the female employees joined in. On the surface, it was all seen as "a bit of fun".

It was only when the consultant was brought in for a wider programme of culture change that his confidential interviews with employees revealed discomfort about the way women were treated. Many of the women felt they could not object for fear of being singled out as a killjoy. They felt they had to swear and drink as hard as the men to be treated as equals. Because the culture was so antagonistic to working mothers taking maternity leave, two women did not tell their boss they were pregnant until the pregnancy showed. It also emerged that the younger men were offended by the verbal abuse perpetuated by the male old guard.

When the results of the interviews were fed back to people in groups of about 20, the problems surfaced publicly for the first time. Some of the most ardent proponents of the behaviour denied it was offensive. They argued that if the work involved tough, down-to-earth negotiations, people had to behave that way. But once these men were confronted by the impact of their behaviour on colleagues and the issue was out in the open, some of the younger men and more courageous women felt able to pull them up when they fell back into old habits. "The biggest effect was achieved by disclosure," the consultant said. "It was cathartic. It made it acceptable to acknowledge something that was like incest in the family" (Author case study).

4 Make it a business issue, not a women's issue
Jump the motivational hurdle:

> "To turn a mere strategy into a movement, people must recognise what needs to be done and yearn to do it themselves. But don't try reforming your whole organisation; that's cumbersome and expensive. Instead, motivate key influencers – persuasive people with multiple connections. Like bowling kingpins hit straight on, they topple all the other pins. Most organisations have several key influencers who share common problems and concerns – making it easy to identify and motivate them."
>
> Chan Kim and Mauborgne, 2003

The person traditionally named to run gender diversity projects is a woman. Often the HR director or one of the firm's more senior women is assigned the responsibility of organising the analysis of the situation and drafting proposals to increase the number of women in management. In most companies that have started a gender initiative, a woman is appointed to head it.

In addition, women are often requested to provide the answers. Most companies start by surveying women, asking them what they think the issues are. Or management asks women's networks to say what is wrong and propose solutions. One educational institution surveyed women students, teaching staff and alumnae – inviting them to share their analysis with the entirely male leadership team. It's like leaning down from above the glass ceiling to ask all the women below why they aren't making it to the top.

This approach unwittingly undermines the solution. By positioning gender as a women's issue, rather than an organisational or business one, it unconsciously communicates that the lack of women in senior management is the responsibility (or fault) of women. So the "minority" is asked to fix the issue. Progressive companies know that women are only partly responsible for their minority status.

The real reasons that women are not moving up do not lie primarily with women. They are embedded in systems that have evolved over decades and reflect the values, motivations and views of a male majority. None of this is done intentionally or even consciously. It is simply the result of history and corporate evolution. But so long as these issues remain unseen, they form an intractable barrier to a more inclusive work environment.

Lessons from Deloitte

Douglas M. McCracken, the former CEO of Deloitte Consulting, wrote that at his company "we came to grips with the fact that women at Deloitte were on the march – out the door ... Only four of our 50 candidates for partner were women even though ... [we] had been heavily recruiting women from colleges and business schools since 1980. We also found that women were leaving the firm at a significantly greater rate than men." He went on to admit that for a long time, they did not really see this as a business issue, but more of a personal choice option. "To be frank, many of the firm's senior partners, including myself, didn't actually see the exodus of women as a problem, or at least, it wasn't our problem. We assumed that women were leaving to have children and stay home. If there was a problem at all, it was society's or the women's, not Deloitte's. In fact, most senior partners firmly believed we were doing everything possible to retain women. We prided ourselves on our open, collegial, performance-based work environment. How wrong we were, and how far we've come" (McCracken, 2000).

Knock over the political hurdle:

> "Even when organisations reach their tipping points, powerful vested interests resist change. Identify and silence key nay-sayers early by putting a respected senior insider on your top team."
>
> Chan Kim and Mauborgne, 2003

Most organisations and managers are profoundly convinced that their systems and cultures are impartial, rational and perfectly fair. Having a woman – or a group of women – stand up and say that they are not is not the strongest guarantee of a mutually enriching dialogue.

A more convincing angle, which a few companies such as Schlumberger, the leading oilfield services group, Bain & Co., the strategy consultants and Nestlé, the nutrition, health and wellness multinational, are starting to experiment with, is to have gender initiatives headed by a senior male fast-tracker. In these cases, the executive's reputation and obvious clout adds credibility to an initiative whose key task is to convince a majority of male managers that gender diversity actually delivers value to the company, and that it presents a strategic business opportunity.

"I was absolutely comfortable pushing it," says Jim Andrews, former Gender Diversity Manager at Schlumberger. "It was easier for me to push the subject with a male-dominated management team. I've been with Schlumberger for 17 years, I've had both HR and operational roles, I've managed countries like Oman and Pakistan. I know our people – and, more importantly, they know me."

In Marshall McLuhan's immortal phrase, the medium is the message. This applies to the choice of leader of a gender programme. Appointing a male star to the gender champion chair sends a clear message – unless, of course, it's a female-dominated firm, in which case the appointment of a woman makes more sense. In either case, the champion should be someone who understands the issue and is seen by the majority as a mover and shaker in the company. It should be someone who would only be assigned to matters of strategic importance.

This needs to be done with extreme sensitivity, however. If the choice is a man, he must both command the attention of the leadership, and be attuned to the views of the mass of employees, both men and women. It would be easy to create resentment. There are many talented women diversity officers toiling inside large companies to bring about culture change. Some have moved on in frustration, having failed to change things in the absence of support from the top, or in the teeth of resistance from managers. The appointment of an influential male executive to the post needs to be accompanied by an open recognition of the obstacles that have prevented progress. (See Schlumberger case study at the end of this chapter).

Around the leader, create a team of high-profile operational heads, both men and women, to steer the initiative. This approach has the advantage of reflecting the kind of organisation you want: one that is gender-balanced and knows how to optimise the talents and listen to the voices of both women and men. It also allows committee members to carry on their operational roles in parallel, supported by HR or diversity specialists. This way, they keep a hand in the business and stay relevant in the eyes of their colleagues, while carrying the gender message deep into the organisation.

In companies for which globalisation and an understanding of different markets and cultures are crucial to future growth, spending a couple of years on the gender committee should be an attractive developmental rite of passage.

The European Aeronautic Defence and Space Company (EADS) did just that. Its management carefully designed a steering committee made up of one operational person and one HR person, usually one man and one woman, from each division. The group met several times to prepare the business case for presentation to the executive committee. During their day-long meetings, they explored and analysed the gender-related opportunities and risks for the organisation, the obstacles, and the targets to be reached in recruiting, identifying high-potential people, and leadership development. They analysed market trends and growing government pressure on the subject of gender across the EU. They commissioned further research and debated who would be the most credible representative to present the issue to the executive committee. By the time they were ready to present, they had all become strong and informed champions of the initiative – convinced that it was of strategic importance.

5 Make changes before making noise

One company's experience illustrates the value of *doing* before communicating. This multinational, dominated by male engineers with only a handful of women anywhere in management, was planning the launch of its diversity initiative. Its first step, after receiving the green light from the executive committee, was to be the announcement of the decision via its internal communications media. After some thoughtful debate within the launch team, however, the company decided an announcement risked backfiring. They realised the dangers in stating baldly to a majority of men that they now wanted to promote women. What surer way was there to elicit a variety of unproductive emotions? So they adapted their approach, and started instead by explaining, in structured sessions, why business imperatives were behind the need for better gender balance. This then prepared the groundwork for a wider communications approach to be better received at a later date.

Before launching any gender initiative, communicate the strategic reasons why gender balance is important for your organisation. Communication has to be done very carefully. It is a delicate subject that can easily annoy both men and women – the former because they don't want to have women thrust onto their promotion path, and the latter because many are convinced that they personally can make it on performance alone.

Communication strategies need to be built for each stage of the initiative and the word should emanate from the top. The first job is to convince senior management as well as key change agents, who should be influencers of opinion and operational heavyweights. This does not require the communications department. More typically, it will require targeted awareness-building sessions. These sessions can first be aimed at the executive committee, then change agents and champions, and then wider groups. After the launch, such sessions can become a mainstream part of management and leadership development programmes.

The arguments about communication also apply to women in the organisation. It does not necessarily help them to trumpet across the company that you will support their advancement, before any action has taken place. Consider who are the leading female role models in the company. Do they understand the gender issues or refute them? Are they acceptable models for younger women? Are they ready to be champions on the topic? It is often assumed that women are automatically prepared to support gender initiatives. This is not necessarily the case. Women have a wide variety of attitudes to the topic, and not all of them are obvious champions. Some can be serious detractors. They need to be as carefully selected as the men to defend the topic visibly.

Finally, once the initiative has been clearly explained to key influencers – male and female – and their input has been incorporated into your strategy and communications plan, you can start communicating more widely to sensitise all managers to the issues. This is often months after having launched.

Going public

Communicating externally on gender is another area that some companies would love to rush into. The pressure on the recruiting front to be known as a female-friendly organisation is growing. Talented women are starting to study companies' track records on gender before they sign a job contract.

Many firms are rushing into external communication and recruitment campaigns making huge and welcoming signals to women. But if relatively little has been done internally, new recruits join companies where they are shocked to discover a big gap between external image and internal reality. When they quit in dismay, it is costly both for them and the company.

External communication campaigns can be planned in parallel with internal ones. It is better not to overstate your case before you are ready. You will alienate not only your newest employees but also your current women employees. They will hoot derisively at promises and pronouncements they may have never seen or heard of internally.

One company took out a double-page spread in a national newspaper on Women's Day (8 March), introducing their top 100 women, complete with photos, without having launched anything about gender internally at all. The communications department had taken the initiative, without even informing the HR people. The backlash from within was almost immediate as the women objected to being used in this way.

Companies can get their messages badly unsynchronised. Deutsche Bank found itself in the media spotlight for the contradiction between its internal efforts to recruit and promote women and ethnic minorities and a series of advertisements for the bank, which featured white men, including super-athletic males under the heading "a passion to perform" (Maitland, 2004). Tess Finch-Lees, a diversity consultant who drew attention to the disparity, says the unwelcome publicity made the bank change tack on its external imagery. "The series of testosterone charged images, all displaying the same male prototype, clearly equated white, able-bodied, masculinity with success. In one fell swoop, Deutsche Bank's marketing department undermined all the work to promote the organisation as a gender inclusive employer," she says.

It is better to go slowly but surely in communications – and be certain you have researched and understood the current awareness levels and openness to gender in the organisation – and in the external national culture – before seeking to address it publicly. Communications on this topic (even more than any other) need to be aligned and adapted to the context.

6 Don't mix up the messages

Gender is not the same topic as work-life balance. Too many companies associate these two issues, often launching work-life programmes within the context or the communication of their gender initiatives. This is not helpful. It simply reaffirms in resistors' minds that women have work-life issues … and that men don't. Balance is an issue that affects all companies and both genders.

Barbara Cassani, who founded Go, the low cost airline, and led London's successful 2012 Olympics bid, gave a personal view on the subject at a McKinsey-organised conference on women as leaders. "Even the issue of childcare, it is not a women's issue; it is a family issue," she said. "And frankly, some of the people who pose those questions to people like me are implying that women should feel guilty about the work-life balance, and should feel more guilty than men" (Cassani, 2007).

Mobility is something else that has been seen as a big obstacle to women's careers. As dual careers have become more common, mobility and immobility have become major issues for both men and women, and a big re-evaluation of what an international career looks like is going on in many companies around the globe.

Flexibility, dual careers, mobility and choice are increasingly important to all current generations in the workforce, as well as those yet to enter, as we explain in Chapter Eight. Progressive companies understand that new ways of working will be an important magnet for the next generation's talent. But it helps initiatives on women if this topic is kept distinct.

Case Study: Standard Chartered's flexible working in Asia[2]

Standard Chartered is not a typical western bank. Based in London, it makes more than 90% of its operating income and profits in Asia, Africa and the Middle East. One of the first efforts on gender was to make working arrangements flexible across markets. "This is kind of passé in markets like the UK," says Jaspal Bindra, the CEO of Standard Chartered Asia. "But until recently, both India and Hong Kong, for example, had six-day weeks and we've brought both to a five-day week. We've also introduced an initiative whereby employees are encouraged to leave work at an earlier hour than normal and avoid scheduling late meetings every Friday (called 'Happy Friday' or, for the Middle East, 'Happy Thursday')."

The bank has actively sought ways to promote flexibility. "We are looking at a range of measures including part-time working and flexible working hours so that not all employees have to work standard nine-to-five days. We also have a large number of people who now work from home."

But the crux of the issue, as for so many international companies, was mobility. "Our biggest issue in this area was around mobility because we had such a geographically

---

[2]Interview conducted by Morice Mendoza for the 20-first.com website, April 2009

diverse company with no home base," says Bindra. "Mobility was a very important criterion in furthering your career and we used to have international mobility listed as a requirement to be "high potential". Because of family circumstances or the fact that men's careers often come first in some cultures, women were more vulnerable to this. Also, the women were probably far more honest in admitting they were not mobile whereas the men would tend to say they were mobile even though they may not have been at the time.

"The combination of these factors didn't support women's progression within the Bank and this was a big issue for us 10 years ago when we had only two to three big markets. It was hard for an individual who didn't move around to develop his or her career in one relatively small market. But now we have 12 big markets and they are of such a size that you could significantly progress your career without having to go to another city."

Is the need for mobility no longer a barrier to women's advancement? "As we've grown, mobility has become less of a challenge," he says. "Previously, we had specific centres for each business and function. But now employees can gain broad experience within the same city. Many global roles can also be done in different locations."

The effect of such changes in emphasis and criteria are clear. "You now have more women labelled as high potential. Now they have more visibility in discussions around promotions and career moves. As they see themselves progressing more quickly, they give more consideration to their career decisions and the trade-offs around family responsibilities become far more balanced. So you are seeing a chain reaction. A significant proportion of the increase in women at senior management has come about as a result." Standard Chartered now has 21% women in senior management across the company, and has been particularly successful in certain countries. So in China, for example, 43% of senior managers are women. In middle management, the pipeline is strengthening, with countries now showing a majority of women at this level (Thailand 64%, Philippines 61% and Brunei 62%).

Part of the company's push on gender has been to ensure that there are relevant role models in its varied operations. The firm promoted SeonJoo Kim, who started as a clerk with the company, to Executive Vice President and Head of CB Operations. She is the first woman in Korea who went from a modest non-management role to become an Executive Vice President in the financial services industry. They also have 13 female CEOs in markets as diverse as China, Afghanistan, Lebanon and Zambia.

These examples help to illustrate Standard Charter's commitment to a three-pronged approach to women: women in the workplace, women as customers and women in the community. This holistic approach helps the bank capture all the opportunities that better gender balance offers.

7   Give it a budget, not just volunteers

For many companies, the issue of gender is seen as simply a redefining of HR priorities and numbers. Once targets have been set, the rest is up to the existing team with existing resources. Very few strategic change initiatives have no budget. The size of the budget and the seniority of the team communicate the importance accorded to the subject. Without a budget, gender initiatives end up as small efforts which create a lot of expectations and reactions without being able to address either properly. This is often the case with women's networks, which remain "voluntary" rather than "business" initiatives, dependent on the personal dedication of already-busy women to sustain them and struggle to gain continued corporate funding after start-up (Cranfield, 2004). If it is not worth investing in, don't bother.

Start smart and avoid the cost of corrections

Launching a gender initiative is a big decision. It can change the culture and context of the organisation more than its leaders may bargain for.

As mentioned above, Douglas McCracken describes this effort at Deloitte – and its payoffs – in an article he wrote, evocatively called, "Winning the Talent War for Women: Sometimes It Takes a Revolution" (McCracken, 2000). Deloitte's Initiative for the Retention and Advancement of Women grew out of a task force headed by then-CEO Mike Cook. "A number of women partners initially wanted nothing to do with the effort *because it implied affirmative action." But Cook drove the initiative with a mixed team of male and female partners, ensuring that it represented a broad range of views, including outright scepticism. It took a methodical approach, first gathering data and understanding before acting and communicating. Deloitte prepared all 5000 of their professionals for change by holding a series of intensive, two-day workshops at a cost of some $8 million. Only once awareness had been raised did the firm move to policy implementation.*

"Resistance was futile," remarked one partner. McCracken himself admits his scepticism about "HR-type programs" and the mental calculations he made of the combined cost of the programme and the lost revenue of having so many consultants in training. But he concludes that "I was dead wrong. The workshops were a turning point, a pivotal event in the life of the firm ... ultimately the workshops converted a critical mass of Deloitte's leaders."

Gender initiatives are change programmes which should start strategically and quietly and gradually pick up strength and steam on people's carefully nurtured support and conviction. Launched incorrectly, gender initiatives are soon seen as management fads with no budget or influence. They end up being objects of derision doing more damage than good to women's reputations and chances. Repairing this kind of negative initial impression is much harder than starting right in the first place.

In conclusion, if you are convinced that gender is a strategic issue for the future of your business, take the time to start smart. Start at the top by getting your executive committee behind it, roll it out quietly by getting credible role models – respected by both men and women – to lead and champion the cause, and communicate with the outside world only when you have something to show, not just something to say. Then you will move beyond just "doing diversity" and start becoming gender-bilingual. It is a lot better for business.

We end this chapter with interviews with three senior male executives about the innovative measures they are taking to addressing the gender issue inside their companies.

Case Study: Nestlé
A ground-breaking approach

In September 2008, Paul Bulcke, the CEO appointed appointed in April, delighted Nestlé's shareholders by announcing a 6.1% increase in net earnings in the first half of the year. Not a bad performance at a time of global financial turmoil and widespread corporate malaise.

At the same time, away from the glare of the media spotlight, Bulcke, encouraged by Peter Brabeck-Letmathe (now Chairman of the Board) was leading a strategic move towards building gender balance at Nestlé.

One of the issues hampering gender balance has been career mobility. Says Bulcke: "We are a multinational company and multinational means quite a lot of people travelling around and having their careers in one country and then moving from one country to another. Maybe we didn't condition the practicality of how we organize this and our approach was based on a 'man's' world".

Nestlé aims to better use talent by changing its corporate culture from a traditional male one into a more gender-bilingual model. "I definitely think that it has everything to do with business, in the sense that gender balance is going to lead us to unlocking the resources that we have, the talent that we have, that we haven't unlocked until today."

The company launched its gender initiative in 2008. But instead of creating a women's network or gathering together its senior women to draft a strategy, it analysed the issue and defined its group action plan at the Executive Board level. It decided, after carefully auditing the current reality on gender around the globe, to launch a change management approach focused on the leadership of the company. Each Executive Board member, along with his direct reports (mostly male executives), spent an entire day in awareness building and action planning workshops.

So the ideas and suggestions of the company's leaders are at the heart of the plan now being implemented. They debated and defined the benefits that better balance would bring the company, and identified the systemic and cultural dimensions that required adapting.

Similar sessions were then run with the Management Committees around the world so that locally relevant strategies could be defined in different markets and countries. It would be rolled out to all managers over the coming year.

Nestlé has given the men currently in power the understanding, tools and responsibility to adapt the corporate culture and systems to 21st century talent and market realities. An early result of this mindset shift was the appointment of the first woman to the Executive Board, Petraea Heynike, a long-time Nestlé executive. A highly experienced and credible appointment, it was seen as underlining a serious commitment by top management to improving gender balance at the top.

Bulcke passionately dismisses the idea that women should try to be the same as men. "Definitely not, because then we would lose what we are looking for … the other angle, the other way of seeing things. It would be going 180 degrees in the wrong direction. It's all about complementarity."

So what is that difference? "I would say that a man is someone who wants to be in the forefront. … I may be wrong but I believe that a woman is driven by a different dynamic. I would say she is more balanced and less aggressive. A woman's style is more inclusive and less 'winner-loser' oriented when compared to men, whose nature is often more competitive."

As with other male leaders such as Carlos Ghosn, head of Renault and Nissan, who has three daughters, personal experience and family life has led Bulcke to arrive at a very different vision for women in business in the future. "Success is linked to women being women and flourishing as themselves. It's only then that you have the complementary elements and that richness coming to the surface."

For a company of 283,000 employees worldwide with annual sales of CHF 110 billion in 2008, Nestlé's gender initiative is a large undertaking. If successful, the impact could inspire many other companies to follow suit. But Bulcke recognises, shrewdly perhaps, that "you cannot change a mindset such as this overnight." The first step, he believes, is to make the leaders at the company aware of the business opportunities that better gender balance creates and of the need for change through "inducing and convincing, rather than legislating."

In this early phase, Bulcke does not want to be too prescriptive about targets. "Let's do it … we have to balance this. But I am not saying this has to be a 50-50 balance or a 90-10 one. But perhaps somewhere in between. I don't want to put a figure on this. Otherwise, we could fall into the trap of fixing it into a time when we might have our 'photo-finish' moment for an annual report, for example, but then everything stops. That's not how we work as a company."

The focus will be on making the current leaders understand how much talent and resources are being squandered by the current gender imbalance. At the same time, Bulcke wants to make sure the process does not become too threatening to men in the company. "It should happen naturally. ... it should not be threatening, otherwise the men will become defensive and when people are defensive they are not successful."

At the core of his message to his top leaders will be the hard business case that a company such as theirs must understand women, who make up the bulk of their consumers. "It is about understanding our consumers ... who can understand female consumers better than women? I am not saying men cannot understand them. But again it is about having a complementary perspective. Above all, it's the business opportunity that will drive the gender balance initiative at Nestlé."

Case Study: Schlumberger
Putting men on the front lines

Schlumberger has a long history of diversity in terms of nationalities. After 40 years of recruiting and training in each of the 80-plus countries in which it operates, the company considers that it has achieved complete cultural diversity at all levels. No single nationality dominates its board or executive committee and among its top 32 managers, there are 12 different nationalities. There are, however, just two women.

Despite a decade's worth of effort, Schlumberger's leadership recognises that similar progress has not been made on women, and that the subject has become a strategic priority for the company. "Gender diversity is business driven," says Andrew Gould, Chairman & CEO. "Why deprive the company of access to half of the world's intellectual potential?"

In an interview, Jim Andrews, Schlumberger's former Gender Diversity Manager, explains why progress has been slow to date. "The problem is two-fold. Firstly, the oil and gas business has not been successful in marketing itself to women. Secondly, we as a company had not fully realized the importance of adapting the working environment to benefit from both genders," he says.

The company decided the issue was absolutely crucial and the timing was right to push much harder. The first decision was to elevate the role of the gender diversity manager. "In the past, the role had been staffed by extremely competent women, but they simply reported too low in the overall organisation. However, when I tried to get our senior women to take on the role, I got push-back from every single one of them. They supported the initiative, but didn't want to be seen as getting promoted because they were women. So I took it on. And I'm absolutely comfortable pushing it. It's easier for me to push the subject with a male-dominated management team. I've been with Schlumberger for 17 years, I've had both HR and operational roles, I've managed countries like Oman and Pakistan. I know our people – and, more importantly, they know me."

Andrews is frank and positive about the personal changes his new role has involved. "I'm finding it very pleasant to work all of a sudden with a majority of women. I've adapted my communication style. I'm marginally less direct and aggressive, although I'm careful not to change too much and I've certainly improved my listening style and become much more conscious of my body language. I was less aware of this before and it is helping me to develop. It is not always helpful for me to automatically take my natural style into a largely female setting where I need women to be completely comfortable. And, no, our women shouldn't change too much the other way – I'm fed up with them all acting like men!

"There are such interesting differences. Almost all women at Schlumberger think it is harder to progress as a woman. And almost all men think that it is easier for women. That means that at least we all have one thing in common – we all think it's easier for the other gender!

"The more I see of other companies on this issue the less I think it is on their Chairman and CEOs' agendas. True top-down commitment to the issue is still rare. Schlumberger is very serious about this. It's not a fad or fashion. We are utterly convinced of the business-driven need to get this right. And we'll continue to invest the time and resources required, just as we did on nationality. The unwavering support from the top makes my job a lot easier.

"We're still struggling with the 'how'. The bit we got wrong was perhaps due to some complacency as a result of having been so successful with nationality diversity. We thought that if we could recruit highly talented women, we could just fit them into a male-dominated culture and let things gradually evolve. The different nationalities we learned to manage over the previous 40 years were all men. We've learned that women are different and because of these differences, we now need to adapt the workplace to their needs.

"A good example is the overalls that our field engineers wear. They are sophisticated, fire resistant, one-piece outfits designed to protect our people even in extreme weather – both hot and cold. The design necessitates that a woman has to remove the top to go to the bathroom and we had a few cases of women not drinking for 24 hours before going out, to avoid this problem and its inherent exposure to the cold. These overalls were designed for men, before there were any women out in the field. Now, we have 2000 female engineers in the field. Is our workplace completely equal? No, and it's time to adapt it.

"The other big challenge is the middle part of careers – the 30s. Women, and perhaps men too, are a bit naïve early on in their careers and we haven't done enough to help them. The basic issue is that we didn't have enough flexibility. We were comfortable with career breaks, but hadn't made it a policy and hadn't particularly applied it to maternity breaks. We were also doing this on a case by case basis, but now we write it down, which in turn helps managers apply it more consistently.

"Women don't necessarily ask for what they want. That doesn't mean they don't expect recognition and rewards. And sometimes they quit because they don't get it – even without ever having asked for it. So one of the first things we did was to stop automatically accepting resignations from women without a serious effort from senior management to understand and fix the underlying issues."

How will Schlumberger know if it has succeeded? "When we have the same gender mix in our senior management team as we have in our new recruits," he says. "The majority of our senior management is home grown and has been developed internally rather than recruited externally. We've moved from 9% to 16% of middle managers being women in the past few years." Two of the company's businesses have recently appointed female Presidents, which is a first for the group. In addition, IT, Health, Safety & Environment, and HR are all now functions headed by women. "Ultimately we should get to around 30%, which is consistent with the percentage of graduating women we will hire this year. It may take us another 20 years to get there completely and across the board, but we are not prepared to let things stagnate in the future."

"It needs absolute management commitment – if you hope to let it happen naturally it just won't. This will give Schlumberger a tremendous competitive advantage. The available population of top female talent to non-women-friendly competitors is ever declining. We're already five years ahead of the game. And we'll be increasing our lead. It's a very hard issue to play 'catch up' on.

"We have little or no trouble recruiting talented women. The challenge is providing them with a career that allows them to balance personal and professional ambitions. When we figure it out for women, we will have created a better workplace for all our employees, the men included. It's not about working less hard. It's about taking the shackles off and letting smart, ambitious people decide how best to work."

Case Study: Bain & Co.
Women hold the key, but men control the lock

Bain & Co, the international strategy consulting firm, appointed a senior male partner in 2006 to head its efforts to increase the number of women in its leadership team in France. Olivier Marchal, Managing Director for Europe, Middle East and Africa, explains the firm's thinking.

"It is not a gimmick. Improving diversity at the highest echelons of a company is both a very smart and a fairly difficult thing to do. The current crisis has not changed our objective: on the contrary. Things just don't move unless there is a clear commitment from the top. When we gave one of our most senior partners this responsibility we achieved three things:

1. "We demonstrated to the men *and* women in our organisation that we were serious."

2. "We provided women with a channel to communicate at the highest level."

3. "We embedded the 'women imperative' at the heart of the management group agenda, through one of its more senior and respected members."

"It is not just about appointing someone to wear the 'women's hat'. The responsibility is linked to clear objectives and performance criteria. His job is to change the management team's attitude toward the gender issue and to identify roadblocks and implement specific action plans. He meets regularly with the women in the organization to identify with them the levers that can improve the situation and to convince them of the seriousness of the initiative. The senior partner's performance will be partly judged upon progress towards these objectives. Our aim is to increase the proportion of women within the leadership team by 40%, in line with the target set by our global Managing Director. Since January 2006, we have more than doubled the number of women in the consulting staff, so we have already secured a good pipeline and it's a major improvement."

Bain & Co. also supported the Women's Forum in Deauville in both 2007 and 2008, and in particular its "Men's Corner" (co-organised by Avivah Wittenberg-Cox's firm, 20-first) – designed for CEOs and other senior executives to discuss the challenge of getting more women into corporate leadership.

"We think the Forum is unique in bringing together two different perspectives: promoting the need for greater gender diversity *and* promoting the opinion of women on the most important issues facing our world," says Marchal. "The idea of the 'Men's Corner' was to have a space reserved for male CEOs and executives. It was to be more than just a safe haven where male leaders, unaccustomed to being a minority, could escape from the perhaps overwhelming dominance of women to a more comforting and secure environment. It also featured experience-sharing sessions, where leaders compared their analyses of the importance and difficulties of responding to the gender challenge. To improve diversity, women may hold the key, but men generally still control the lock."

Why does he believe CEOs should get serious about sex? "CEOs have constant quarterly hurdles to jump, but also a more important and longer term responsibility for the company they lead: to plan and prepare for the future. This requires the ability to develop and communicate a vision, and to strengthen the team and the culture that will carry it forward.

"Not integrating the gender dimension into this agenda will mean failing this longer-term responsibility; one should not be too frivolous about gender ... The reasons why diversity in senior executive circles is crucial are now increasingly accepted. It is a solution to the growing war for talent; an enrichment of the leadership team's collective intelligence; and a social responsibility imperative.

"In other words, getting serious about sex is now an accepted necessity. But those who have thought about it and already worked at it know that beyond the easy communication phase lie the rocky difficulties of implementation, and all the associated cultural barriers. Change in this area takes leadership, patience and conviction. That's why it is the CEO who must be the first to get serious about gender."

Chapter Six

CULTURE COUNTS
What Countries Can Do

"Countries that do not capitalise on the full potential of one half of their societies are misallocating their human resources and compromising their competitive potential."

World Economic Forum

Making bosses and babies

Ageing populations and falling birth rates pose serious problems for many economies, especially in the developed world. One obvious, but still often overlooked, solution is greater female participation in the workforce. Many cultures, and governments, still seem to believe that this conflicts with the goal of making more babies. In reality, the opposite is the case. Economic growth – through better use of women's talents and skills in the workplace – goes hand in hand with population growth.

This happy combination has been receiving growing recognition and endorsement from respected economic quarters. At first rather cautiously, the OECD noted back in 2003 that the evidence "suggests that an increase in the level of female participation does not necessarily come at the cost of a reduction of fertility." It went on: "When the increase in female participation is supported by appropriate work-family reconciliation policies, women tend to achieve a higher level of labour force participation without reducing fertility, and even perhaps with a small increase in fertility" (Jaumotte, 2003).

In 2005, in a report called "Babies and Bosses", the same august institution stated that "high female employment rates are not incompatible with fertility rates close to replacement levels ..." (OECD, 2005). The following year, *The Economist* magazine followed up by pointing out that "the decline in fertility has been greatest in several countries where female employment is low (*The Economist*, 2006)."

Then in 2007, Goldman Sachs, the leading investment bank, pronounced confidently in a study on gender, growth and global ageing that "in countries where it is relatively easy for women to work *and* have children, female employment and fertility both tend to be higher" (Daly, 2007).

About the same time, the European Union added its weight. "It is clear that countries that favour family-friendly policies in areas such as equal access to employment, parental leave for men and women, and equal pay, generally have higher birth rates and more women in work. They are also some of the best performing countries in terms of jobs and growth" (Europa, 2007).

Norway is a pioneer of gender equality in parenthood. "Both women and men must be able to take part in working life, social life and family life," said Kjell Erik Øie, state secretary of the Norwegian Ministry for Children and Equality, in a speech to the United Nations Economic Commission for Europe. "It is a matter of democracy, and to be honest: It should be a matter of common sense ... Europe faces two

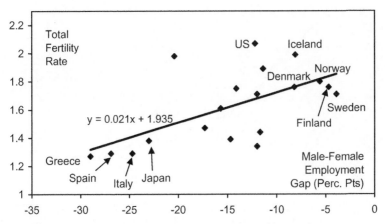

Fertility is Positively Correlated with High Female Employment[1]

---

[1]Source: Eurostat and Goldman Sachs calculations

main challenges in the years ahead. Firstly; to ensure that more children are born. Secondly; to ensure that more people work and work longer ..." (Economic Commission for Europe, 2007).

Women no longer want (or can afford) to be forced to choose between work and family. They want both. Countries, and their politicians, need to understand that if women find work does not accommodate family, then it is the babies who get left out of the equation. This phenomenon is still poorly appreciated, but it is scarcely revolutionary. It was once again the OECD, when advocating more family-friendly

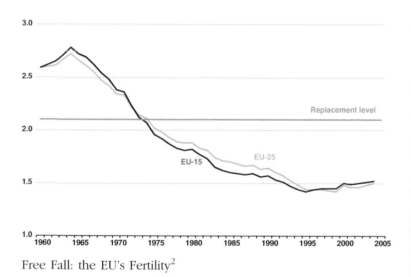

Free Fall: the EU's Fertility[2]

---

[2]Source: Eurostat.

employment policies, that pointed out in 2004: "Declining fertility rates are a concern in most countries, particularly in Japan, where birth rates are dropping as more people put jobs before childbearing. In Switzerland, as many as 40% of women at age 40 with university degrees are childless." Strong economies and manageable pensions systems, it warned, depend on both higher fertility rates and higher employment rates (OECD, 2004).

Best and worst: surprising results

An understanding of the economic opportunities that women represent for countries and companies would be incomplete without an examination of the important role of national culture and public policy in realising – or stifling – their potential. "No country in the world, no matter how advanced, has achieved true gender equality," says the influential World Economic Forum (World Economic Forum, 2005).

Which countries do best, and which do worst? The answers, it turns out, are sometimes surprising.

Goldman Sachs, in its analysis of national policies affecting women's participation in the workforce, finds that "the US – often considered the benchmark for structural economic comparisons – does not represent 'best practice' in terms of female employment." (See table overleaf)

Policies Affecting Female Employment (Daly, 2007)

Country	Gender Gap* (with one child)	Women's Employment Rate**	Public Spending on Childcare (as % of GDP)	Maternity Leave (weeks) Paid	Unpaid
Denmark	3.5	88.1	2.7	42	54
Sweden	9.8	80.6	1.9	40	85
US	17.4	75.6	0.5	0	12
France	18.7	74.1	1.3	73	162
Germany	21.2	70.4	0.8	38	162
Italy	40.9	52.1	not available	30	65
Spain	44.7	47.6	0.4	16	164
Japan	not available		0.3	8	58

Key to Table:

*Gap between % of men with one child who have jobs and % of women with one child who have jobs

**Percentage of women of working age who are in paid work

The World Economic Forum made a similar discovery in its first Global Gender Gap report in 2005 and its subsequent annual rankings. The rankings measure educational, health, economic and political gaps between women and men in different countries. In the overall 2008 index, the US was in 27th place, behind countries such as the Philippines (6th), Sri Lanka (12th), South Africa (22nd) and Cuba (25th). Even on economic participation and opportunity, the US came in 12th, behind countries including Mozambique, Moldova, Tanzania, Azerbaijan and the Philippines (WEF: The Global Gender Gap Index 2008 rankings).

World Economic Forum global gender gap ranking 2008
Focus on economic participation and opportunity

1 Mozambique	12 United States
2 Moldova	16 Russia
3 Tanzania	42 United Kingdom
4 Azerbaijan	43 China
5 Sweden	45 Germany
6 Norway	85 Italy
7 New Zealand	102 Japan
8 Philippines	110 South Korea
9 Barbados	125 India
10 Mongolia	130 Yemen

Not only do America and Britain not have a monopoly on women's economic opportunity. On this count, they are actually trailing behind some considerably less developed countries. We examine this more closely later in the chapter.

In the developing world, too, public policy choices have a huge impact on the opportunities available to women, and on the societies that these choices help to foster. As Danny M. Leipziger, World Bank vice president for poverty reduction and economic management, puts it: "The economic empowerment of women is not a women's issue, it is a development issue. Under-investing in women's economic opportunity limits economic growth and slows down progress in poverty reduction" (World Bank, 2007).

The Arab world has one of the lowest participation levels of women working (33% compared to a global average of 56%). "Full participation and empowerment of women, as citizens, as producers, as mothers and sisters, will be a source of strength for Arab Nations and will allow the Arab World to reach greater prosperity, greater influence and higher levels of human development," said Kemal Derviş, Administrator of the United Nations Development Programme (UNDP, 2006).

A tale of two countries

Annika is a successful young German IT entrepreneur. She runs her own company with her husband. The couple share the management of their internet business, which has eight employees and was founded nine years ago. He looks after the technical and financial side while she is responsible for marketing and account management.

They dearly wanted children, but Annika was convinced this was impossible if they were to keep the company going. She had no examples of successful work-and-family balancing acts anywhere around her. She also ran a community website for professional women where debate raged about choosing between family and work. So she had pretty well renounced having children. Then she got involved in a pan-European project, working with a group of French women. They were all senior and successful professionals, and they all had several children. They were astonished when she said she could not have a family and work. They assured her she could, with a bit of organisation. She took their word for it, and a year later, her first child was born, then three years later her second.

Balancing her entrepreneurial and familial roles was tougher for her than for her French counterparts. The delegation of childcare and household services was not easy to arrange, and her culture and social environment made her uncomfortable with handing over the whole day's childcare to others. While she struggles with care issues for her children, her company's business model – targeting online communities – is increasingly successful. She wonders how she will survive all the different demands on her time and feels unhappy at being an exception in Germany, which leaves her isolated from other mothers and families. She is, however, happy to be able to have achieved financial and professional success without renouncing a family life.

Contrast two neighbouring countries, France and Germany, to understand some of the multitude of issues affecting women's progress. They represent culturally different attitudes about women, work and families. They have taken almost diametrically opposite approaches since the 1950s. Today, France has the highest birth rate in the European Union after Ireland (where Catholicism still weighs heavily on the statistics), while Germany has one of the lowest.

France is also at the higher end of the European Union league table for the percentage of women combining work and motherhood. Germany is close to the bottom. In France, 67% of women with children under 12 are in paid work, while the figure in Germany is 56% (European Commission, 2007).

Germany would desperately like to have more children. The current fertility rate of 1.3 is nowhere near the required population replacement ratio of 2.1. At these levels, the country's population will be cut in half in a couple of generations. Germany has traditionally sought to encourage mothers to stay at home, offering child benefit allowances, and until recently has not provided the infrastructure, child-care and educational services to facilitate their combining work and parenting.

Significant changes are now underway in Germany, however, which are likely to narrow the gap with France. In 2007, the government introduced a new parent's salary, called *Elterngeld*, that pays parents between €300 and €1800 a month to stay at home. It was a woman minister – who herself has six children – who pushed the legislation through. The initiative opened up the option for fathers to take some of the leave, reserving two months for their exclusive use, in line with Swedish policy. If fathers take this time, the family is entitled to two additional months of leave. The old system of low flat-rate pay for parental leave has also been replaced by earnings-related compensation up to two-thirds of income.

The new German approach is beginning to see results. "After its introduction in early 2007 the number of fathers taking leave quadrupled to 12% in the fourth quarter of that year. Sixty per cent of fathers taking leave opted for two months, while 18% used the full 12 months' leave entitlement," says a report published by Britain's Equality Commission (Equality and Human Rights Commission, 2009).

In a further effort at change, Germany has instigated 'Family Pacts' encouraging cooperation between employers, unions, local government and service providers on things like child-care provision and training for women returning to the workforce.

These are positive reforms. It is very hard for women to work and have children in Germany, as Annika found. In addition to the lack of logistical support, the social pressure on mothers to stay home and take care of children is intense and comes from both men and women. Mothers who work are still referred to as *rabenmütter*, or crow-mothers, on the (mistaken) belief that crows make bad mothers because the chicks leave the safety of the nest before they can fly. Actually the mothers continue to feed the chicks on the ground! (Deutsche Welle). School hours are complex, varied and short. Children are tossed out of school after lunch, with the expectation that they will be caught in waiting, maternal arms. Many will respond that it is a cultural issue – that German women want to spend time at home with their children. But the falling birth rate does not support this interpretation. Nor is it supported by OECD data that found that only 6% of German couples with children under six wanted the father to be working full time and the mother not working – even though this was the actual division of labour for 52% of couples (Jaumotte, 2003).

Chancellor Angela Merkel has recognised that the situation whereby 40% of German women with university degrees are childless is unsustainable, as is women's absence from the country's boardrooms. "I do not believe that more people will want to start a family unless childcare is available and compatibility of career and family is assured," she said in a speech in early 2007 (*Knowledge@Wharton*, 2007).

By contrast, neighbouring France now boasts a birth rate of 2.0, the much sought replacement ratio. Although the Nordic countries grab the headlines on gender, France is an interesting model in its own right.

Half the graduates of the country's elite *grandes écoles* business schools are women. Surveys show that these alumnae actually have more children than the national average (2.2) and that over 80% of them work full time throughout their careers (Grand Ecoles au Féminin, 2005, 2007). An IDC report about the skills shortage facing the European high-tech industry noted that "the French government has been proactive in creating more of a gender balance in many professions ... Challenging careers, such as those in the networking industry, are more likely to be filled by full-time employees, regardless of gender" (Kolding and Milroy, 2001). Indeed in France, only 31% of employed women work part time, an option typically associated with poor career progression, compared with 43% in the UK, 46% in Germany and a massive 75% in the Netherlands (European Commission, 2007).

France has not yet cracked the matter of women in leadership, although the numbers are inching up. Only 7% of the country's *dirigeants*, or senior executives, are women (Les Femmes en France, 2007). But the talent pipeline is well stocked with highly educated women who have substantial professional experience in a variety of sectors and professions. Women in France account for the highest proportion of managers – 38% – of any EU nation apart from Latvia and Lithuania. The figure for female managers in Germany is 26% (European Commission, 2007).

The Anglo-American media have often treated the French economy with incredulity, particularly its combination of shorter working hours, inflexible labour markets and high youth unemployment. Nicolas Sarkozy was elected president in 2007 on a platform that included major labour reforms. Yet there is another side that is rarely highlighted, except in the stereotyped image of France as a hedonistic nation of wine, cheese and long-weekend lovers. It has accomplished what very few others have: a non-judgemental social norm of full-time, dual-career couples, complete with numerous children (three is currently the fashion). The French are well known for their emphasis on family meals and gatherings. There is no talk of choosing between career and family. They are not seen as antagonistic forces. If anything, there is a negative social judgement in affluent circles on women who do not work. (French dinner parties can be ruthless on the "uninteresting".) The government supports working parents in a variety of ways – daycare, tax breaks, parental leave, after-school clubs and subsidised training for babysitters.

Parents contentedly tuck their children into excellent, full-time state-funded schools at the age of three. Guilt is noticeably absent.

"French family policy shows a more comprehensive commitment to offering choices to all working mothers than many other European countries," says a BBC report. It points out that paid maternity leave was introduced in 1913. Generous parental leave and family allowances were brought in to replace wages forgone, rather than as "wages for motherhood", as in Germany. A quarter of children aged two and under, and 95% of three- to five-year-olds, were in public childcare, it said. Almost 80% of women aged 25 to 39, the main childbearing years, were employed in 1995. "The French have never set out, in the way that other countries have, to restore the place of women in the home" (BBC, 2006).

Judith Warner is a former *Newsweek* journalist who worked and had her children in France before moving back to the US. In the book she wrote upon her return, *Perfect Madness, Motherhood in the Age of Anxiety,* she says of her time as a working mother in Paris that "I used to live in paradise, and I didn't even know it" (Warner, 2005). She compares the mothering styles of the two countries and says much of the pressure on modern American mothers comes from themselves. She describes a generation of professional American women who decide to "opt out" of work and then transfer all their considerable ambitions to their progeny and their performance as mothers.

Frenchwomen are comfortable demonstrating that womanhood and power are not incompatible – even if the country is itself not yet entirely comfortable with this combination. In her presidential campaign, Ségolène Royal, Nicolas Sarkozy's defeated Socialist rival, made great play of being a woman and of her ability to understand people's everyday concerns (although both she and Sarkozy attracted much media attention for their respective, turbulent personal lives). Sarkozy half-filled his new government with some of the country's best female talent (such as Michèle Alliot-Marie as Interior Minister and Christine Lagarde, swiftly promoted from Agriculture Minister to Finance Minister.) In a notable turnaround from the usual media views, a May 2009 cover story of *The Economist* featured France as the leading economic model in the midst of economic crisis, well ahead of Germany, and even further ahead of the UK (*The Economist*, 2009).

France is rarely cited in the literature on women or gender. Yet it shows how successfully public policy initiatives can support women in their various roles. What is lacking is a concerted attempt by the private sector to take advantage of the highly educated women that a high-quality, egalitarian state education has produced. French companies have woken up to the potential of women only very recently. It will be interesting to see, over the next decade or so, if the country's public policy pull is matched by a more active private sector push, and whether France will be a pioneer in benefiting fully from the talents and strengths of women as leaders as well as mothers.

Times are changing very quickly in Europe. France's new government, formed in May 2007, is not the only one to have been crafted with parity as policy. It followed in the footsteps of José Luis Rodriguez Zapatero's Spain. A traditionally macho, southern European country, Spain is being dramatically transformed with gender as a catalyst. Zapatero's socialist government is pushing companies to give women 40% of the seats on their boards within the next eight years. There is even a movement afoot to change Spain's business working hours, full of late lunches and even later dinners, to make them more family-friendly, spearheaded by Nuria Chinchilla, an activist professor at IESE Business School.

Finland and Iceland also boast governments with real gender balance. What all these countries have in common is that, typical of Europe's approach in many areas, the driving force behind parenting and work issues is public policy. The private sector in Europe has been relatively absent from the debate until now. This is a key reason why women are still lagging behind in leadership positions in Europe. Grooming women for private sector power depends more on internal corporate initiatives than on government work/

life facilitation. But France and the Nordic countries show how far societies can evolve with strong and thoughtful public policy, namely, that it is possible for women to work full time, and for families to have children, without exhausting the one, nor breaking the other.

Imperfect deal in America

This is very different from the American model. Here, as in most areas, the impetus for change comes from the private sector. Several companies have tried very hard and quite successfully to bring women fully into the workforce. IBM, HP, Procter & Gamble, Xerox and Johnson & Johnson are companies which have for decades supported and encouraged women's employment and ascent into leadership. They understand the issues well, and have taught their managers to learn how to maximise the most diverse forms of talent – including the female kind.

Still today, and around the globe, American companies lead in promoting women all the way to the top, often proving to other countries that it can be done. The first, and for a long time the only, female CEO to feature in the UK FTSE 100 was Marjorie Scardino, the American head of Pearson. She was eventually followed in 2006 by a compatriot, Cynthia Carroll, the new boss of Anglo American. The first female CEO of a company in France's CAC 40 was Pat Russo, the (now-departed) American head of the newly created Alcatel-Lucent merger. IBM's first head of the North-ern European region was a woman, as is Microsoft's country manager in Spain, and the head of Intel France, then Europe, was Bernadette Andrietti.

However, data coming out of the US do raise questions about the costs and sustainability of this one-sided, private sector-only, approach. (See table on page 198, Policies Affecting Female Employment.) It was not until President Bill Clinton that the US's first legislation for (unpaid) maternity leave was voted in, so it is perhaps no surprise that women wanting to climb the corporate ladder have been faced with a very personal choice, echoed by feminist leaders. It was at a women's conference in Europe that Sheila Wellington, the then-head of gender think-tank Catalyst, told a sceptical audi-ence that women had to choose: family or career. After her speech came Gro Harlem Brundtland, the feisty Norwegian who then headed the World Health Organisation. She insisted that women's leadership was strengthened and informed by motherhood – and that this should never be seen as a choice or trade-off (WIN, 1999).

Corporate America has let women into the game – and allowed them to scale the heights – as long as they play by the existing rules. So women adapt. The costs seem high to cultures less convinced that work is life. Sylvia Ann Hewlett of the Center for Work-Life Policy in New York has found that 49% of women earning over $100000 do not have children. Forty-three percent don't even have a spouse. This is in striking contrast to men in the same position, who have both. Only 19% of men earning over $200000 do not have children, and only 17% aren't married. "Across a range of professions," concludes Hewlett, "high-achieving women continue to have an exceedingly hard time combining career and family," and face "brutal trade-offs" (Hewlett, 2002).

So where men make it to the top, complete with spouses and offspring, the women in America make it to the top, half of them childless. No matter how much one likes power and its influence on the world, the costs seem a bit steep. And it is taking its toll. The next generation just isn't buying it. Depending on people's perspective, there is lamentation or celebration about the "opt-out revolution" among well-heeled professional women.

Without formally admitting it, some top US business schools whisper about the fact that a majority of their alumnae do not "work" at all. This is no wonder, if they marry their business-school boyfriends. America's 24/7 version of workaholism, combined with an absence of public policy on the subject, pretty well guarantees that if children are on the agenda, one parent will have to gear down to find some time to have – and to hold – them. Add to that the competitive pressures put on perfectionist parents by a culture of excess, described in Judith Warner's book *Perfect Madness*, and the whole idea of balance is blown apart at the first sign of a nappy – or diaper.

As Joshua Holland, an independent American political journalist, wrote, it is not just the 20% gender wage gap that is the problem, or that white men comprise under a third of the workforce but hold nearly 95% of the top corporate jobs. "The real problem facing working women in the US is that we have the most inflexible workplaces in the developed world" (Holland, 2006).

The US is the only developed country – and one of only four countries around the world – which does not provide women with any paid maternity leave, according to the 173-nation Project on Global Working Families. This extraordinary fact puts the world's only superpower in a league with Liberia, Swaziland and Papua New Guinea. Ninety-eight of the countries studied in the project offer 14 or more weeks of paid leave (McGill University, 2007) (see table on page 198).

It is interesting to compare the sacrifices made by successful corporate women in the US with the results of a 2005 French study of a comparably élite group, the alumnae of the country's top *grandes écoles*. The survey, carried out by an association of alumnae, *Grandes Ecoles au Féminin*, showed that 97% of these French schools' former students worked, 88% of them full time. On average, 63% of these women earned at least half their household income, two-thirds of those over 30 had children, and 80% of these had two or more. In addition, they worked the same amount as their male colleagues at all ages (over 50 hours per week) (Grandes Ecoles au Féminin/IPSOS, 2005).

By looking back at a half-century of this transatlantic divide, with the US promoting private sector initiatives and Europe pushing public sector policy, it is clear that either/or approaches do not suffice. European companies, facing huge demographic challenges and talent shortages, have only recently woken up to the issues of women. It will be interesting to see whether they can build on the strong female talent base created in countries like France and the Nordic countries to achieve both greater opportunities and balance.

In contrast with US non-interventionism, the European Union sees a vital role for government. Vladimír Špidla, EU Commissioner for Employment, Social Affairs and Equal Opportunities, says that "far too many men and particularly women in Europe still have to make difficult choices between family life and a successful career. We must create the conditions for people to have both." He adds that "women continue to bear the lion's share of care responsibilities, so unless we put a stronger emphasis on gender equality and equal opportunities, low birth rates will persist, Europe will not meet its employment targets and we will not achieve our goal for a more prosperous and inclusive Europe" (Špidla, 2007).

The election of President Barack Obama in the US has created the opportunity to address these issues head on. We would like to think this opportunity will not be missed. In his book, *The Audacity of Hope*, Obama discussed the dilemmas and sacrifices facing parents – usually mothers – who work. He pointed out that most American workers cannot take a day off to look after a child without losing pay or eating into their vacation days. Obama threw the arguments of social conservatives back at them. "If we're serious about family values, then we can put policies in place that make the juggling of work and parenting a little bit easier," he wrote. "We could start by making high-quality day care affordable for every family that needs it" (Obama, 2006). The economic crisis may delay sweeping reforms, but it is time more Americans – women and men – became involved in the discussion.

Continents of contrast

We have already looked at western Europe, in particular France and Germany. One of the less-reported aspects of the gender question, however, is the egalitarian environment and relatively powerful social and economic position of women in the former Soviet Bloc countries of eastern Europe. The International Labour Organization says that "countries in central and eastern Europe … are among the highest ranking for women in management" (Wirth, 2002). Under Communist rule, for all its oppression, women worked and had children,

How the US trails the world

- Sixty-five countries grant fathers paid paternity leave or paid parental leave, with 31 offering 14 or more weeks. The US guarantees fathers neither paid paternity nor paid parental leave.
- At least 107 countries protect working women's right to breastfeed – breastfeeding breaks are paid in at least 73 of these countries. The US does not guarantee the right to breastfeed, even though breastfeeding is demonstrated to reduce infant mortality by between one-and-a-half and five times.
- At least 145 countries provide paid sick days for short- or long-term illnesses. The US provides unpaid leave only for serious illnesses through the Family & Medical Leave Act, which does not cover all workers, and it has no federal law providing for paid sick days.
- 137 countries require employers to provide paid annual leave. The US does not.
- At least 134 countries have laws fixing the maximum length of the working week. The US has neither a maximum working week nor a limit on mandatory overtime per week.
- At least 126 countries mandate that employers provide a day of rest each week so workers are not required to go for long periods without a day off. The US does not.
  "The US has been a proud leader in adopting laws that provide for equal opportunity in the workplace, but our work/family protections are among the worst," says Dr Jody Heymann, who is lead author of the study, founder of the Project on Global Working Families, and director of the McGill University Institute for Health and Social Policy. "It's time for change."

Source: "The Work, Family, and Equity Index: How Does the U.S. Measure Up?" (McGill University, 2007) and there were well-organised and highly subsidised schools and day care to take care of the children. It is no surprise that Germany's first female Chancellor, Angela Merkel, is an East German. She was raised in a system that taught her to think she could lead.

When the Wall fell, East German women discovered what "freedom" meant, as all their support mechanisms were discarded as relics of a backward Communist past. Once they learned the new West German rules of the game, the birth rate tumbled. The percentage of women in management has also gone into decline in recent years in countries like the Czech Republic, Poland, Slovenia and Romania (Wirth, 2002). The ex-Communist countries now have some of the "lowest birthrates in the world – and the lowest sustained rates in history: 1.2 per woman in the Czech Republic, Slovenia, Latvia and Poland" (Rosenthal, 2006).

Like Germany, the Czech parliament voted unanimously to double the payment given to women on maternity leave. The population of the Czech Republic is projected to drop by 20% over the next 40 years (from 10 million to 8 million). "In this year's election, every political party had a platform on family issues," said Professor Jitka Rychtaríková, a demographer advising the government (Rosenthal, 2006). The country is not likely to shift the statistics if it adopts German policies.

There are other big contrasts on gender and work policies between countries across Europe. While more than 40% of women work part time in Sweden, Austria, Belgium, the UK and Germany, very few women workers are part time in Bulgaria, Slovakia, Hungary, the Czech Republic and Latvia (European Commission, 2007). Holiday allowances – which impact on family life – diverge greatly too, according to Mercer, the human resources consulting firm. In France and Lithuania, full-time employees have an average of 40 days' holiday, including statutory leave and public holidays. But workers in the UK, the Netherlands and Romania have just 28 days, against an EU average of 34 (Mercer Human Resource Consulting, 2007).

The diversity in attitudes and policies is even greater across Asia. Where the Philippines boasts one of the higher percentages of women in management in the world (56% in 2003), (Caparas, interview with author) Japan has one of the lowest (9%) (Goldman Sachs, 2005). Women are Japan's "most underutilized resource", says Goldman Sachs.

Interestingly, the Philippines is one of the very few countries in the world where women are more active in starting businesses than men (Center for Women's Leadership, 2007). What makes it so different, in addition to having a female president, Gloria Macapagal-Arroyo?

"The Philippines is a matriarchal society," says Rhodora Palomar-Fresnedi, the Filipina former Global Head of

Diversity at Unilever. "Men pretend they run the show, but it's actually the women. There are a lot of jokes and puns about being afraid of the wife, the mother or the mother-in-law. It's the fun side of respect.

"A lot of women run the financial side of the household. It's common for husbands to hand all of their income to the wife and then get an allowance. So the concept of women in leadership positions is not alien. It's socially acceptable. Well-educated women have a lot of options to 'off-ramp' and 'on-ramp' again because there's a support system of maids and drivers and extended family. It makes working hard and delivering results easier, by taking away all the chores" (Interview with author, 22 February 2007).

Japan is at the other end of the spectrum, along with South Korea. Both countries lie at the developed nations' bottom end on several rankings related to gender. Japan has one of the lowest percentages of women in management, along with one of the lowest birth rates in the world (1.29). In a culture where women are traditionally expected to stop working upon marriage, or after the birth of their first child, not too many policy makers have realised that there might be a link between the two.

Goldman Sachs economists estimate that Japan's workforce will shrink by 10% over the next 20 years. "The Japanese government has attempted to raise the fertility rate by

offering everything from child-rearing subsidies to gifts …
but none of these have proven effective," says a Goldman
report entitled "Womenomics: Japan's hidden asset" (Goldman
Sachs, 2005). Japan still suffers from the traditional M-curve
of women's careers, where women enter the workforce in
their 20s, but leave between the ages of 30 and 44 to raise
their children, only returning afterwards, and usually into
part-time roles.

Strong cultural roles and expectations make Japan in some
ways comparable to Germany, although more extreme.
Women are putting off marriage and children, according to
Professor Mariko Bando, former head of Japan's gender
equality bureau. More than 17% of women in their 40s are
single, she told Britain's *Daily Telegraph* newspaper. "It's not
so bad in the civil service, but business remains the last stand
culturally for the Japanese man" (Evans-Pritchard, 2007).

Japan has much to gain from better use of women's talents.
"Increased female participation implies higher income and
consumption growth which we estimate could lift trend GDP
growth by 0.3 percentage points to 1.5% from 1.2% and boost
per-capita income by 5.8% over the next 20 years," says
Goldman Sachs (Goldman Sachs, 2005).

The government has tried to change things over the years.
It introduced an Equal Employment Opportunity Law in
1985, which prohibited discrimination against women in

employment and urged employers to treat women equally in terms of recruitment, job assignment and promotion.

In 2004, it improved matters in favour of women by changing the tax code, eliminating a special dependent exemption. Previously, the head of a household could claim both a dependent exemption and a special dependent exemption for a wife as long as she earned an annual income of less than ¥1.03 million. After the special dependent exemption was eliminated, this disincentive to work was taken away.

More could be done to provide good childcare facilities for working mothers. Goldman Sachs noted that the proportion of Japanese children at daycare centres stood at just 13% for children under the age of three and 34% for those between three years and the mandatory age for enrolment in school. The respective ratios in the US were 54% and 70%. The investment bank also pointed out that the government could relax immigration rules to enable foreign workers to enter Japan as nannies, a much more affordable option for most Japanese women than having to hire Japanese workers for the same role.

Long ingrained social attitudes need to change too. A Japanese government report, Gender Equality in Japan, referred to an opinion survey gathered in 2003–2004 which asked people to agree or disagree with the following statement,

"The husband should be the breadwinner; the wife should stay at home". Over 40% of respondents agreed with this statement (some strongly, some less so) compared with 18% in the US.

The same report suggested that attitudes were beginning to shift. Men who supported uninterrupted work for women had risen from 20% to 40% between 1992 and 2007, for example. However, data from 2001 showed Japanese men more averse to doing any work around the house than their counterparts in other countries, even when their wives were working. In a 24-hour period, Japanese men said they did 24 minutes of work in the house; American men said they did two hours' worth.

Awareness of the female talent that is being lost to the corporate world appears to be rising. A government White Paper published last year announced an objective to have 30% of women in all fields of business. A new buzzword in Japan is "daiba-shitii", alias diversity, as the *International Herald Tribune* explained in a colourful report on how large Japanese companies are beginning to pay attention to the need to break down barriers which force high-potential women to leave the corporate world. It quoted Hiroko Amemiya, a diversity officer at Tokyo Electric Power, as saying: "There is a whole generation of women employees who joined after 1987 that are missing, who would be eligible for management jobs by now" (Tanikawa, 2007).

China, by contrast, is in some ways comparable to the former Soviet bloc countries on gender. The burgeoning market economy is affecting the more egalitarian roles that women had previously, says Fanny Cheung, head of the Gender Unit of Chinese University of Hong Kong. The pressure to cut costs and boost productivity is eroding investment in child-care support and infrastructure. Relatively few reliable data exist about the situation of women in management in China. In large cities, some sources cite levels of 35% in senior management. Cultural norms are very different from those in Japan as women are used to working full-time and exercising leadership roles in a more matriarchal country.

Four Chinese business women appear in *Forbes Magazine*'s 2008 list of the World's 100 Most Powerful Women: Zhang Xin, co-founder and CEO of SOHO China; Yang Mian Mian, President of the Haier Group; Eva Cheng, Chief Executive of Amway (Greater China and Southeast Asia), and Jing Ulrich, Chairperson and Managing Director of JP Morgan Chase (China Equities). Success in promoting women is in part dependent on the share of women in the workplace. Mainland China, with 42% of its workforce being female, is well ahead of countries like India, where the share is only 25%.

Yet the wage gap between men and women in unskilled factory labour has worsened for women since the transition to the market economy, as companies have more power to set their own pay schemes, says McKinsey in an interview with the economists Li Bo and Chi Wei from China's Tsinghua University on current conditions for women workers in China. Closures of factories following the economic recession will hit women hard. Men are more likely to benefit from government investment in construction because they dominate in that industry (McKinsey Global Institute, 2009).

The World Economic Forum's 2008 gender gap index put China in 43rd position in terms of economic opportunity for women, far ahead of Japan in 102nd place. The country's one-child policy has, perhaps unintentionally, lessened the impact of motherhood on women's participation in the labour force. Yet it is storing up huge problems in the form of an ageing population and severe gender imbalance. Demographers have highlighted China's millions of missing baby girls, the result of infanticide, sex-selected abortion or neglect and abandonment. Chinese state media reported in 2007 that there would be 30 million more men of marriageable age than women in less than 15 years because of the one-child policy. In a front-page report, the *China Daily* said social instability could result from the inability of tens of millions of men to find wives (Associated Press, 2007).

China is one of the countries covered by a fascinating survey of medium-sized, privately owned businesses, which reveals women's prominence in senior management in many Asian countries. Grant Thornton, the business advice firm, compared the results with the UK, to striking effect.

Its International Business Report (Grant Thornton, 2007), covering 7200 companies in 32 countries, put the Philippines in top place, with 97% of businesses employing women in senior management. In China, 91% have women in the top echelons. This compares with only 64% of UK businesses.

The Asian region also showed the biggest growth in the percentage of women in senior management – from an average of 17% to 23% – in the three years to 2007. The highest numbers are in the Philippines, where women make up 50% of senior management, in Thailand (39%) and in Hong Kong (35%).

"At first sight it may seem staggering that our supposedly enlightened western democracy lags behind countries such as the Philippines, mainland China and Thailand," commented Alysoun Stewart, head of Grant Thornton's strategic services group. "This clearly challenges the commonly held perception that East Asia is less developed than the UK both economically and in the area of gender equality" (Grant Thornton, 2007).

In the table overleaf, we summarise the situation in the countries and regions we have examined, in relation to private and public sector approaches.

Different approaches to gender, work and families across the world

US	Europe			Asia	
Advances by women have been driven by well-organised and active women's groups and by private sector initiatives	Huge differences between countries			As in Europe, huge differences across countries, but even more extreme	
Equal rights legislation helped push women into the workplace in large numbers, but the US is now seriously behind on public initiatives to enable parents to combine work and family	Progressive policies largely pushed by government and not, until very recently, the private sector			In terms of enabling women's participation in management, Philippines leads the field, but China, Hong Kong and Thailand also do well	
Progress in certain forward-looking and/or talent-hungry companies but the bulk of work-life management is left entirely to individuals and families to work out	The UK is an exception in having public *and* private sector approaches; however, a high proportion of women work part time and there is a persistent gender pay gap			Japan stands out for the minuscule representation of women in management, and high female dropout rate	
Significant "opt-out" by professional women	Progressive	Middle of the Road	Conservative	High female participation	Low female participation
	France, Nordics, some ex-Communist countries, Spain (under Zapatero government)	Belgium, Netherlands, UK	German-speaking Europe (e.g., Germany, Switzerland) and South (Greece, Italy, Portugal)	China, Philippines, Thailand	Japan, South Korea

Public policy pull, private sector push

What can countries do? One of the items on the list must be to drop the exclusive link between mothers and children – just as companies would benefit from treating flexibility and work-life balance as part of business, rather than "a working mother's problem". If countries want people to have children, they need to enable them to combine dual careers with parenthood. This means investing in day care and all-day school rather than paying parents to stay at home. Studies show that subsidising childcare boosts the labour supply of women.

An essential lever in lessening the impact of maternity on women lies in greater involvement by men. The Nordic countries have tried to make parental leave neutral by letting parents share the allotted, paid year off for childbirth between them as they choose. In Scandinavia, fathers can take most of the time instead of mothers. Most other countries that have considered fathers have introduced paternity leave timidly, usually limiting it to a couple of weeks, which many men still do not take because of competitive corporate pressures. Whether mothers or fathers take time off for childcare, the costs and impact of their decisions on their employers should be the same.

As studies such as Sylvia Hewlett's "Off-ramps and on-ramps" (see Chapter Two) have shown, taking a break for children puts women at a disadvantage in getting back onto the career path. The longer the break, the harder it becomes. We are not suggesting that women or men should be told how much leave to take – this is an intensely personal matter – but simply that they should not be penalised in career and financial terms for the choices they make. If more fathers were able to share parental leave, this would be a big step towards reducing the damage to women's career prospects. It would also allow men to be fathers and make it the organisational norm for parents to take some time off for the important job of caring for their young children.

Progressive public policy is not enough to optimise women's talents, however. As the International Labor Organization has put it, "even Scandinavian countries, which stand out for their high level of women's participation in political decision-making and generous family-friendly policies, rank relatively low [on gender equality in the labour force] due to the low participation [of women] in private sector management jobs" (Wirth, 2002).

In an article on boardroom quotas in Norway, Pilita Clark of the *Financial Times* pointed out that Norwegian men were financially penalised if they did not take their allocated "papa leave" for new babies. "This [increase] will be excellent, a businesswoman said over a glass of wine one night, because until employers look at male staff and think 'he's going to disappear when the baby comes,' nothing will really change for women in business" (Clark, 2005). In a recent budget proposal, the Norwegian government presented a plan to increase the parental leave period reserved for the father from six to 10 weeks, effective from July 2009. Anniken Huitfeldt, the Minister of Children and Equality, explains that the objective is to help parents to become more gender balanced in their work and family roles. Huitfeldt says that sharing the parental leave period helps anchor the sharing of childcare responsibilities throughout childhood.

Countries grappling with these issues have other policy tools to consider. "Governments could do much more to narrow the gender employment gap: reducing tax distortions that discourage female employment, eliminating differences in retirement policies and subsidising childcare are three obvious examples," says Kevin Daly of Goldman Sachs (Daly, 2007). Other economists have suggested reducing tax distortions and boosting women's employment by lowering income tax for women and raising it slightly for men, an idea we cover in Chapter Eight.

So far, no country in the world has successfully combined progressive public policy with strong corporate initiatives to optimise women's skills. As the parallel pressures of demography, skills shortages and global competitiveness grow, a better conjunction of private and public sector forces will allow both parents to work and care for their families.

Otherwise countries could find themselves losing out on both economic growth and sustainable population growth.

The final word goes to Britain, which in recent years has witnessed public and private sector initiatives to help women advance in the workplace. In more than a decade of Labour government, sweeping initiatives have included the right for parents of young children to request flexible working, extended paid maternity leave, and help with childcare costs through tax credits for lower income working families. However, the Equality and Human Rights Commission called in 2009 for a radical overhaul of parental leave provision to make it more "gender-neutral", as in other parts of Europe. It argued that the UK government's focus on extending maternity leave risked entrenching the "career penalty" that women pay at work and not enabling fathers to play their full role in parenting. (Equality and Human Rights Commission, 2009)

Some leading employers, meanwhile, have taken part in private sector initiatives such as benchmarking their gender practices through the Opportunity Now campaign, and mentoring women for directorships through the FTSE 100 Cross-Company Mentoring Programme.

Still, the progress of women into the senior ranks of companies remains painfully slow, even stagnant. At the current rate, it will take 60 years for women to win parity in FTSE 100 boardrooms, the Equal Opportunities Commission calculated.

Further government measures on childcare, making it both more flexible and less costly, would do much to help women maintain and pursue their careers – currently more than 50% of women who work part time are in roles which under-use their skills. The Labour government pledged that all schools would offer extended hours for pupils from 8am to 6pm by 2010.

The economic potential of using women's talents to the full is huge, as Meg Munn, then deputy minister for women, underlined in 2007. "Enabling women to move into higher-paid occupations and roles could be worth between £15 billion and £23 billion a year to the UK economy." Munn also pointed out the crucial role of employers in tackling the under-representation of women in senior management.

What still holds women back from reaching leadership positions in the corporate world? Professor Susan Vinnicombe, director of Cranfield University's International Centre for Women Business Leaders, says focusing on motherhood and career breaks misses the bigger point that women are often alienated by prevailing corporate behaviour and expectations.

"A number of findings come out of all our research studies," she says. "One is that it's clear that women *do* want to make partner level or CEO, but they are very reluctant to engage in the process of 'impression management'. They feel very uncomfortable with it. They don't like promoting themselves. It's difficult to network, there are sexual innuendos and it's not easy for them to hang out with the men. So they're not looking up and saying: 'I don't want that job', they just don't want to engage in the process that gets them there. Also, they feel that if you're a very good manager or leader then it's your job to spot talent, not to require talented people to have to promote themselves to you."

It is not just a case of women not wanting to engage in "impression management", she says. "It's also that the selection of directors/leaders/partners is a very subjective process in which the clear bias is to choose individuals that look like the existing directors/leaders/partners. Inevitably this ends up being a very masculine model of leadership which excludes many women."

Vinnicombe believes it is time for the UK to move on from corporate benchmarking exercises and awards for diversity. "I think these benchmarking studies have deluded organis-ations into believing they have made progress. We're now into a culture of just winning awards. It's all about getting ticks in boxes for policies and processes, not about whether these things are actually having an impact and changing the numbers. Companies have made some progress, but not very much. The numbers of women at the top haven't changed" (Interview with author, June 2007).

A promising new initiative began in 2009 when the Pro-fessional Boards Forum, an organisation started in Norway by entrepreneur Elin Hurvenes, launched events in the UK to bring together chairmen of leading companies with highly qualified, aspiring women board directors. "There are not very many natural arenas where these two groups ... have an opportunity to meet," Hurvenes explained in a *Financial Times* article (Maitland, 2009).

Shifting the numbers will take a concerted effort on the part of companies, and of the men and women inside them, particularly those at the top. This is a universal requirement, not peculiar to one country or one industry sector. Changing the current trends requires a deeper understanding and appreciation of each other's ways of thinking, working, behaving and leading. The next chapter opens the door to this deeper understanding. It takes a closer look at 21st-century women, their careers, their expectations of work, and their attitudes to leadership and power.

Chapter Seven

FIGURING OUT FEMALES

" 'Powerful women': I must admit that phrase took a little getting used to. As a group, I think we've been taught that power is bad or scary. It needn't be either. Power is an opportunity – if we have the courage to use it. You're not given power. It doesn't come with position or title or wealth. To exercise power over the long haul – to sustain power – you have to earn it and you earn it by developing 'followership'. Power is a privilege, not a right. You have to use it in the service of others – or lose it. You have to have the interests of the institution at heart, not your own celebrity or ambition. Power demands integrity. The role of power is to have the courage to decide – to influence – and then to take responsibility for the consequences."

Anne Mulcahy, CEO, Xerox[1]

What companies need to know about women

Do women really want power? Are they ready for the top executive job or the seat in the boardroom? These questions

---

[1]Fortune conference, 2005

are rarely voiced openly, but they form an uncomfortable undercurrent through discussions in senior teams about how and when to promote women. Men who want power usually push for it, navigating organisational politics as natives of a familiar homeland. They look at women and think that if they wanted power they would do the same. But most women do not thrust themselves forward, especially if it means trampling on the opposition. They need to be pulled, or coaxed into it, and given some breathing space to acclimatise when they get there.

Rhodora Palomar-Fresnedi has seen this happen at Unilever, when she was Global Head of Diversity. The leadership team was considering appointing a woman to a senior role heading one of the businesses but decided that she was "not ready". Palomar-Fresnedi challenged this perception. "I said to them: 'I know when she's going to be ready – when she becomes a man.'" The woman in question got the job, and, at Palomar-Fresnedi's suggestion, was given support and protection from the limelight in her early days so that she could find her footing without feeling that people were waiting for her to fail.

This kind of intervention is important if more women are going to take the risk of running for the top corporate jobs. Women are not yet natives of the business world. They are like second-generation immigrants, with one foot in the culture of business and one foot in the culture of "women". They have arrived en masse and are seemingly fluent in the language of business, but are not as familiar or as comfortable with the unwritten codes and rules as men are. Most women retain their own ways of speaking and behaving. Or as one female managing director of a large American multinational put it: "It's just so tiring trying to be yourself. You have to fight so hard to resist attempts to modify your behaviour."

The current assumption is that only those who visibly want power are ready to exercise it. We question that assumption, with regard to both men and women. Perhaps those best able to exercise the responsibility and service of leadership (as defined by Robert Greenleaf, the author of the newly relevant *Servant Leadership* (Greenleaf, 1977)) are those not particularly hungering after power. Promoting more "power-reluctant" women could open the way for a greater variation in accepted male leadership styles as well.

We explore the differences which women bring to the corporate world in this chapter. They are differences that companies need to assimilate, rather than ignore, if women are to thrive and if companies would like men to demonstrate a variety of leadership styles too.

Discomfort with "politics"

Women in the business world look and sound resolutely modern, yet many still struggle with the internal stereotypes and expectations of an earlier era. They often lack self-confidence, and believe it is a personal weakness, not realising that lack of self-confidence is a general trait of the out-of-power, and even of very senior women. They are not yet convinced that they deserve all the opportunities open to them. This is not entirely surprising. A sense of great opportunity, tinged with insecurity, is a sign of the times: overt discrimination is less common today, but most women who make it into corporate power have stories of the farcical attitudes they faced not so long ago.

Anne Lauvergeon, CEO of French nuclear group Areva, who often features at the top of *Fortune*'s international Most Powerful Women list, likes to tell the story of when she was interviewed for an early job. To her amazement, her boss-to-be said: "You're a woman, why are you here and not at home?" Three months later, she reminded him of the remark, asking if he didn't agree that she was up to the job. He answered: "Yes, but you're not a woman."

When she chaired Qantas, the Australian airline, Margaret Jackson recalled how men in various walks of life seemed to find a conflict between her sex and her seniority. She told the *Financial Times* about an incident when she was on the board of BHP, the Anglo-Australian mining group, interviewing potential directors. "I walked into the room and this candidate handed me some papers and asked me to photocopy them. I explained to him who I was and he went puce.

It still happens. People look at me and they say 'but you're a woman'. It makes me laugh" (Tucker, 2007).

Catharine Furrer-Lech, a managing director and head of business development and strategy at UBS investment bank in Switzerland, remembers the 60 interviews she had when she joined Swiss Bank Corporation 18 years ago. "They told me I was far too overqualified for any job they would ever offer a woman, and then asked if my husband knew that I was out looking for such a job." When she worked her way up to the Executive Committee, the CEO asked for her help in suggesting what they should talk about over lunch. "They usually talked about the military or women, and with me there, they felt they couldn't do either but were at a loss to know what else to discuss" (Furrer-Lech, 2006).

Many of these more obvious barriers have now been dismantled. What women are still working on are more deepseated and harder-to-eradicate issues below the surface – both in others and in themselves.

Right from their first job, research shows that women do not negotiate their salary (or much else) – and that men do (Babcock and Laschever, 2003). So women end up with the salaries they are offered and men launch their professional lives by getting more. This simple matter of not asking, compounded by a less acute angle of salary trajectory from the outset, can amount to hundreds of thousands of euros or dollars over the course of a career. Eva, a Swiss entrepreneur running a high-tech firm, needed to hire 200 people. She was struck by the difference in interviewing and negotiating styles of the men and women she saw. "Women tried to prove why they deserved the job and how much they could deliver, while the men asked what the company could do for them and their careers" (Author's case study).

There is a deep-rooted belief among women that if they do a good job they will be promoted, recognised and rewarded. Telling them this is not true is an unsettling eye-opener. But companies would be doing them a service if they made clear to women that moving into leadership roles (as opposed to expert functional roles where women are better represented) takes more than doing things right. It also takes doing the right things, making sure that the right people know about them and having the political and communication skills to get others to support your ideas and objectives.

Women do not usually feel comfortable with the power structures in their organisations. Hierarchy itself, and its implicit positioning of people into one-up, one-down posi-tions, is actually far from women's search for establishing series of relationships between equals, as Deborah Tannen has effectively documented (Tannen, 2001). So they refuse to get involved. They disdain "politics" as being about self-promotion and power-grabbing, or they go to the opposite extreme, getting so involved that they fight more bloodily than men and leave casualties, male and female, in their wake.

Wanda Wallace, chief executive of Leadership Forum, a consultancy working with top teams and women leaders, says women can do a lot to help themselves. "I talk to senior men and women every day who are frustrated at the inability of women to make the organisation work for them," she says. "I think women struggle with how to use power, and how to compete without trying to kill someone. Competition is often more personal for women. Rather than saying: 'You win this one and I'll maybe win the next one?' they see it as black and white. Women need some understanding of the middle ground."

Does she believe companies have a responsibility here too? "I'm not saying it's women's fault. I do believe that you can't be a victim, and that you have to take some ownership, power and responsibility for your career and interactions with the organisation. The organisation has a responsibility too, to increase people's skills and to improve the ability to give quality feedback. Men are terrified to give women feedback because they are afraid it will become part of a lawsuit – that's probably more fear than it is rational. Companies also have a responsibility to make the talent succession and promotion processes more transparent. That could stop some of the biases that get in the way of women. It could stop this tendency to say of a woman: 'She's not strategic enough,' and substitute that with 'How do you know she's not? What's the evidence? What does she need to do to show strategic capability?'" (Interview with author, 20 February 2007).

When women condemn politics and stay away from it, they effectively remove themselves from the game, without consciously acknowledging it. They spend all of their time on carrying out the content of their job description. Smart employers know this – and love them for it – which is why women are so appreciated in middle management. They make great worker bees. But the worker bees become frustrated when they see that the colleagues who get promoted are the ones who have spent a lot of time networking, building alliances and "managing up", and a lot less time, at least from a woman's perspective, actually getting things done.

In recruiting interviews, women who are unable to take on international assignments tend to say so if they are asked. At a meeting about gender issues with an HR director and her young male colleague in a large Norwegian company, the ambitious and successful young man said that doing this was "just stupid". "It hurts your image and potential. My wife works and I'm not really mobile, but I certainly said that I was. When the time comes, and if I'm proposed for a move, I'll simply decline it." His female boss was shocked at discovering these "rules of the game", realising that she, like other women, had been transparent about her lack of flexibility in job interviews.

Women value authenticity. According to a survey of 516 executive and professional women by Aspire, a UK coaching and leadership development firm, the top things that motivate them are, in order of importance:

- making a difference;
- being challenged;
- believing in their company's direction;
- a sense of satisfaction in their team; and
- recognition.

Just under half said "flexibility". Money came bottom of the list (Aspire, 2006).

The women were asked how they would improve diversity programmes in their company. Many of them said they would put greater emphasis on appreciating "individual uniqueness". Separate research from the Center for Creative Leadership, which operates campuses in North America, Europe and Asia, put authenticity at the top of women's list of values (Ruderman and Ohlott, 2002).

The head of a large American company was giving a keynote speech to a high-profile gathering of his top women. He insisted that mobility was a key part of leadership development in the firm and described the ideal female career of the future, showcasing a young woman called Juliet. Juliet had a fast-paced and brilliant career, moving countries every few years. His audience was incredulous. He neglected to mention that he himself had never moved, and was actually still living in the same neighbourhood of the city where he was born.

How, then, should women align the need for "political" competence, which often requires hiding thoughts and feelings, with their deep-seated need to do just the opposite?

Let us start with the politics. Being politically savvy can help in setting priorities and managing time. One of us first heard about the 80/20 rule – as applied to organisational politics – from a very young male colleague, flush from his MBA. The concept is simple, he said. You spend 80% of your time doing your job, and 20% of your time telling others what a good job you did. When women hear about this application

of the rule, generally they hate it. They are much more comfortable, particularly in their 30s, with doing things their way:
to spend 100% of their time on the specifics of their job,
preferably behind the closed door of their office, and then
rush home to take care of the rest of life.

Globalisation and corporate restructuring have ensured that
almost everyone in business today has too much work. Managers have little time to manage anyone any more, especially
people who do not make any demands or remind their
bosses of what they have accomplished. In this high-intensity
environment, those who keep their heads down and simply
work are appreciated when something needs doing, but
passed over when the search is on for people to promote.

One woman executive described it beautifully. She was
senior director in her division of a big consumer goods
company. When a new country manager was appointed, he
moved into his office four doors down from hers. She was
so busy with her work that she never quite made it down
the corridor. One day, a month after he arrived, he knocked
on her door and said: "Why don't I know you?" She raised
her head from her over-brimming desk and sighed: "Because
I'm so busy doing my job." He said: "Then you'd better
rethink your job definition."

This is where management and leadership training tailored
to women's needs is useful. As Linda Babcock and Sara

Laschever outline in their book *Women Don't Ask*, training is one of the great ways to improve women's sense of control and readiness to negotiate. It helps them understand the reality of the workplace and produces "dramatic results, completely eliminating the gender gap in [negotiating] performance" (Babcock and Laschever, 2003).

We agree with Warren Farrell, the author of *Why Men Earn More* (Farrell, 2005), that a better understanding of the workplace, its rules and its opportunities helps women make choices to correspond with their ambitions. Training specifically designed for women is an effective mechanism for waking them up to the reality of the business world. We also agree that it is preferable not to recreate same-sex ghettos internally to combat the informal same-sex networks that exist. Which is why we recommend that organisations use external leadership programmes for women. It is a complicated reality that women benefit from these courses but that they can create unfortunate backlash or resentment if they are delivered internally (especially since men are not usually offered similar treatment). Outsourcing women's training is a compromise that allows companies to reap the benefit of empowered women while reducing the negative impact on men.

Programmes of this kind are just beginning to emerge in Europe after having been launched by business schools like Harvard. A host of private companies have offered courses across North America for the past decade. Several business schools (Harvard, IMD, INSEAD, Cranfield University in the UK) and private companies (Aurora, Aspire, 20-first, women's associations) have created tailored development opportunities for women since the turn of the century.

Even the most sceptical women are usually converted, delighted to discover that the issues they face are not theirs alone. Probably the most striking feature of such programmes is the sense of relief that permeates the room. For many senior women still working in largely male environments, it is the first time in their careers that they can let their hair down, relax and behave naturally, surrounded by a group of empathetic peers.

The growing popularity of women's conferences and leadership training is testament to the fact that women find value in learning and developing in an environment specifically designed for them. Here, self-effacing communication styles are not interpreted as lack of ambition. Women can express themselves in their own language, and be heard. They can step back and get a wider perspective of their situation and how they can advance their own careers. They feel energised and strengthened.

In Chapter Two, we looked at what business schools are doing to increase the low numbers of female students and staff. The learning environment which many women prefer is utterly different from the typical business school model. Sharing vulnerabilities, exchanging stories, swapping advice, and thinking together in non-competitive ways contrasts with the bell curves, case studies, self-promotion and competitive team structures that are the building blocks of the typical MBA.

As we noted in the section above, however, women can still feel insecure in the corporate world – and men can feel they are walking on eggshells around women. It may be hard for a woman to explain to her boss why women-only leadership courses matter. She may think it is dangerous to be explicit about issues of self-confidence because it could feed the view that she is not quite up to the harsh realities of a competitive world. He may doubt that differences matter, and see any focus on them as discrimination or condescension. Some women also buy this argument. If they have succeeded themselves, they do not see that others may have more difficulty or need a little coaxing and support. It can sometimes be men who are first to spot that there is an issue.

Close Up: The conversations that matter

Women can miss out on the informal conversations men have at work, which can ultimately identify who has real influence on the business. "These are informal, deep, off the record conversations," says Austin Hogan, head of human resources for operations and technology at AIB Group, Ireland's largest banking group. "These are the most important conversations that we have and they usually result in great decisions or interesting avenues to follow. As males, we're very comfortable having them. My observation is that women aren't as comfortable with this. And most of my male colleagues aren't comfortable having them with women. Both parties have to 'learn' the value of informal sharing of ideas that build trust and confidence – the very things that help to identify leaders."

He says conversations of this kind between senior men often take place very early or very late, outside the normal working day, and at a time when women are often occupied with other commitments – mostly essential family time. "I have four women managers working for me who are absolutely fantastic. But they don't naturally get a chance to take part in these informal conversations at work. I make a point of taking them along when I'm going to see a senior male colleague so that they get an opportunity to hear how these conversations go, and to get asked and give their opinion on the business. It's really important that everyone has every opportunity to shine – my managers have the best ideas and that must be true in most organisations. Perhaps it is a backhanded compliment, but I think I have the managers that I deserve and more than just me needs to know that directly – that's what these conversations are all about."

Careers are not linear

One of the biggest and least managed differences between men and women is that of their career "life cycles". Like many of the other differences between genders, this one is largely socially and culturally constructed, but identifying its historical source does little to alleviate its consequences. Recognising the realities of modern life, and the many personal and professional responsibilities increasingly shared by both men and women, will help companies minimise these consequences. "Divided responsibilities," writes Warren Farrell, "are the wave of the future – not just for women, but for many men, too ... making use of the gift of working women, then, involves treating women as pioneers in helping companies adapt to the divided responsibilities that will be a twenty-first-century reality" (Farrell, 2005).

Colleen Arnold, General Manager of IBM Europe, a company that has invested more than most in diversity, described an archetypal "female career moment". She was competing with a male colleague for a promotion to vice-president. Pregnant at the time, she did not dare announce her pregnancy to her boss until he had made his promotion decision. So she held off, working hard and wearing increasingly large and loose-fitting outfits. One day, he called her into his office to tell her that she had the job. He was horrified to see his newly appointed VP faint at his feet. As he bent over her in concern, he asked: "Is there anything I can do for you?" Having recovered, she cheerily answered: "No, but I'll need the summer off" (Arnold, 2006). That women still feel the need to take on these kinds of disguises, even in the most enlightened companies, shows how much progress still needs to be made.

Women, particularly if they have children, have what has been described as an M-shaped career curve. This reality differs from country to country, depending on the amount of support for working parents the environment offers (see Chapter Six). They start out strongly, encounter some turbulence in their 30s which often makes their career progression plateau or dip, then pick up again somewhere in their 40s. Men traditionally start out in their 20s, rise in a straight line, then stop abruptly at retirement. Of course, both men and women may plateau at some point, or be "downsized", "delayered" or "re-engineered".

These broad differences in career and work cycles may help explain why women and men differ when it comes to naming the decade of their lives they consider best. According to HSBC's "Future of Retirement" surveys, being in your 20s is the best decade for both sexes. What is interesting, however, is that more men than women choose the teens, 20s or 30s as their best decade, while more women than men choose the 40s or 50s.

Women's careers often peak a decade later than their male peers. Retaining 30-something women who leave to balance life is a big issue, as is an understanding of how to manage their return after a career absence. A growing number of companies are launching programmes to lure former employees back from career breaks.

In 2005, *Harvard Business Review* published an article by Sylvia Ann Hewlett and Carolyn Buck Luce called "Off-Ramps and On-Ramps" which has elicited much attention and interest, and which we cite in Chapters Two and Six (Hewlett and Buck Luce, 2005). It was followed by Hewlett's book of the same name. The terminology was not universally appreciated by women, however, highlighting important differences between the US and Europe in perceptions of gender and careers. At a small lunch of senior women leaders in Paris, hosted by then-French Trade Minister and subsequently Finance Minister Christine Lagarde, there were objections to the implication that having babies was "off-ramping". What was needed was simply a redefinition of what careers look like, not an image of women "leaving" and then "returning", with the inevitable costs in terms of earnings and reputation. They felt the terminology reinforced the belief that the "normal" career path is an upward ramp with no bumps.

Getting the metaphors right may seem like quibbling but, in this area, vocabulary and language are extraordinarily important. In altering attitudes, language is one of the more powerful tools available. It can reflect an acceptance of, and adaptation to, an existing system, or it can signal an entirely new way of approaching the issue.

For a future in which 40- or even 50-year working lives are likely to encompass multiple, flexible and non-linear careers, getting a grip on new terminology is essential. A good metaphor is one of building blocks, not the old-fashioned, square, wooden kind that need a solid, wide base, but rather those new, colourful, Frank Gehry-style systems, which clip into each other in endlessly creative ways. They can be built upwards, sideways or star-shaped in an infinite number of individual patterns, crafting new concepts that move beyond "career as pyramid" to a more exciting notion of "career as snowflake".

As our societies age, and people work longer, the career experiences of burned-out men in their 50s and 60s may well start to resemble those of women in their 30s – full of a desire for flexibility and balance. Women in their 50s and 60s may start to resemble men in their 30s and 40s – set on promotion and power. Successful older women may be delightedly wading deeper into the world of work while their husbands are just as delightedly dreaming of sailing off to sea or retiring gently on a golf course in the South of France.

This is not fantasy. Some of the most powerful women in the corporate world have partners who have taken a back seat or early retirement. Moreover, a study of mothers' and daughters' attitudes to retirement, commissioned by the MetLife Mature Market Institute in the US, found that most of the younger women expect to retire later than 65; 17% expected to retire at 70 or later, and 6% said they may never retire (MetLife, 2007). Here, as in so many other areas, large companies stand to gain by managing these complementary cycles rather than suffer the rather costly consequences of ignoring their existence.

Below we describe the three key phases of female career cycles.

Phase 1: ambition

Alison is 28, British of Chinese origin, and going places. Born of modest immigrant parents, she is ambitious, energetic and attractive. With low expectations from her parents (who reserved their ambitions for their son), she has run headlong into success at every turn. Since grade 1 she has excelled at school, working hard and playing by the rules. After an excellent degree from Oxford, she went into consulting. A few years later, like most of her peers, she flew off for a graduate degree. Upon finishing her MBA, she joined a top investment bank because that was the highest-status, highest-salary job, considered the top of the b-school punching order. The best of the best, competing with her cleverest peers for the spot she got.

She sees no barrier or cloud on her horizon. She has been recruited and rewarded at every turn. She is supremely convinced that the world is hers to discover, that she has only to continue excelling at her job, bringing in the numbers and delivering value to her firm. When she hears older women speak of women's issues, or sees some of her colleagues organising women's networks in the bank, her judgement is quick and absolute. They are complaining about an obsolete issue and are probably just not good enough to get ahead. She will prove – with her brains and will – that she can get to the top. No problem.

In this sense, the women's movement has created what it set out to achieve: a level playing field, where women, completely unconscious of their gender, can go out and win. Alison is unencumbered with stereotypes or notions of limits or hang-ups about ambition.

But precisely because she has had so much success and so little trouble, she is completely unprepared for the rather sudden and perplexing culture shock just around the corner. She does not want to listen to – or even associate – with older women. They make her uncomfortable, with their choices and compromises and advice. She does not want to be like them, so she keeps her distance.

The 20s is an important and rewarding decade for the modern woman. It is a time when women can fully flaunt their potential. They need to make the most of it, getting the best education possible, the most international travel, and as much job experience as they can.

Companies also need to make the most of this decade with their female talent. Some have realised this, and now cram a lot of early training and travelling into this decade. Energy companies, in particular, which require international mobility of their managers, have started to move their staff much earlier.

Phase 2: culture shock

Rebecca has just celebrated her 33rd birthday. She is a brilliant, slightly brittle over-achiever. She has played the consulting game, worked round the clock and learned to swear like a sailor. But all of a sudden, having married a former colleague, her top priority in life has dramatically shifted: now she wants to start a family. She is agonising over the consequences for her chances to make it to partner. After a decade's round-the-clock investment in the firm, she'd like to hedge her bets. There is not a single woman partner in her office – in fact there are hardly any in Europe. Most women before her have chosen to leave or have taken a staff role after having children.

Rebecca suspects this is not just an issue of maternity. She has been in the potential partner pool now for a couple of years, but the feedback she is getting is, suddenly, less flattering. After having had rave reviews and top performance evaluations, the tone has shifted. Partners are suddenly suggesting that she may not be quite up to joining them. She does not have quite the presence and gravitas required, and has not demonstrated her ability to sell. These are issues she had never heard of and never expected. The shock is absolute, and the fury not far behind. She decides to have her kids, downgrade to second-class administrative status at work, and leave the company when she is ready to gear back up.

So what happened to Rebecca? The same thing that happens to many ambitious women in this decade. Squeezed by the simultaneous pressures of personal and professional life, they suddenly experience culture shock. Typically, they delay having children into their thirties. The average age for first children has been in continuous rise and is now around 30 in many European countries (Rosenthal, 2006). Most start to dream of motherhood some time after their rather late marriages, and usually between the ages of 30 and 35.

When do most companies formally identify the high potential pool of employees to receive all the attention and development and be groomed for power? When do professional service firms start to turn up the heat in their "up or out" policies? Between 30 and 35. Many of them even have those particular ages written in black and white in their personnel policies. If companies had tried to design a system to exclude women – which they have not – they could not have done a better job of it.

Babies aren't the half of it. The real issues lie hidden and unacknowledged in the much harder to reach recesses of gender incomprehension. Even women without children bump into the complexities of managing this decade at work because all of a sudden, and without any warning that most women are aware of, the rules of the game subtly shift.

Success in the 20s was simple, and based on the same rules and behaviours that served women so well at school: be a good student, work hard and do what you are told. But in the 30s, this kind of attitude keeps women firmly glued to a rather sticky floor of junior roles. Where "productivity" is the key word of the 20s, "people" is the key word of the 30s. Potential is measured not just on how well they perform (that's the assumed minimum) but on how well they manage people, build networks of influence and start convincing others that things could be done better if people followed their brilliantly innovative ideas – and, by the way, that their extraordinary last quarter achievements merit a major promotion to a job overseeing a big chunk of profit-and-loss. The kind of ambitious young men who get ahead seem to be innately endowed with the skills to manoeuvre through this maze. Are political realities hardwired into their genes or is the organisational maze designed to respond to ambitious men's ways of relating to each other, competing and jockeying for position? The current system is dominated by what are commonly referred to as alpha males. Is this best for business?

"The business world swarms with alpha males (and females). Although there are no hard numbers to support this approximation, we estimate that alphas comprise about 75% of top executives ... The healthy ones are natural leaders trusted by colleagues, respected by competitors, revered by employees and adored by Wall Street. But other alpha males are risks to their organisations – and sometimes to themselves (Ludeman and Erlandson, 2006)."

Women can find alpha male rules incomprehensible – assuming they can see them in the first place. These men are generally informed and helped by the networks of peers and mentors who often hang out together after work in a bar, or meet on the golf course or in management retreats for exotic pursuits, such as boar-hunting in Nordic forests.

These networks are not generally constructed to exclude women, but most men are still surprisingly uncomfortable inviting the girls along. They worry about all kinds of things: how the invitation will be perceived, the potential lawsuits they risk, what their wives would say, and frankly, whether they wouldn't just be happier in all-male company.

Women, and gender research, repeatedly cite the lack of informal networks as one of the major barriers to progress in their careers. These become increasingly important with age, starting in earnest in the 30s. Miss this boat, and you lose the foundation on which promotions are built: who you know, and who knows you.

During the 30s, these issues of networks, visibility and over-work too often combine in an overwhelming wave which washes women from the fast track, almost without their knowing what hit them. The challenge for women – with or without children – is to learn the reality of organisation rules early, to see the wave before it hits and build a raft which will let them surf rather than sink.

For companies, it means being prepared to give parents, not just women, a breather. Focusing parental policies on women reinforces all the stereotypes and disadvantages tripping women up today. As careers lengthen, giving mothers and fathers (and other 30-somethings in danger of burn-out) a few years' grace to coast, to be an internal consultant, or to take up a new skill, need not be an unprofitable exercise but a useful investment in the future.

Companies are feeling the full brunt of dual-career partner-ships. Where once they could send employees around the world at a moment's notice, with a "trailing spouse" picking up the pieces, the planning and the kids, today both men and women are increasingly immobile because of their part-ner's careers. Imaginative solutions are required, such as the British Foreign Office's job-sharing deputy heads of mission in Slovakia, a husband-and-wife team who swap with each other every four months the roles of full-time diplomat and full-time parent (Maitland, 2006).

Companies' reluctance to adapt to women's and men's needs for flexibility stems partly from a fear of opening a Pandora's Box. We may think we live in a global, networked economy of knowledge workers, but many organisations still focus too heavily on the hours put in, rather than the outcomes achieved. As women (and many of the new Generation Xs and Ys) push for more flexibility about where and when they work, managers are not necessarily ready to let go. The belief in total commitment is deep. The generation now running most big companies gave their lives to their careers. They expect others to do the same. Most expect their executives to put their jobs ahead of their kids. *They* did. Younger generations are starting to reject this paradigm and women never really accepted it in significant numbers. Forced to choose, and with no back-up at home, most human beings will put their kids before their company. Companies which still force parents to choose between family and work will find the talent wars give employees the upper hand in their growing demands for flexibility and autonomy.

This vicious circle can be broken to everyone's advantage. Bernadette Andrietti heads Intel France. She has introduced changes to the company's culture, and to industry practices. She has allowed her entire staff of a couple of hundred people including secretaries to go on flextime. Typical of people in the high-tech sector, she knows that fixed ideas of how, when and where people work are largely obsolete and that technology allows huge amounts of flexibility. She also recognised that it was the application of technology to the pragmatic realities of life that would have the greatest impact. Instead of marketing to the converted, she took technology into the home: in 2004, Intel France displayed its products at the Home show in Paris, in addition to the more traditional Technology show (Andrietti, 2004).

Case Study: flexible leaders at Booz Allen Australia

Sarah Butler and Vanessa Wallace are partners in the Sydney office of Booz Allen Hamilton, the global strategy consulting firm. Butler was elected partner in 2000 after 10 years at the firm, while she was on maternity leave with her first child. She has since had three more children. She has typically taken six to 12 months' maternity leave and returned to working at 60% of full time. "At times I've flexed this, some-times working longer, then making up time later on. I tend to find some weeks I need to work four or five days, others I work less or take longer holidays – driven by how many clients I am serving at the same time," she says. "Vanessa has three children and worked part time earlier on, and restricted her travel so she could be in Sydney, and is now full time as the children are all a little older" (Interview with author, April 2007).

Women represent three out of 10 directors and three out of 12 principals in the firm in Australia – comparing very favour-ably with Booz Allen globally, where women typically account for less than 10–20% of these senior posts, she says.

In Australia, flexible work arrangements are open to men and women and there has been take-up of part-time deals at most levels. At one stage, take-up was split pretty evenly between men and women. However, the overall numbers working flexibly are still small and a harsher market environment has helped to depress levels of take-up. The firm is looking at other models, from working a set number of hours a year to buying extra time off, to working on a retainer or contractor basis, to tailoring arrangements to an individual's needs.

So is this an exception, or an example of culture change? "Probably a bit of both," says Butler. "I think Booz Allen is far ahead of many on having a good set of part-time policies and more importantly the culture to encourage this. I firmly believe I could not have done what I have done anywhere else. In particular for Vanessa, who was the guinea pig, the managing director strongly sponsored her – and this set an example. Now our directors in Australia are all mostly Generation X and all have children – many young, some teenagers – and also many have spouses who have worked or are still working, so they see the 'other side' of juggling, which helps on the culture change."

On the other hand, flexibility varies between the firm's offices globally. "We tend to see that a few offices have lots of women and more take-up of flexible working arrangements, so there are microcosms – and in particular this is linked to the potential to cut out travel in certain geographies, a key issue in commercial strategy consulting. Also, the practices serving government clients have been much more successful at retaining and advancing some great women, and this also reflects a higher proportion of women in their clients. I have always had absolute support from clients on working part time. If questions have been raised it's more often been internally at corporate level on the sustainability of a 60% model, but luckily this has dropped off!"

Phase 3: self-affirmation

After 40, women have either weathered the 30s acceptably and find renewed ambition and opportunity, or have decided to leave, either physically or mentally. Provided they have managed to navigate the first two phases described above, they are in a position of relative strength. They have established their expertise, woven their networks, and built a credible track record. At home, they have got over the most exhausting part of parenthood, and they and their partners have tucked the littlest into full-time school. Many are ready to reinvest professionally and at a time when success, self-confidence and maturity combine to ignite or augment ambition.

The fashionable idea, prominent in MBA programmes, is that to be marketable you have to change companies every five years. This can work for some people. But for many women, particularly those who want to combine career and family, finding the right employer at the start is a strong element in their career chances. It is commonly believed that long careers with companies went the way of the telex machine, but this seems not to be true. An interesting study by Ann Huff Stevens shows that many people in the US stay with the same employer for a long time. "In 1969, average tenure in the longest job for males aged 58–62 was 21.9 years. In 2002, the comparable figure was 21.4 years. Just over half of men ending their careers in 1969 had been with a single employer for at least 20 years; the same is true in 2002" (Huff Stevens, 2005).

Similarly, a study by the International Labour Organization has found no evidence that long-term employment relationships are dying out in Europe. Job tenure in Europe averaged about 10.5 years between 1992 and 2002, with a slightly rising trend, according to Peter Auer, one of the authors. The figure for Japan was 12.2 years (Auer, Berg and Coulibaly, 2006).

Women can be intensely loyal to companies which treat them well, partly because they know there are not yet that many of them but also because longevity works for women. It makes sense for women to invest big in their 20s, negotiate some flexibility in their 30s and then gear up into leadership roles in their 40s and 50s.

This is often when companies can reap the benefits of their investments in women and derive a great deal of value.

Take Vivienne Cox, who was BP's head of gas, power and renewables until 2009. She was with the company for over 25 years. In 1998, Rodney Chase, deputy chief executive, offered her a promotion to head a division in the company's downstream division. She was 39, had just had her first child, and turned the promotion down on the grounds that she did not want to travel all the time, work weekends and put in the constant late nights she assumed that the job required. He rejected her refusal, and promoted her because he wanted to show that the job could be done on her terms.

Cox has since become one of the *Financial Times*'s top 25 businesswomen in Europe, and received a host of other accolades. The company benefited from her loyalty and her distinctly different way of managing and seeing the company's future. A regular organiser of unconventional meetings, with themes like "Whither democracy?", Cox thought, early on, that many things her company did were unsustainable. In 2005, it was under her leadership that the company launched its renewables business, investing some $8 billion in finding new sources of energy (Interview with author, 30 November 2006).

Catharine Furrer-Lech of UBS argues that women often go to places which men do not consider worthwhile, career-wise. She was interested, years before it was considered fashionable, in the issue of Islamic financing. Her CEO agreed that she could, if she wanted to. With all the advantages of working for a non-American bank in the Middle East, she researched and developed the beginnings of what would become a large business for UBS, settting it up as a pioneer in a new area (Furrer-Lech, 2006).

The same is true of Marie-Claude Peyrache, the first woman appointed to France Télécom's executive committee and now president of the European Professional Women's Network in Paris. Early on in her career, and long before "international" was a necessary rite of passage, she headed off, with three children aged nine, seven and two, to set up the company's business in Japan. She had no competition for the job, and no one else really wanted to go. But the resulting success launched her into a high-profile career in the group. "It also," she notes, "gave France Télécom strong visibility as the first company in the sector to appoint a woman to head a subsidiary" (Interview with author, June 2007). So she not only weathered the 30s, but used that time as a platform for greater things.

The lure of entrepreneurship

Unfortunately, Peyrache is not typical. Many women are not aware that it might be easier to have children in Japan on an expat package than in their home country. After 40, struggling to be recognised and promoted internally, or just ready to be more naturally who they really are, many start dreaming of faraway opportunities … outside the company.

Sandrine Tézé-Limal was a Vice President at Bain & Co. in Paris. After a couple of decades in consulting in several countries around the globe, she decided to leave to renew an old passion, architecture. With four children at home, she returned to university for five years to become an architect and then started her own business. She did not really aim to stop consulting, but rather to start something more meaningful in mid-life. "Consulting is very exciting and very rewarding in many ways. However, there is not much room in the business world for aesthetics and/or feelings. There comes a point when helping large multinationals improve their bottom line does not get you up in the morning … Our architecture business is thriving. My associate and I have the luxury of choosing the clients we want to work for. We work with men and women I consider gifted, passionate craftsmen, to design and build for people we appreciate, a space that they can be happy in. That gets me up very early!" It is this passion and renewed ambition that many corporates are losing, just as their experience and networks could be most useful.

Entrepreneurship can also be hugely attractive to women at this age who see little opportunity for advancement or recognition. This is often a different kind of business ownership, bigger and more ambitious than the "lifestyle" options they tend to go for in the 30s. In the US, between 1997 and 2007, "privately held businesses owned by women grew at three times the rate of all American privately held firms," writes

Margaret Heffernan, author of an informative book about female entrepreneurship, *How She Does It* (Heffernan, 2007) "Every *day*, 420 women go out and start their own businesses – twice the rate at which men do ... And these businesses are growing revenue, profits and jobs faster than business as a whole. The explosion in women-owned businesses explains why women's companies now employ more people than America's largest 500 companies combined. Women now own 46% of the private businesses in the US."

For Heffernan, the growing popularity of entrepreneurship among women, poses some important questions: "If women are so successful working for themselves, why aren't they just as successful in traditional corporations? Why do they have to leave in order to prove just how good they are?" For her, there are two main answers from women: "No one would take me seriously, and I wanted more control over my life. Both themes are important. Much of the growth of women-owned businesses is fueled by ideas that fell on deaf corporate ears" (Heffernan, 2006).

While entrepreneurship is an excellent and viable alternative for some women, it is not for everyone. And given the power that large companies wield today around the world, it is worrying if too many women abandon their efforts at moving into corporate power. For some firms, losing experienced women at this stage means not only losing their wisdom and contacts but also gaining a potent new competitor. Like political power, corporate power is a hard nut for women to crack. But the impact of their rise to the top of business could be huge, as we explain in the next section.

Alternative views of "power"

One of the aphorisms about power is that it is taken and not given. In order to "take" power, you have to start by wanting it. Few women would say they "want power" in those terms. They are much readier to accept ideas of leadership, particularly if the concepts are couched in the context of serving others *à la* Peter Senge and Robert Greenleaf (author of *Servant Leadership*) rather than as Caesar's army coming in conquest. Women are full of ambitions and desires for change and revolution, but they are generally not as motivated by the trappings and status of power.

Part of their reluctance to claim power wholeheartedly stems from the role models who have it. They have seen too often how power corrupts, and have thought less often of how powerlessness also corrupts, a concept described decades ago by Rosabeth Moss Kanter (Moss Kanter, 1977). They have not yet been told by other women what the pleasures of power can be.

What they are likely to focus on is the intense scrutiny that the few women at the top have to endure. The media seem more enamoured with stories of women losing power than acquiring it. Martha Stewart and Carly Fiorina are better known than the rather more successful Meg Whitman (eBay) or Anne Mulcahy (Xerox).

Sex, success and the media

When a woman lands a really big job, her gender is still a major part of the news story, as it was with Cynthia Carroll's arrival as chief executive of Anglo American, or the appointment of Drew Gilpin Faust to the presidency of Harvard.

This is understandable. Female firsts are still newsworthy. Nonetheless, there is growing discomfort with the way that society and the media react to women who make it in corporate life. Barbara Thomas Judge, an American businesswoman who chairs the UK's Atomic Energy Authority and sits on many boards, believes attitudes need to change. She notes that when women have business reverses – and men have business reverses all the time – it gets a much bigger spotlight. "I think that successful women have a really hard time. If you stumble, there's a magnifying glass on you, and if you do well, people are always questioning how you got there, 'was it a token appointment', 'who did she know?' Even today, when I give a big speech, people are always surprised, especially the men. They say: 'That was really wonderful.' They have that lilt in the voice, as if to say: 'I didn't know you knew that much about the subject.'"

271

Judge believes men are more comfortable dealing with people who look like them. "I always feel, when I put my make-up on, that it's like putting on armour. You don't have a second chance to make a first impression. If you look serious and a little bit formidable, that helps."

She asks people to question their assumptions. "I haven't ever thought that my failures or my successes were because I was a woman, but I've felt that the fact that I was a woman was from time to time really difficult. I have had a reasonable career, but it hasn't been easy because of all the 'stuff' around it. I'd like people to lay off successful women. I like being treated like an 'old boy', rather than a 'new woman'" (Interview with author, February 2007).

Barbara Cassani, who launched Go, a low-cost UK airline, and led London's successful 2012 Olympics bid, even goes to the lengths of warning women to be wary of accepting a high profile in the media. "At the airline, I tried to be careful about courting the media's attention by keeping quiet unless talking to the media helped us to sell more seats on our aircraft. I used the same principle in the Olympic bid. Don't let yourself be seduced into the whole media cult of personality thing" (Cassani, 2007).

Successful women know it is a double-edged sword. Many feel uncomfortable being featured as "women". In many countries, news coverage of women stays locked in a ghetto of "women's stories". This is somewhat less true in the UK and North America, where newspapers have recognised that readers appreciate hearing the point of view of women. The *New York Times*'s Maureen Dowd and the *Toronto Globe and Mail*'s Margaret Wente are strong voices addressing the major issues of the day from a female perspective. They are still rare.

Despite all this, we have witnessed a slow shift over the past decade in women's private reactions to the word "power". Asked behind closed doors at one of the authors' leadership programmes to free-associate with the word, women a decade ago produced mostly negative or sarcastic terms – from "corruption" to "man", "tie" or "tan". Now, they have begun to associate power more positively with "autonomy", "money", "influence", or "charisma".

For all the lists of "powerful women" that have sprung up across the world, little is known about what actually turns these women on at work. Some are so intent on distancing their success from their gender that they would prefer not to pronounce on the issue. Yet the women in the room are avidly awaiting role models.

The most appreciated bit of women's workshops and confer-ences are speaker panels made up of different women with varying definitions of success and the choices that accompa-nied them. Women want to know how these women managed their climb, their kids and their careers. They usually do not personally know anyone up there who is able to bring a message back down the mountain about how the system really works.

Having power can be fun, exhilarating, liberating and empowering. It allows people to craft their lives, their organisations, and their priorities their way. But women's culture, aside from a few superstar women attracted to the limelight, is one of relative modesty. Women do not enjoy self-promotion and as Deborah Tannen has noted in *Talking 9 to 5*, the feminine language is one of egalitarianism, a refusal of one-up or one-down positioning, a preference for a philosophy of "all the same".

Interviewed for this book, Helen Alexander, the former CEO of the Economist Group, and the first female president of the UK's CBI employers' group, was interested by the association of the words pleasure and power. Upon reflection, she said that her role brought her satisfaction in terms of "making profits and adding value, status, interest, the people I meet, and the team that I have built up. We've weathered recessions, we employ good people, and we help spread ideas round the world. I love doing something well, and enjoy making a difference" (Interviews with author, November 2006 and June 2007).

As we said at the beginning of this chapter, women are often deeply motivated by their values and talk a lot about making a difference. Lena Olving is the Swedish senior vice president of quality at Volvo. "Power gives me the opportunity to prove to the organisation and to myself that I can do it. I love being able to deliver, to have a voice, to push for everything that is important to me. To protect my company's core values. My voice is loud and clear and listened to" (Olving, 2006). Catharine Furrer-Lech of UBS agrees. "The satisfaction that comes of making a difference is made much easier with power," she explains. "It opens doors and gives you the resources."

Marie-Christine Levet was CEO of the French subsidiary of German telecoms company T-Online. She has had a fast-paced career, moving up through big consumer brand-names like EuroDisney and PepsiCo. She leapt into the high-tech world, propelled by her belief in the potential of the internet. At 39, while CEO, she had her first child. She runs the show, so her team has adapted to her schedule, and she has worked from home when she needs to, her performance undiminished. Asked about her ambition, she laughs at the advice that she has been given. "I manage 500 people, so head-hunters tell me my next job should be managing 3000. But I don't evaluate myself on how many people I manage. I'm mostly motivated by learning, interest and opportunity" (Interview with author, December 2006).

Levet is not driven by conventional ideas of status and power. Her power resides in part from this kind of independence and readiness to take positions that others might describe as risky. Her mission at the company was to make technology-driven engineers deliver products to mass retail customers (54% of whom are women, says Levet) who are not interested in the minutiae of bits and bytes.

Change agents on their own terms

Earlier in this chapter, we asked how women could combine being politically savvy with being true to themselves – for example, in being open and honest about their feelings. A lot of advice is expended on the first part of this equation, much less on the second part. Cranfield University School of Management, for example, has an internationally respected Centre for Women Business Leaders that has published extensively on the importance of "impression management", or self-marketing, skills. It runs tailored workshops which help women learn to communicate more comfortably about themselves in a corporate setting.

Alex Tosolini, general manager for Procter & Gamble in Poland and the Baltics (Tosolini, 2005), says men typically oversell their abilities while women undersell theirs. It is, he says, up to the leaders in any situation simply to know this and to adjust men's claims about themselves downwards and women's upwards to get close to an accurate reading of reality. That ability, he admits, is rare today. His advice to women? "Strive to be arrogant, because you may *just* succeed in coming across as confident" (WIN Conference, 2005).

Perhaps companies should ask themselves if they really want to train the other half of the population to become more "assertive", in other words, more like men. Do they want to encourage more people to spend significant amounts of time perfecting skills that will help them vie for visibility? Would it not make more sense to spend equivalent sums on more objective performance evaluations?

As for women, perhaps they would do better to focus, not on themselves, but on their ideas. Women can also be highly progressive agents of change in companies. When they forget about themselves and focus on their proposals for change, they become far more comfortable – and far more convincing. Immediately.

Women tend to feel more at ease defending their proposals for others than seeking promotions for themselves. They are more effective at networking and readier to "manage up" and contact senior people if they feel it is for "a good cause", such as the success of the company.

They also become more strategically adept at:

- identifying key stakeholders and their interests;
- approaching "enemies" and seeking common ground;

- building coalitions on shared ideas;
- networking and developing the number of people they know, and who know them;
- lobbying for their proposals with senior management or external bodies;
- packaging and communicating progress and achievements.

Women are naturally strong in all the aspects of political and influencing skills that they are said to be lacking, on one condition – that it isn't all about *them*. Organisations would be wise to recognise this and to stop expecting women to promote themselves.

To summarise:

If companies want to benefit from women's talents they first need to recognise the differences that affect their careers. This does not require reading psychology or debating nature versus nurture. It means acknowledging that a majority of women have different career cycles, communication styles and career motivations from the majority of men who hold corporate power. It is time to move on from our 20th-century concepts of careers, success and leadership.

Men ask: Does this mean introducing positive discrimination? The answer is clearly no. No one is in favour of discrimination. Companies simply need to remove the positive discrimination that is currently in place, and that favours the dominant group.

Tips for managing gender differences

Recognise that most women are different from most men in a few crucial ways that affect their careers, and that these do not just involve having babies:

- non-linear career cycles;
- communication styles;
- career motivation and management;
- power and political networks

Adapt HR systems to these differences:

- Recruitment processes – check the design and language of job ads, as well as hidden biases in the corporate "types" they project.
- Career and succession planning – support women through the 30s, making career choices and their consequences more transparent.
- Performance evaluations – help managers to understand women's more modest and relationship-oriented communication style for what it is, a valid communication style.
- Reward systems – money and status are not big motivators for many women. Recognition, learning, making a difference, and meaningful work are.

- Promotion realities – make more transparent the rules of the game on promotion, and communicate early the importance of networks and political competence
- Train managers to become familiar enough with these differences so that they can manage them bilingually.

Chapter Eight

TOMORROW'S TALENT TRENDS ... TODAY

"Women-friendly" Means "People-friendly"

"Increasingly, the management of people is a 'marketing job.' And in marketing one does not begin with the question: 'What do we want?' One begins with the question: 'What does the other party want? What are its values? What are its goals? What does it consider results?'"

Peter Drucker (Drucker, 1999)

Up to now, this book has focused on women in the corporate world. However, companies which adapt their culture, language and career models to women are likely to reap benefits across a wide gamut of employees in western societies.

Globalisation, changing demographics and social attitudes are causing a shift in people's relationship with work. The established concept of retirement is dying, loyalty is an alien notion for young people entering work, and parenthood is a role that men increasingly want to share.

The dominant, linear career path is under pressure from many sides. Working lives are extending and changing shape as older people work beyond retirement age and younger people take bouts of "time out" to study, travel or work for non-profit organisations. It is not only women who want more flexibility, choice and control in relation to work: increasing numbers of long-serving male employees, new entrants and mid-career executives would like a new deal too.

Companies that want to attract and keep this talent are more likely to do so by following the steps we set out in Chapter Four, to create an inclusive culture for women. These are:

- understanding that flexibility is a desire of men as well as women;
- recognising that careers no longer have to be linear and unbroken;
- raising or abolishing narrow age bands for spotting "high potential";
- making the language of corporate leaders more inclusive;
- avoiding assumptions about what women – or men – want from careers.

"Increasingly, people of both sexes are seeking spatial and time flexibility – doing the same work but at different times and in different places, for the same pay," said the UK's Equal Opportunities Commission in a 2007 report (Equal Opportunities Commission, 2007).

In a world where customers expect 24/7 service, and the supply of skilled workers is expected to get tighter, large companies that pay attention to people's changing expectations of work should find themselves at a distinct competitive advantage. Redesigning work would aid recruitment and retention, tackle absenteeism and work-related health problems, and increase employee engagement and thereby customer satisfaction.

This holds true in tough as well as benign economic conditions. During the global downturn, some employers have found that flexible working offers them ways to retain staff, for example on temporarily reduced hours, rather than making them redundant and losing their experience and knowledge outright.

This has resulted in some interesting trends. The number of US teleworkers – employees using technology to work remotely, often from home, at least one day a month – jumped by 39% to 17.2 m between 2006 and 2008, according to the global human resources association WorldatWork. Rose Stanley, work-life practice leader at WorldatWork, said:

"With employees taking home smaller pay cheques, the employer has to pilot new programmes to motivate them."

Getting this right will enable companies to keep up with the demands of their clients because they have a willing and motivated workforce. If companies do not respond to these long-term trends, they will see more of their best women *and* men walking out of the door.

New models of work

Princeton-educated Troy Smeal had all the credentials of a corporate high-flier. He was a partner at Marakon Associates, an international strategy consulting firm, and then a director of strategy at Diageo, the global drinks group. But he quit the corporate world at the age of 36 to become an independent consultant. The long hours at Marakon and the non-stop travel at Diageo left him no room to be the kind of father he wanted to be to his two young children.

"I think very highly of Marakon and the people who work there, but we had a very different approach to things," he said. "I wanted a work-life balance which meant working fewer hours. While the firm sympathised with it rationally, emotionally they never believed that in the consulting world you could work less because of client demands."

At Diageo, the job he took on quickly changed and he found himself travelling every week between key markets in Asia and Latin America and sleeping off the jet lag at home at weekends. "I wasn't able to give to Diageo what I wanted to give to someone because I was miserable and tired."

Then he heard about a new London firm, Eden McCallum, that he thought might be the answer for him. Launched by two former McKinsey consultants, Liann Eden and Dena McCallum, it has a different business model from traditional, pyramid-shaped consultancies. Instead of directly employing large numbers of consultants, it draws on a core group of 150 freelances, and a wider network of 350 other specialists when needed, matching their expertise to the strategic consulting requirements of its corporate clients.

This way of working might be expected mainly to attract female consultants. In fact, 70% of Eden McCallum's consultants are men, choosing what projects they take on to suit their interests and lifestyles, while not sacrificing their income. A survey by the firm showed the consultants' top reason for wanting to be independent was the flexibility it gave them – followed by the earning power.

"It allows me to use my skills and do what I find exciting in consulting – working with chief executives and their teams on very interesting issues," said Smeal. His established reputation and earning capacity meant he had to work for no more than 100 days a year, including 40 to 50 nights away from home. "That's a very small price to pay in comparison to having a full-time job," he said. "I can take months off at a time."

Eden McCallum, with its lower cost, flexible business model, was launched in the difficult post-dotcom market of 2000, when many companies were cutting their budgets for consulting. The founders were unsure whether it would prove as attractive to high-flying consultants when the market improved and competition for talent became tougher. In fact, it continued to draw clients and consultants, the latter typically in their late 30s and 40s. In 2007, its turnover hit more than £12.5m, and even in the depressed consulting market of 2008, it maintained revenue at the 2007 level. New models of working such as this pose a challenge to traditional firms, which have struggled with how to meet client demands while responding to employee demands for greater flexibility.

"It's a model which many other consulting firms are watching with a mixture of interest and concern," says Fiona Czerniawska, a leading authority on the industry (Interview with author, February 2007). Consulting is a cyclical business, and firms have to be able to grow without becoming too flabby. "The single most important challenge consulting firms face is how best to match supply to demand. The war for talent makes things harder because firms often have to recruit ahead of it to be sure of having the resources to meet client demand."

To lure back talented consultants like Smeal, large firms need to become more responsive to both sexes' desire for greater flexibility and choice. Wayne Henderson was in his 40s and a prominent member of the "inner circle" of consultants at Eden McCallum, having left Booz Allen Hamilton to have more time for his family. He was contemplating a possible return to a "more corporate-type career" but was very choosy. "Work-life balance will be a strong determinant of what I do," he said. "I couldn't imagine going back into a big corporate consultancy right now. It's still not appropriate to be spending four nights a week away from home. But I don't want to be in my 50s and feel I've forgone my career" (Interview with author, February 2007).

As for Smeal, he had no immediate plans to return. "I do miss the interaction and part of me says: 'Wouldn't it be nice to walk into an office and have a conversation over a cup of coffee?' But I'm quickly brought down to earth when I realise everything else that goes with it. I wouldn't consider that when my kids were young. Maybe there will be a happy middle ground somewhere, which is still part of the corporate world, with its perks and responsibilities, but is much more flexible than it is today" (Interview with author, February 2007).

Fathers count too

In some countries, there is a big cultural shift towards fathers wanting to play a greater role in their children's upbringing.

We discussed the approach of Nordic countries to men's role in parenting, and the growing uptake of paternity leave by German fathers, in Chapter Six, Culture Counts. In the UK, where full-time men work some of the longest hours in the European Union, recent research has found that 52% of men and 48% of women would like more flexible hours (Holmes et al., 2007).

Surveys of new parents show that most new fathers no longer see their key role as breadwinner, according to the Equal Opportunities Commission. Four out of five say they would be happy to stay at home alone to look after the baby (Thompson et al., 2006). The proportion of fathers working from home more than doubled from 14% to 29% in the three years to 2005 (Smeaton and Marsh, 2006).

Another UK poll of working parents recently found that 60% believe fathers should spend more time with their children. "Research shows that early, active involvement by fathers can lead to a range of positive outcomes for children and young people," says *Working Better*, a report by Britain's Equality and Human Rights Commission. (Equality and Human Rights Commission, 2009)

Companies welcoming women as full contributors and part-ners at every level in the workplace will make it easier for men to fulfil their responsibilities as parents. The same applies the other way round. Those which accept that men are full partners in parenthood will make it easier for women to fulfil their potential at work.

The British high street bank Lloyds TSB (now part of Lloyds Banking Group) found that its male employees wanted their role as parents to be better understood by the company. Employee surveys showed that men at all levels were less satisfied than women, said Fiona Cannon, head of diversity. "It was men who came back and said: 'We want more recognition of our role as fathers.' They still feel it would be frowned upon if they phone in to say: 'My child is sick.' They're looking for more discussion about men as fathers."

The bank started working with Fathers Direct, a national information centre on fatherhood, to investigate the barriers to men being better recognised for their share in parenting.

"Everything in parenthood is focused on the woman, from the moment she is pregnant," said Cannon. "Internally, we're working with a group of fathers to look at things we might do, such as a booklet for fathers in the parental leave pack" (Interview with author, February 2007).

Collaboration between companies could also play a role in shifting attitudes. A white paper from a French insurance company, headed by a woman (Nicole Rosa), has proposed setting up a fund to which companies could contribute, sharing the cost of parental leave between the employers of both parents. That would go a long way to neutralising the impact of maternity on women's careers by emphasising that most children have two parents, not one mother.

Another radical idea comes from two economics professors at Harvard and Bologna universities. Alberto Alesina and Andrea Ichino have proposed a reform of the tax system that would cut income tax on women and raise it – by less – on men (Gender Based Taxation; Alesina and Ichino, 2007). This, they argue, would achieve the public policy goal of increasing women's participation in the workforce and would reduce tax distortions. It would make it more expensive for employers to discriminate by gender and it could be an alternative to affirmative action and subsidised childcare. "In the long run, gender-based taxation may contribute to changing the traditional division of labour within the family, which currently encourages men to work more in the market and women more often at home," the economists say.

The motivations of men like Smeal and Henderson appear to be shared by large numbers of international executives – even if many of them hesitate to take such radical steps to realise their wishes. While travel and relocation are currently an inevitable part of the upward path of the global executive, 87% of them are concerned about their work-life balance, according to the Association of Executive Search Consultants, a worldwide professional body (Association of Executive Search Consultants, 2007).

Technology as enabler

The demand for greater flexibility is not only about parenting. Highly skilled people have been choosing to work independently because they want to nurture other aspects of their lives that the big-company, long-hours model does not permit. They are being assisted by technology, which allows people to work as dispersed affiliates of networked organisations, rather than having to be tied to a desk in a traditional firm.

One example of this kind of flexibility is Resources Global Professionals, a fast-growing, California-based business employing an international network of 3200 legal, finance, IT and human resources specialists who work on a project basis with corporate teams. In describing what kind of organisation it is, the company says: "With a focus on collaboration across functional and industry networks, and across practice groups, we are not unlike academic and scientific communities who have created forums for dynamic teaming and cooperation." In an interview with the *Chicago Tribune*, Donald Murray, the company's founder, explained his approach to managing people flexibly: "We don't monitor hours, we monitor results (Kleiman, 2005)."

Another case is Axiom Legal, a virtual law firm established in the US in 2000. Its revenues reached $56 m in 2008, up from $1.5 m in 2002. Named one of the 50 most innovative US companies by *Fast Company* magazine, it employs a pool of experienced lawyers who choose their engagements and work from their homes or clients' offices, using only a laptop connected to Axiom's "extranet" and service centre.

The 200 attorneys, half of whom are men, are typically in their late 30s and have worked for big name law firms and in-house corporate teams. They take on short- or long-term projects with clients that include Goldman Sachs, Cisco, American Express, Reuters, Virgin Mobile and Google. Having started in New York, Axiom has opened offices in San Francisco, Chicago, Washington DC, Los Angeles and London.

Staff turnover is lower than for the average law firm, and almost no one returns to work in a traditional firm, says Alec Guettel, co-founder. Those who leave tend to take up in-house posts at client companies, where the hours are more predictable than at a typical law firm and the work more fulfilling. He adds that the economic downturn has given the business an advantage. "It has opened up new categories of work we couldn't compete for in the past because clients are so motivated to find more efficient ways to operate." (Interviews with author, May 2007 and May 2009).

Axiom lawyers' reasons for choosing independence are many. Some like the variety of the work, some are passionate followers of outside pursuits – scuba diving and screenwriting are just two of those mentioned – while some want time for their young families. What they have in common is a desire for control over their work and careers. In an interview with Forbes Sky Radio, Mark Harris, the other co-founder, said their main guiding principle was "treating people, whether clients or colleagues, as human beings, not as instruments of growth or profitability".

Large firms could take a leaf out of these start-ups' books. Many companies fret about how to keep their employees "engaged". Giving them greater flexibility and choice would be a good start. Just as companies need to wake up to the potential of women, so they could be more alert to the potential of technology for humanising the way we work, and making it more productive. Why persist in irrationally rewarding long hours in the office, regardless of whether work is accomplished or not, when there is a plethora of technology – mobile phones, BlackBerrys, videoconferencing – that allows flexible, location-independent working to be built into even the most senior jobs?

The new model of decentralised but interconnected working used by the youthful consulting and legal businesses we have described above is part of a shift that has been dubbed "disorganisation" by Demos, an independent UK think-tank (Miller and Skidmore, 2004). Demos argues that there are two countervailing forces: hyper-organisation and disorganisation. Hyper-organisation has seen corporate operations first re-engineered, then rationalised and now outsourced, at each stage stripping out processes and people in order to stay competitive and improve the bottom line. Disorganisation, on the other hand, is something that people once only dreamed of but that is now being enabled by technology.

"Technology unleashes new possibilities for organising work in ways that are more aligned with other priorities, from family life to civic duty," says Demos. "Employees want more human organisations with greater autonomy and flexibility. They want an experience of work that is aligned with their values. They want a workplace forged in the image of their identities, not a workplace that tries to define them. They want organisations that can let go, and grant them a greater say in how things are run."

Case Study: WL Gore's empowered communities

WL Gore & Associates, the privately-held US multinational manufacturer of waterproof gear, fuel cell technology, cables and surgical products, is an unusual example of an old-established yet non-hierarchical business. The company, which regularly wins "best workplace" awards and has annual revenues of around $2bn, is akin to a commercial network of expert individuals, working in close communities.

Since its foundation in 1958, it has avoided hierarchy and chains of command. Instead it operates a "lattice" structure in which people communicate directly with each other and are accountable to the other members of their teams. All of its 7500 people are "associates" and new recruits have "sponsors", not bosses, who guide them to projects that match their skills. This encourages individual freedom to invent new products, though always based on consultation and cooperation.

Leaders are sometimes appointed but they often just "emerge" through special knowledge or skills that are useful to the business. People are ranked by their team members for their contribution to the company and are compensated accordingly. Teams are kept to about 150 people to foster self-organisation, autonomy and individual responsibility.

The authors of the Demos study, Paul Miller and Paul Skidmore, argue that the current model of work in organisations is unsustainable – as demonstrated by high levels of stress, falling job satisfaction and "foreboding about the future of working life". Companies, they say, need to "loosen up".

The logic of "disorganisation" is that work can and should be built around people, not the other way around, says Demos. It commissioned polls from MORI and NOP to look at people's desire to work for smaller rather than larger organisations. This desire was strongest in the most educated and affluent social groups. Interestingly, among business leaders, 71% wanted to work for a smaller company and only 7% for a larger one.

The wish to work for "human scale" organisations was most pronounced among people in the 45–54 bracket – the age group in which business leaders are most likely to be found and in which people are starting to look ahead to retirement.

"This is the generation at the leading edge of the shift away from the traditional 20th-century career structure," says Demos. It is also the generation with 30 or more years of accumulated knowledge and experience that companies will increasingly need to retain.

The value of "grey" brainpower

Flexibility played an important part in the working life of Heikki Poutiainen, a production manager for Assa Abloy, the world's largest lock-maker whose global brands include Chubb and Yale.

Poutiainen had hit 60. But far from wanting to lose him, the Abloy plant where he worked in Joensuu, near the eastern Finnish border, was keen to keep his skills and knowledge for as long as possible. The demographic profile of the factory reflected that of the country as a whole (and many other parts of the developed world): an ageing workforce of baby-boomers approaching retirement, and too few young people coming in to take their places.

As an incentive to stay on, Poutiainen and his fellow over-58s at the factory were offered extra days off each year, rising in number with age. This time off for rest or leisure activities was part of a novel programme, launched in 2001 and called Age Masters. It also provided special events, health and well-being courses, ergonomic changes to the workplace, and opportunities to adapt jobs to encompass mentoring of younger colleagues. The psychological boost from raising the status and profile of mature workers (those aged 55 and over) as they approached retirement was deemed at least as important as the practical measures.

Poutiainen, who recalled being written off as "past it" by some of his former colleagues when he was in his 40s, planned to stay on for five more years. The Age Masters scheme had been a major factor in his decision. At 60, he was granted 10 extra days' holiday a year, rising to a maximum of 20 days when he reached 64. He and fellow participants in the scheme said they felt they had gained greater control over their lives.

"The best parts are the extra days off and the fact that your work colleagues ask about and admire your experience," said Poutiainen, a keen golfer in his spare time. "For the past

18 months I have been guiding three people – a production manager, a foreman and a testing engineer – with preparations for their examination in leadership skills. I helped them to understand leadership and supervised their final examination along with their teacher (Interview with author, February 2007)."

This is a great example of a company that has redesigned how work is done, how people are rewarded and what the job actually entails. The aim: to achieve a strategic business objective by responding to the changing career priorities and needs of its workforce.

Abloy tackled the challenge of its ageing employees in much the same way that we suggest companies should approach the issue of gender.

- It analysed the composition of its workforce and found two age clusters: one between 25 and 35, the other, much bigger, between 50 and 60.
- It recognised that the average retirement age was 59. In the next 10 years, it would lose a large chunk of the skills that lay behind its unique brand and market share unless it took action.
- It looked at the opportunities offered by effective action that would retain these people's experience for longer: increased turnover, better sharing of skills and knowledge, new training and development programmes, and

an overhaul of the prevailing culture and attitudes towards mature workers.

- It instituted a programme, led from the top and with input from key executives, that spoke directly to the attitudes, concerns, needs and wishes of this older population.

This is the kind of thing that more companies will have to do as demographic changes take their toll and skill shortages worsen. Not only will more women be working in the future, so will more people in their 50s and 60s.

Finland happens to be ahead of the game on age because it had an exceptionally big baby boom after the Second World War. With fewer young people entering the work-force, looming labour shortages and no tradition of immigration, the government, employers and unions have been working hard over the past decade to extend working lives. An important incentive introduced by the government is that people may choose to work until 68, receiving a 4.5% rise in state pension for each year they work past 63. Given these collaborative efforts to humanise working life, it may not be entirely coincidental that Finland has a female-dominated cabinet, a woman president, Tarja Halonen, and the world's fifth highest representation of women in parliament.

Finland is, of course, not alone in facing stark demographic reality. By 2050, one in five people in the world will be over 60. In 1950, the figure was one in 12.

The challenge is becoming acute in many parts of the world. In China, the dependency ratio – the number of people of working age for each retired person – is expected to fall from 6:1 to 2:1 over the next 30 years (Gimbel, 2007). In the OECD, the number of retired people per worker will double over the next 50 years if nothing is done to keep people in work longer. "This will threaten living standards and put enormous pressure on the financing of social protection systems," says the OECD. "To help meet these daunting challenges, work needs to be made a more attractive and rewarding proposition for older workers" (OECD, 2006).

An IBM survey of human resources directors pointed to the consequences for the business world. "When the baby-boomer generation retires, many companies will find out too late that a career's worth of experience has walked out the door, leaving insufficient talent to fill the void" (IBM, 2005).

In the European Union, the number of workers aged 50 to 64 will grow by 25% over the next two decades and the number of those aged 20 to 29 will fall by 20%. Despite this, early retirement remains common and attempts to reform pensions and raise, or abolish, retirement ages can meet heavy resistance from employers, labour unions and the media.

This state of affairs is out of sync with changing attitudes to retirement around the world. The views of the "age masters" at Abloy's Finnish plant mirror those held by ordinary people globally. The vast majority of people want to see an end to mandatory retirement ages, according to a survey commissioned by HSBC, the international banking group (HSBC, 2006).

Three out of four people see work as part of their ideal existence in later life. They do not want to be forced to work, but many envisage a mixture of work and leisure, family time and voluntary activities. Above all – and this is the key factor in our case for a big shift in corporate culture and attitudes – they want flexibility and choice.

They want this for a wide variety of reasons. It may be to have more time for grandchildren, for study, for community work, or for leisure pursuits. Many men and women are involved in caring for elderly relatives and this is set to increase with the ageing population. In the UK, for example, it is projected that nearly 10 m people will be caring for an older relative by 2010 (UK Dept of Work and Pensions Figures).

Employers know there are benefits in retaining mature employees: in general, they say they are more reliable and loyal than younger workers and just as motivated and productive, although less technologically able (HSBC, 2006). As is the case for women, however, companies have not yet learned how to grasp these benefits and make full use of "grey brainpower". Adopting the approaches we recommend to make workplaces attractive to women will help them do so, as we outline at the end of this chapter. Doing so should also make it easier to capture the best talent in the new generation moving into the world of work, or soon to join it.

Making the most of the "Me" generation

Predicting what young people not yet in work will want from it is a slightly hazardous exercise. Their views may be strongly held but subject to change. Their expectations may be unrealistic. Their aspirations and priorities will certainly change over time, and perhaps as soon as they find out what work is really like.

Nonetheless, there are enough so-called "millennials" – born between about 1980 and 1995 when birth rates increased in the developed world – already in work to indicate whether forecasts about their younger counterparts carry weight.

What do the predictions say?

- That the new generation – also known as "Echo Boom" and "Generation Y" – will move not only between jobs but also between careers through their working lives, reinventing themselves possibly many times over.

- That technology is not a tool for them but a part of who they are – as shown by their use of social networking websites such as MySpace, YouTube and Facebook.
- That they want challenges and development opportunities from work, but also choice and flexibility in order to accommodate their personal lives.
- That they value employers who demonstrate a responsible approach to society and the environment.

Not an easy generation to please, then. For this generation in particular, with its assumptions of perpetual prosperity, the 2008–09 economic downturn was a rude awakening. But companies also need to look ahead, to economic recovery and beyond. Willingness to rethink career models and tailor opportunities to individuals' abilities, needs and priorities will be instrumental in attracting and retaining high-performers in this cohort over the longer term, as it will for the other groups already described in this chapter.

PricewaterhouseCoopers, the global professional services firm with 140 000 people, has as big an incentive as any organisation to be "an employer of choice". An internal research study on "21st-century human capital", carried out by its Genesis Park leadership development programme, found that millennials value the human touch in their bosses, have a strong desire to belong, and want the chance to be creative and to have a say in mapping their career.

The study recommends better networking tools within PwC to keep this generation connected, a more flexible career model, greater choice over jobs, and new ways to achieve work-life equilibrium, such as bonuses that can be redeemed for leave rather than pay. "Millennials need to be engaged early by their employer and feel like their contributions are heard [in order] to be satisfied," it says.

PwC in the UK recruits about 1000 graduates every year and sees these trends showing up in their expectations of work. "For young people coming into the world of work there is no preordained loyalty to their first employer," says Sarah Churchman, director of diversity (Interview with author, May 2007). "The majority don't expect to be with their first employer for more than four years. They assume they will move and they work for themselves. It's all about 'Me plc'. That's the biggest shift in mindset. They are very focused on doing things that will develop them."

For those at the starting blocks of working life, parenthood seems a long way off. Many want to travel. Yet these young men and women are also looking for a good work-life balance and flexibility, says Churchman. "They're quite interested in PwC and what it's doing as a socially responsible business, especially in terms of how much time they could have off to work with charities."

Another threat to traditional, linear career paths is that more young people are studying for longer. Once they have completed their degrees, their professional studies can continue for years into their working lives. Not surprisingly, they want to take longer breaks, such as a sabbatical, whether to travel or to gain leadership experience in a different environment.

Case Study: MSN's switch to a flexible culture

Microsoft's MSN portal has a predominantly young workforce. A survey of its UK employees revealed the shocking statistic that 64% were considering leaving the company because they disliked its long hours culture.

Stung into action, the UK management shifted to measuring performance on output rather than input. This "culture change" programme was deemed so successful it was rolled out to the whole of Microsoft's UK operations. Most of the 2400 employees now have some flexibility to suit their lifestyles, as long as they meet their objectives, keep clients and co-workers aware of their availability, and are adaptable to the needs of the business, said Dave Gartenberg, former human resources director.

Most of MSN's staff at the time of the initial experiment were at the pre-family stage, and they used their newfound flexibility for leisure interests. But employees, including senior executives, with families have since benefited from the changes. Gartenberg said he leaves the office most evenings in time to have a meal with his young children before sitting down at his laptop to finish work. Once a week he leaves at 4pm to lead a "den meeting" of the Cub Scouts' group to which one of his sons belongs.

Crucially, he said, the changes have benefited the business, resulting in an increase in productivity and customer service. Employee turnover has fallen and most staff now plan to stay for at least four years (Maitland, 2007 and interview with author).

A lot of the resistance inside large companies to new ways of working is based on fear that it will cost more and be difficult to manage. Some of the resistance is also due to inertia. The evidence from businesses that have gained a head start by measuring results, rather than the hours spent in the office, is that it reduces costs and improves job satisfaction. Trusting people to get on with the job makes them feel more valued.

BT, a UK-based international telecommunications group, has an "Anytime, Anywhere" work programme which allows employees to control the hours and location of their working day – once they have completed a self-selection questionnaire that determines whether their personality and work role is suitable for the scheme. The proven benefits include (BT, 2007):

- increases in productivity of 15% to 31% across functions;
- absenteeism 20% below the national average;

- 1000 people retained who would have left;
- a 55% increase in job satisfaction;
- the equivalent of 1800 years of commuting avoided, a saving of £ 9.7 m a year;
- a boost to reputation: BT has come top of its sector in the Dow Jones Sustainability Index for six years' running.

In addition to these benefits, the scheme helped keep the business running after the 2005 London bombings because so many of BT's people worked remotely and were unaffected by the chaos.

The future is already here

As we have seen, companies are preoccupied with the competition for talent. Even after the global credit crisis had battered their confidence in late 2008, CEOs said that finding and retaining top talent remained a major priority. Nearly 70% cited the shortage of candidates with essential skills as a key challenge, according to a PwC survey. "Other human resource concerns included recruiting and integrating youngevr employees, providing attractive career paths, and competition for talent within their sector," it said (PricewaterhouseCoopers, 2009).

We believe that companies which adapt to women, and make them feel truly welcome, will be able to draw on the widest pool of talent from all sources. To do this, they need to:

- understand that everyone's work priorities change at different life stages;
- recognise that the linear, unbroken career model is unsustainable;
- broaden narrow definitions of the career path to the top;
- abolish age limits for spotting and developing "high potential" people;
- treat flexibility and work-life balance as issues for everyone;
- measure performance by results, not hours.

Multinational companies need executives who are willing to travel. While technology, and the dangers of climate change, should lead to far greater reliance on virtual communication in future, companies could also rethink the demands that constant travel places on executives in mid-career. Why not match foreign assignments more closely to the early and late phases in people's working lives, when they may have fewer family responsibilities? While many of today's male executives are thinking of winding down in their 50s and 60s, their female counterparts may be entering their work prime – and revving up for international assignments and leadership challenges.

There are other important lessons from the huge changes in working patterns we have described in this chapter. Old hands still want to be appreciated. Young ones want organisations with a human face. Women want these things too. If corporate leaders can personalise the conversation in the ways we suggest they do for women, they will be offering the rest of their employees a better deal as well.

Some companies have introduced programmes to encourage women to return after breaks of several years. They have realised how important this female talent is to their future. Keeping in touch with *all* the talented people, men and women, who leave is a sensible course in this networked age. Some of them may want to come back one day – or they may become important customers.

For businesses that make themselves attractive places for women to work and progress, wider benefits will derive. The social and demographic trends we have highlighted are not somewhere out there in the future. They are happening now. Wise companies will be responding now, too.

Chapter Nine

CONCLUSION

From Better Business to a Better World?

"Courage is what it takes to stand up and speak. Courage is also what it takes to sit down and listen."

Winston Churchill

It was a weighty gathering. Chairmen and senior executives from some of the world's largest companies were launching the findings of an 18-month inquiry into the future of global business. The speeches by the all-male panel touched on the challenges facing the world – climate change, poverty and pandemics, economic and political upheaval, the clash of cultures – and how business could help to address them.

The inquiry's report called on companies to "redefine success", "embed values" and "create better regulatory frameworks" that would allow them to meet their environmental and social responsibilities while generating wealth and providing improved goods and services.

Ulf Karlberg, a former senior executive at AstraZeneca, the pharmaceutical company, and founding chair of the Amnesty International Business Group in Sweden, then took the podium as a member of the inquiry team, which comprised 17 men and two women.

To general surprise, he began by asking whether the outcome would have been different if the gender balance on the team had been the other way round, with women heavily out-numbering the men. "It would perhaps have been more brave," he suggested, "more intuitive, and more practical, with some very clear action plans." He added later that it would also have been a smarter team, because its delibera-tions would have had more dimensions and "less politics" (Karlberg, 2007 and interview with author).

There are both men and women today who imagine that the world would be better run *à deux*, with women taking their place alongside men in the seats of political and economic power, not as exceptions or tokens, but as full partners with their own identifiable voices.

New voices, new choices

What will women bring to the international table? We would not yet claim to be able to answer that question definitively. However, as a new generation of women begins to move into political power, it is possible to start examining some of the approaches and ideas they contribute.

The political world is already producing more and more examples of gender balance in leadership. On a single day in Europe in mid-2007, the media carried images of Angela Merkel, the German chancellor, receiving flowers, a tribute and a kiss from José Manuel Barroso, president of the European Commission, after she had overseen difficult negotiations on a new EU treaty; and Christine Lagarde, France's newly appointed Finance Minister, cheerfully leaving a meeting alongside Nicolas Sarkozy, the French president.

Merkel in Germany, Hillary Clinton in the US, and Ségolène Royal in France have all changed perceptions. Initially viewed as improbable political leaders, each succeeded against tremendous odds to make the image of women in the highest political office more acceptable in their countries – whether or not they were finally elected.

It is not always *what* they have proposed in terms of policies and reforms that is different, but more *how* they have gone about it. Merkel, the research physicist from former East Germany, erupted on the German political scene and was elected to chair the Christian Democratic Union in 2000. By 2005 she was Chancellor. "Merkel's leadership style," wrote Henry Kissinger in *Time* magazine, is "the art of accomplishing great goals through the accumulation of nuance" (Kissinger, 2007).

In Europe, she won a strong reputation as a diplomat and consensus-builder, managing the complexity of relations among often bickering member states with unexpected skill. She used Germany's six-month presidency of the European Union to push through difficult deals on climate change and on the outlines of a new treaty to reform the 27-nation bloc.

Royal cut a very different, overtly feminine and fashionable, figure in her ultimately unsuccessful French presidential bid against Nicolas Sarkozy. Among her achievements was to challenge the country's traditional left-right divide. She was also the first to push for what she called "participatory government", side-stepping the old-fashioned Socialist party structure to connect directly with voters through innovative use of online technology such as blogs and discussion forums.

In America, with its strong tradition of a loyal First Lady supporting her President-spouse, it was perhaps even harder for a female contender – let alone one who was a former First Lady herself – to strike a comfortable balance between the difference she brought as a woman and the seriousness of her policies and experience. Clinton certainly emphasised the latter. She played the political game as a clever professional, too busy for "motherhood and apple pie"-style baking.

She did, however, surround herself with a tight-knit team of loyal women. "Never have so many women operated at such a high level in one campaign," reported the *Washington Post*. Noting that opinion polls suggested voters saw her as cool and aloof, the newspaper said that "among her own staff, she has cultivated a nurturing culture of collegiality and loyalty, a leadership style based in teamwork, and often favored by women, that values consensus over hierarchy" (Romano, 2007). After her defeat by Barack Obama in the thrilling Democratic presidential contest of 2008, Clinton was generously offered, and graciously accepted, the post of Secretary of State in her former rival's new government.

All three of these women, in Germany, France and the US, were deeply unsettling to part of their potential electorate. Some competitors did not appreciate the change and damaged their own prospects by revealing outdated attitudes, like the French politician who asked Royal who would take care of her children.

Of course, there have been female political leaders before them, some more famous, such as Golda Meir and Margaret Thatcher, both of whom were fearsomely tough. One of the jokes about Thatcher, the "Iron Lady", was that she was the only man in her government.

The new generation of female political leaders is breaking that mould. Laura Liswood, secretary general of the Council of Women World Leaders, believes some voters, if not all, want women to bring a different style of leadership (Hill, 2007). The financial meltdown in Iceland brought a historic change of government when Social Democrat Johanna Sigurdardottir became the country's first woman prime minister in 2009. The arrival of leaders like Merkel, Royal, Clinton, Sigurdardottir and Chile's Michelle Bachelet on the political stage in the early 21st century has allowed a generation of girls and boys to see that it is plausible, even normal, for women to run for president.

New measures of success

In Chapter One, we wrote about the three Ws – Weather, Women and Web – that are changing our lives, our economies and our future prospects. Josephine Green, a "future thinker" and director of Trends and Strategy at Philips Design, says "there may prove to be interconnections between these Ws." In other words, women may turn out to have an important, and different, impact on the challenge of global warming and on the way technology is developed and used. There are already pointers to this: in Europe, it was Merkel who pushed through new environmental standards; in France, it was Royal who used the internet to reach out to voters and render democracy more accessible, something which Barack Obama did subsequently in the US presidential election to great effect.

Former US President Bill Clinton told a Fortune Magazine conference in 2009 that educating and empowering women would help fight global warming, because it would slow population growth, which in turn would moderate climate change. (Fortune, 2009) Other commentators also base their optimism for the future at least partly on the positive influence of women. Dominique Moïsi, a senior adviser at France's Institute for International Relations, sees four "forces of hope" for Europe amid what he describes as passivity and pessimism. "In order of importance and influence, they are: women, businesses, new European Union member states and immigrants," he wrote in the *Financial Times*. "What brings these groups together is a combination of hope and will, self-confidence and, above all, energy. They share a positive outlook and a sense of progress" (Moïsi, 2006).

The inquiry report described at the start of this chapter talks about the need for companies to redefine success in terms not only of profitability but also of lasting positive impacts on individuals, communities and the environment. The rise of women is likely to contribute to this redefinition of progress and success. The microfinance revolution demonstrates how empowering women can transform the prospects of developing world economies by pulling them out of poverty.

Micro-credits – tiny loans repaid in instalments, made on the basis of trust and requiring no collateral – go primarily to women, who have been found to be the lever to enriching and educating children and families. Nobel peace prize winner Muhammad Yunus, who created this revolutionary model of finance with his Grameen Bank in Bangladesh, has said his country is on track to the Millennium Development Goal of halving its poverty rate by 2015. Of Grameen's customers – people shunned by the traditional banking system because of their extreme poverty – 97% are women.

Essma Ben Hamida is executive director of Enda Inter-Arabe, a Tunisian micro-credit institution with a loan portfolio of $ 11 million, which she started in the 1990s with $ 20 000. She works with women across the country and knows how successful the process is, with 99% of loans repaid. "Tunisia has been transformed. Before, there were hardly any women on the streets," she told a conference. "Now, there is an explosion of women's micro-enterprises across the country. They find joy and fulfilment in the exercise ... it improves the image of women in the eyes of their children, their families and their communities" (Ben Hamida, 2006).

She said the fund had been reluctant to lend to men, "not because we don't like them, but because women use the money better. Their family is the first to benefit, they use it to educate their children, to send their girls to university. Men not only tend to fail to reimburse loans, it's almost a matter of pride not to do so as it means they've rebelled against the system." Increasingly, however, the fund is lending to both sexes on the grounds that money is power and the best way to ensure harmonious families is for both men and women to have access to financing.

Men involved in micro-credit are blunter about the attitudes of their own sex. Cheikh Tidiane Mbaye, managing director of Sonatel, the national telecoms company in Senegal, told the same meeting: "Women want to make things work locally for themselves and their families, while men simply dream of escape to other countries."

A challenge for business

An estimated 70% of the world's poor are women. Barbara Stocking, director of Oxfam in Britain, has said more would be done to tackle poverty if there were more women leaders. That applies particularly to business leadership, according to Stocking. On visits to the annual gathering of top business people in Davos, Switzerland, she encountered women from the political world and from NGOs but very few from business. "If there were more women leaders across the board, it would make a difference," she told the *Financial Times* (Maitland, 2003).

As in the political world, there are early signs of the kind of difference women leaders can make in business, if they have the will and courage to stand out from the traditional mould. Some of the very few women who have made it to the top of the world's biggest companies were at the fore-front of reforms to create a more sustainable model of capi-talism. Three global companies, PepsiCo, Pfizer and Xerox, were among the first signatories in 2007 of the Aspen Prin-ciples, which encourage business to switch from a short-term focus to long-term value creation. The US initiative, also backed by institutional investors, business groups and labour unions, was prompted by concerns about the corrosive effect of market pressure for short-term performance, and by growing popular resentment at the size of executive remu-neration, an issue that was thrown into sharp relief by the subsequent credit crisis and global downturn. The CEOs of two of those three signatory companies, PepsiCo and Xerox, are women.

The gender gap in leadership is nowhere more apparent than in the corporate world, as we have documented in this book. Yet we see signs of movement here too. Progressive com-panies are learning not just how to market themselves better to women, but also how to make the women in their own ranks feel more welcome and better valued. There are, as yet, few companies that have got this completely right, although we highlight examples of those which have accepted the challenge head on, made significant breakthroughs and learned positive things about themselves in the process.

They know that they have every reason to do so. Women are outperforming educationally, and there is now a wealth of evidence that links better gender balance at the top of companies to stronger financial performance.

We have examined the opportunities for companies in adapting their strategies to become "gender-bilingual": that is, to demonstrate an understanding of the different ways that men and women talk, think and behave. Doing so will enable them to benefit from some of the extraordinary changes taking place in the female market: the fact that women in the US, for example, will control $ 22 trillion by 2010, or that there are more female than male millionaires in the UK between the ages of 18 and 44.

We have pointed to the added value that companies will gain by becoming "women-friendly". They will find themselves employers of choice for a host of talent, among the younger and older generations of knowledge workers whose skills they wish to acquire (and possibly not to retire), and among the increasing number of men looking for a new deal from work that allows them to embrace their dual roles as parents and breadwinners. As we show, this is no idle fancy – technology is moving faster in enabling this to happen than most big companies can keep pace with.

We have analysed the different approaches to gender and work in countries around the world. Although women face serious obstacles, even in some of the most developed countries, our message is surprisingly positive: that rising birth rates can go hand in hand with women's full participation in the workforce. For the sake of economic recovery and sustainable growth, countries would do well to learn from each other which economic and social policies work best in enabling parents of both sexes to combine family life with work.

Along the way, we have explained why many gender initiatives to date have failed to achieve their desired objectives. Traditional approaches – including an unfortunate insistence that being equal means being the same – have affected our ability to craft a more balanced future. We do not expect positive measures in favour of women. We ask for recognition that the dominant model of work and career path favours a now outmoded division of labour between the sexes – and for a willingness to adapt it for the future that is already upon us.

We have given readers a step-by-step guide to manage the gender question successfully. We do not pretend it is easy. It requires the careful dismantling of what we call "gender asbestos": values, systems and processes designed for a different era, which can cause barely detectable but long-lasting damage to women's career opportunities. There will be resistance from some people – women as well as men – who prefer the corporate structure built the old way, or who say the problem lies outside the workplace rather than inside, or who deny there is a problem even.

There are senior managers who think that women will only make it in the professional sphere once they have learned to set clearer priorities at home – in other words getting their partners to do more than the average 20% of household tasks currently attributed to them. It appears that robots that mow the lawn, wash and iron the clothes and clean the house are still at least 20 years' away from being in general domestic use, which strikes us as too long to wait.

In any case, the truth is that the power and confidence to negotiate at home comes from success, recognition and salary earned at work. A time-use study carried out in Canada found that men spend more time on housework, and women less time, as the women's income rises. "When women's pay cheques hit $ 100000, the division of paid labour and housework within couples is more likely to be split equally," noted Chrystia Freeland in the *Financial Times* (Freeland, 2006).

Progressive companies are realising that it is in their own interests to have women better represented throughout their ranks, and that to do this they have to stop forcing women to adapt. Women have already done plenty of adapting to the corporate world. Now it is for companies to change the rules to fit women too. It is not women who need help in adjusting to the new reality so much as the men who unconsciously perpetuate and benefit most from the status quo.

Since this book was first published in 2008, we have been encouraged by the growing number of male business leaders who are willing to talk publicly about the importance of gender balance and the need for change. We have spoken to many of them and have included a special feature called "CEOs Who Get It" on the website published by one of the authors.

There is Michel Landel, CEO of Sodexo, which provides food and facilities management services to clients around the world. Landel has made gender balance a top priority and says he has to keep up the pressure all the time in order to bring about reform in the company.

"The world is driven by men, if we don't push them to yield power, it will take generations," says Landel. "You need to develop managers' awareness – awareness is the fundamental key to improvement. They need to realise that rebalancing gender requires doing some work on themselves. There is a certain degree of willingness to put oneself into question that is required. For some people, that is harder or takes a bit more time than for others" (Wittenberg-Cox, 2009).

Then there is Roger Carr, chairman of two large UK companies, Cadbury and Centrica, who is deeply involved in initiatives to increase the number of women on boards. "Having a mixed gender board is invariably better than a single gender board," he says. It encourages men and women to air their different perspectives. "If half the people you're serving are women and you have no women on the board to offer a view, that's a very distorted picture you risk creating" (Maitland, 2009).

There is also Piyush Gupta, CEO of Citibank in South East Asia Pacific, who, at an Insead debate in Singapore, amusingly followed this book's three 21st century Ws – weather, women and web – with his own three 20th century Ms: "Men, myopia and mayhem".

Gupta recognises that women are the majority of the bank's customers in Asia. "We've found that women respond better to women bankers," he says. "Women bring something different to business, and you need to leverage both genders. It's a substantive business issue. It is not about being kind to women. It is about ensuring the success of our business in the future" (Wittenberg-Cox, 2009).

In French, there is a word, *mixité*, which means a balanced mix of the sexes. It is a helpful term with which to change the tone of the gender debate, trapped as it is in concepts of glass ceilings, sticky floors and other apparently insurmountable obstacles.

Olivier Marchal, managing director of the French office of Bain, the international strategy consultancy, offers a vivid metaphor to add to the new vocabulary. Women may hold the key to a better gender balance, he told us, "but men generally still control the lock" (see Olivier Marchal interview, Chapter Five).

This book has brought together overwhelming evidence that women do indeed mean business. Their fast-growing influence in the workplace and the marketplace is changing everything. These changes represent a desirable, not a threatening, revolution. Rather than thinking that men and women are from different planets, we have the more amusing challenge of learning how to run this planet together.

Understanding, harnessing and working with the formidable force that women have become can propel companies into a sustainable and profitable future. It will take courage, conviction, a willingness to learn. As Winston Churchill said: "Courage is what it takes to stand up and speak," and "courage is also what it takes to sit down and listen."

The answers now lie in your, the reader's, hands. The signs are that a balance of power between men and women will be better, not just for individual companies and countries, but for the planet – and *all* its people.

REFERENCES AND FURTHER READING

Adler, R.D. and Conlin, R. (2009) "Profit, thy name is ... woman?", *Miller-McCune*, 27 February.

Alesina, A. and Ichino, A. (2007) "Why women should pay less tax", *Financial Times*, 18 April.

Alimo-Metcalfe, B. (2002) *Leadership & Gender: A Masculine Past; A Feminine Future?* Thematic paper for CERFE Project.

Alliot-Marie, M. (2006) speaking at the Women's Forum, Deauville.

Amalou, A. (2006) "Le bricolage est devenu un jeu", *Le Monde*, 12 October.

AMM Finance announcement (2007).

Anderson, J. (2007) "Wall St firm will settle sex bias suit", *The New York Times*, 25 April.

Andrietti, B. (2004) Speech at a EuropeanPWN Paris lunch, May.

Antoine, C. (2005) General manager, country & business internet marketing services EMEA, speaking at the WIN Conference, Geneva.

Arnold, C. (2006) Speech at the European Catalyst and Conference Board Conference, Prague, May.

Aspire (2006) "The 2006 Aspire Survey of Executive Women", www.aspirecompanies.com.

Associated Press (2007) "China's gender gap widening", Beijing, 12 January.

Association of Executive Search Consultants (2007) Press release, May.

Auer, P., Berg, J. and Coulibaly, I. (2006) "Is a stable workforce good for productivity?" *International Labour Review*, vol 144/3, ILO, Geneva, 2005; and ILO online interview, 20 January.

Babcock, L. and Laschever, S. (2003) *Women Don't Ask: Negotiation and the Gender Divide*, Princeton University Press.

Bakewell, J. (2006) The *Independent*, November 10.

Barclays (2007) "Boom in female wealth creation driven by business success: and money can buy you happiness after all", Press release, 11 June, referring to "Barclays Wealth Insights: a question of gender".

Barletta, M. (2006) *Marketing to Women, How to Increase Your Share of the World's Largest Market*, Dearborn Publishing.

Baron-Cohen, S. (2003) *The Essential Difference*. Allen Lane.

BBC (2006) "Right time for a baby, UK vs France", 14 June.

Bell Burnell, J. (2007) Speaking at Women as Leaders conference, organised by McKinsey with Oxford Women in Politics, 2 February.

Ben Hamida, E. (2006) Speaking at panel discussion on microfinance at the Women's Forum for the Economy and Society, Deauville, France, October.

Blair, C. (2005) Keynote speech at the Women's Forum, Deauville.

Brabeck-Letmathe, P. (2006) Speech, Women's Forum Conference, Deauville, www.womens-forum.com.

Bradshaw, D. (2007) "Stepping stones to top careers", *Financial Times*, 5 March.

Brizendine, L. (2006) *The Female Brain.* Broadway.

BT (2007) Case study from "Enter the timelords: Transforming work to meet the future", final report of the Equal Opportunities Commission investigation into the transformation of work, June.

Business Week online (2001) "Tyson takes on London", 14 August.

Caparas, A., Assistant Professor, Master of Science in Management Programme, University of Asia and the Pacific, in interview with author.

Carter, S. (2006) Speech at Women's Financial Adviser Group Awards, London, January.

Cassani, B. (2007) Speaking at Women as Leaders, a McKinsey conference with Oxford Women in Politics, February.

Catalyst (2004) *The Bottom Line: Connecting Corporate Performance and Gender Diversity.*

Catalyst (2005) Bureau of Labor Statistics, quoted in Catalyst Census of Women Corporate Officers and Top Earners of the *Fortune* 500.

Catalyst (2005) *Women "Take Care", Men "Take Charge": Stereotyping of US Business Leaders Exposed,* October.

Catalyst (2006) Census of Women Corporate Officers and Top Earners of the *Fortune* 500, July.

Catalyst (2006) *Different Cultures, Similar Perceptions: Stereotyping of Western European Business Leaders,* June.

Catalyst (2007) *The Bottom Line: Corporate Performance and Women's Representation on Boards.*

Catalyst (2007) *The double-bind dilemma for women in leadership: Damned if you do, doomed if you don't,* July.

Catalyst (2008) *Advancing Women Leaders.*

Catalyst (2009) *Engaging Men in Gender Initiatives,* May.

Center for Women's Leadership at Babson College and London Business School (2007) "Global Entrepreneurship Monitor, 2006 Report on Women and Entrepreneurship".

Chan Kim, W. and Mauborgne, R. (2003) "Tipping Point Leadership", *Harvard Business Review*, April.

Chan Kim, W. and Mauborgne, R. (2005) *Blue Ocean Strategy: How to Create Uncontested Market Space and Make Competition Irrelevant*, Harvard Business School Press.

Clark, P. (2005) "Europe's Top 25: The accidental feminist", *FT Magazine*, 15 October.

Cranfield School of Management and Opportunity Now (2004) "Making Good Connections".

Cunningham, J. and Roberts, P. (2006) *Inside Her Pretty Little Head*, Cyan Communications.

Daly, K. (2007) "Gender Inequality, Growth and Global Ageing", Goldman Sachs Global Economics Paper No. 154, 3 April.

Datamonitor (2007) "Targeting Women in Private Banking 2007".

Dempsey, J. (2006) "For the working mothers of Germany, an incentive", *International Herald Tribune*, 30 December.

Deutsche Welle, www.dw-world.de.

Development Dimensions International Inc (2009) "Holding Women Back", ddiworld.com.

Dezsö, C. and Ross, D.G. (2008) "Girl Power: Female Participation in Management and Firm Quality", Working Paper, Columbia Business School, August.

DiPiazza, S. (2006) Speech given at the Women's Forum, Deauville, France, 7 October.

Drucker, P.F. (1999) *Management Challenges for the 21st Century*, HarperBusiness.

Economic Commission for Europe (2007) "Gender Equality: a key component of a modern growth strategy", keynote speech to UN, 27 April.

Equal Opportunities Commission (2005) *30 Voices*, Equal Opportunities Commission, www.eoc.org.uk/PDF/30voices_booklet.pdf.

Equal Opportunities Commission (2007) "Working outside the box: changing work to meet the future", January.

Equality and Human Rights Commission (2009) "Working Better: Meeting the changing needs of families, workers and employers in the 21st century", March.

EU (2006) "She Figures 2006".

EU (2007) "Women driving EU job growth – but still face barriers to equality", Press Release, 7 March.

Europa (2007) Press release, 10 May, IP/07/643.

European Commission (2007) Report on equality between women and men, 7 February.

Evans-Pritchard, A. (2007) "Japan leads world in demographic decline", *Daily Telegraph*, 1 June.

Farrell, W. (2005) *Why Men Earn More: The Startling Truth Behind the Pay Gap*, Amacom.

Ferenczi, T. (2007) "Angela Merkel à petits pas", *Le Monde*, 20 April.

Financial Times (2007) "The *FT*'s guide to the best of Davos 2007", 23 January.

Financial Times (2007) "Young women are web's biggest audience", 17 May.

Financial Times (2009) MBA 2009 Rankings.

Fortune (2009) 25 May.

Fragale, A. (2006) "The power of powerless speech", Kenan-Flagler Business School, University of North Carolina, March, www.sciencedirect.com.

Freeland, C. (2006) "Women are the hidden engine of world growth", *Financial Times*, 28 August.

Furrer-Lech, C. (2006) Speech at the GBG Women's Leadership Forum, Barcelona, November 2006.

Gender Based Taxation working paper, www2.dse.unibo.it/ichino/#papinprog.

Ghosn, C. (2006) Speech given at the Women's Forum, Deauville, France, 7 October.

Gimbel, F. (2007) "Asia grapples with its high-speed ageing", *Financial Times*, 9 April.

Gladwell, M. (2000) *The Tipping Point*, Little, Brown and Company.

Goldman Sachs (2005) "Womenomics: Japan's Hidden Asset", 19 October.

Grandes Ecoles au Féminin/IPSOS (2005) "L'ambition au féminin".

Grandes Ecoles au Féminin/IPSOS (2005, 2007) "Etudes sur les Carrières au Féminin".

Grant Thornton (2007) "Growth of women in UK boardroom stagnates as Asian counterparts go from strength to strength", UK press release, 8 March, www.grant-thornton.co.uk.

Grant Thornton International (2007) "International Business Report", conducted by Experian Business Strategies and Harris Interactive www.internationalbusinessreport.com.

Greenleaf, R. (1977) *Servant Leadership: A Journey Into Legitimate Power and Greatness*, Paulist Press.

Harvard Business Review Online (2007) "How to manage the Most Talented", March.

Hay Group Global Employee Pay and Staffing Survey (2008), December.

Heffernan, M. (2004) *The Naked Truth.* Jossey-Bass.

Heffernan, M. (2006) "Are women better entrepreneurs?" Forbes. com, 27 June.

Heffernan, M. (2007) *How She Does It, Redefining power and the nature of success for the 21st century*, Penguin.

Helfat, C., Harris, D. and Wolfson, P. (2006) "The pipeline to the top: women and men in the top executive ranks of US corporations", *Academy of Management Perspectives*, November, 20(4).

Hewlett, S.A. (2002) *Creating A Life: Professional Women and the Quest for Children*, Hyperion.

Hewlett, S.A. and Buck Luce, C. (2005) "Off-ramps and on-ramps: keeping talented women on the road to success", *Harvard Business Review*, 28 February.

Hirschman, L.R. (2007) *Get to Work: A Manifesto for Women of the World*, Viking.

Hill, M. (2007) in "Madam President?" *Baltimore Sun*, 6 May.

Holland, J. (2006) "Womenomics 101", 16 March, www.AlterNet. com.

Holmes, K. et al. (2007) cited in "Working outside the box: Changing work to meet the future", interim report of the Equal Opportunities Commission investigation into the transformation of work, January.

HSBC (2006) "The Future of Retirement, What Businesses Want".

Huff Stevens, A. (2005) "The more things change, the more they stay the same: trends in long-term employment in the United States, 1969–2002", National Bureau of Economic Research Working Paper 11878, December.

Ibarra, H. (2004) *Working Identity*: Unconventional Strategies for Reinventing your Career.

Ibarra, H. and Obodaru, O. (2009) "Women and the Vision Thing", *Harvard Business Review*, January.

IBM (2005) Survey of human resources directors.

Inter-Parliamentary Union (2009) 31 March, www.ipu.org/wmn-e/ classif.htm.

Jaumotte, F. (2003) "Female labour force participation: past trends and main determinants in OECD countries", OECD Economics Department Working Papers No. 376, December.

Johnson, L. and Learned, A. (2004) *Don't Think Pink: What Really Makes Women Buy – and How to Increase Your Share of This Crucial Market*, AMACOM.

Karlberg, U. (2007) Speaking at the launch of "Tomorrow's Global Company, challenges and choices", a report by Tomorrow's Company, 18 June, and interview with author.

Kissinger, H.A. (2007) "How Germany found an Iron Lady of its own", *Time*, 14 May.

Kleiman, C. (2005) "Given job flexibility, working moms deliver, CEO says", *Chicago Tribune*, 3 May.

Knight, R. (2006) "Top business schools woo young students to foil rivals", *Financial Times*, 14 September.

Knowledge@Wharton (2007) "Falling Behind: Working Women in Germany Grapple with Limited Child-Care Options".

Kolding, M. and Milroy, A. (2001) "The Networking Skills Shortage, How Women Can Narrow the Gap", IDC (International Data Corporation), November.

Kowaleski, T. (2006) "Time for business to mature", *World Business*, September.

Les Femmes en France, http://www.quid.fr/2007/Femmes/Les_Femmes_En_France/1.

L'Oréal-Unesco (2007) Press release on Awards for Women in Science, 23 February.

Ludeman, K. and Erlandson, E. (2006) "The alpha male syndrome", *World Business*, October.

MacGregor, H. (2006) "Mixed Blessings", *Financial Times*, 25 February.

MailOnline (2009) "Would we be in this mess if our money was managed by women?" 28 March.

Maitland, A. (2003) "Oxfam must get things done", *Financial Times*, 24 December.

Maitland, A. (2003) "Unilever hits at the glass ceiling from above", *Financial Times*, 17 June.

Maitland, A. (2004) "A mixed workforce can open up markets", *Financial Times* report on Business & Diversity, 10 May.

Maitland, A. (2005) "The puzzle of the lost women", *Financial Times*, 1 March.

Maitland, A. (2006) "Friends in high places", *FT Weekend Magazine*, 7 October.

Maitland, A. (2006) "Learn the masculine imperative", *Financial Times*, 2 August.

Maitland, A. (2006) "Our innovative 'man' in Bratislava", *Financial Times*, 30 December.

Maitland, A. (2006) "Women are rising to the top of heavy industry", *Financial Times*, 25 October.

Maitland, A. (2007) "Companies make time for flexible hours", *Financial Times*, 23 January.

Maitland, A. (2007) "Top women tip the scales", *Financial Times*, 10 October.

Maitland, A. (2009) "Female talent takes to the boards", *Financial Times*, 30 April.

Martin, P. (2003) "Sustainable migration policies in a globalising world", ILO, March.

McCracken, D. (2000) "Winning the Talent War for Women: Sometimes it Takes a Revolution", *Harvard Business Review*, November.

McGill University (2007) "McGill study: US protections for working families worst of all affluent countries", McGill University press release, 1 February.

McGill University (2007) "The Work, Family, and Equity Index: How Does the U.S. Measure Up?" from The Project on Global Working Families, Harvard School of Public Health, and the Institute for Health and Social Policy, McGill University. Available online at www.mcgill.ca/ihsp.

McKinsey & Company (2007) "Women Matter: Gender diversity, a corporate performance driver", October.

McKinsey & Company (2008) "Women Matter 2. Female leadership, a competitive edge for the future", October.

McKinsey Global Institute (2009) "China's 'sticky floor'", May.

Meece, M. (2006) "What do women want? Just ask them", *New York Times*, 31 October.

Megalogenis, G. (2009) "Women grabbing more of jobs pie", *The Australian*, 11 April.

Mercer Human Resource Consulting (2007) "Holiday entitlements – large disparities between EU member states", press release, London, 4 June.

MetLife (2007) "It's not your mother's retirement", MetLife Mature Market Institute, May.

Miller, P. and Skidmore, P. (2004) "Disorganisation, Why future organisations must 'loosen up'" www.demos.co.uk.

Moïsi, D. (2006) "Four good reasons to have faith in Europe's future", *Financial Times*, 29 January.

Morello, D., Raskino, M. and Harris, K. (2006) *Women and Men in IT: Breaking through sexual stereotypes*, Gartner Symposium ITxpo, Orlando, Florida, October.

Moss Kanter, R. (1977) *Men and Women of the Corporation*, BasicBooks.

Mulcahy, A. (2005) quote given to the authors, based on comments she made at the *Fortune* Most Powerful Women conference, November.

Munn, M. (2007) Speech at Opportunity Now Awards, 24 April.

New Europe (2009) "EU campaigns to bridge the gender pay gap", 9 March.

Newswise (2006) "What men think they know about executive women", www.newswise.com, 1 November.

Nielsen/NetRatings (2007) "Young women now the most dominant group online".

Obama, B. (2006) *The Audacity of Hope*, Crown.

O'Brien, T.L. (2006) "Up the down staircase", *The New York Times*, 19 March.

OECD (2004) "Babies and Bosses".

OECD (2005) "Babies and Bosses".

OECD (2005) *Health at a glance: OECD indicators 2005.*

OECD (2006) *Live longer, work longer.*

OECD (2006) "Women and Men in OECD Countries", Paris.

OECD (2007) "Babies and Bosses".

OECD (2007) Diafora OECD gender awareness seminar, 31 May.

Olving, L. (2006) speaking at GBG Women's Leadership Forum, Barcelona, November.

Opportunity Now Awards (2009).

Peters, T. (2006) foreword to *Marketing to Women*, Dearborn Publishing.

PricewaterhouseCoopers (2007) Tackling the issues of diversity, www.pwc.com/extweb/aboutus.nsf/docid/41C70EA4016E823F8 525720C0007E66D, June.

PricewaterhouseCoopers (2008) "Closing the gender gap".

PricewaterhouseCoopers (2009) 12th Annual Global CEO Survey.

Rampell, Catherine (2009) "As Layoffs Surge, Women May Pass Men in Job Force", *New York Times*, 5 February.

Ricol, Lasteyrie & Associés, Capitalcom and Christian & Timbers (2006) "The presence of women in executive committees and on boards of directors", October.

Romano, L. (2007) "Gatekeepers of Hillaryland", *Washington Post*, 21 June.

Rosa, N. La Compagnie des Femmes, http://www.comdesfemmes. com/.

Rosenthal, E. (2006) "Europe, East and West, wrestles with falling birthrates", *International Herald Tribune*, 3 September.

Ruderman, M.N. and Ohlott, P.J. (2002) *Standing at the Crossroads: Next Steps for High-Achieving Women*, Jossey-Bass.

Saatchi & Saatchi (2007) "Lady Geek".

Sapphire Partners (2009) "There is a silver lining".

Smeaton, D. and Marsh, A. (2006) cited in "Working outside the box: Changing work to meet the future", interim report of the Equal Opportunities Commission investigation into the transformation of work, January 2007.

Špidla, V. (2007) Commissioner for Employment, Social Affairs and Equal Opportunities quoted on EU website, Europa.eu, "Support for families is key to reach Lisbon targets", press release May 10.

Stephenson, C. (2004) "Leveraging diversity to maximum advantage: The business case for appointing more women to boards", *Ivey Business Journal*, September/October.

Tanikawa, M. (2007) "Japan Inc. embraces diversity", *International Herald Tribune*, 2 June.

Tannen, D. (2001) *Talking from 9 to 5: Women and men at work*. Harper Paperbacks.

The Conference Board of Canada (2002) "Women on boards: not just the right thing ... but the 'bright' thing", June.

The Daily Telegraph (2008) "Now more than ever, we need women on boards", 20 October.

The Economist (2005) "The conundrum of the glass ceiling", July.

The Economist (2006) Corporate Executive Board survey, cited in "The battle for brainpower", 7 October.

The Economist (2006) "The Battle for Brainpower", 7 October.

The Economist (2006) "Womenomics" 12 April.

The Economist (2009) "A new pecking order", 7 May.

The Female FTSE Report 2003 (2003) November, Cranfield University School of Management.

The Female FTSE Report 2004 (2004) December, Cranfield University School of Management.

The Female FTSE Report 2006 (2006) November, Cranfield University School of Management.

The Female FTSE Report 2008 (2008) "A Decade of Delay", Cranfield University.

The Times (2009) "Women in the boardroom help companies succeed", 19 March.

Thomas Yaccato, J. (2003) *The 80% Minority: Reaching the Real World of Women Consumers*, Viking Canada.

Thompson, M. et al. (2006) cited in "Working outside the box: Changing work to meet the future", interim report of the Equal Opportunities Commission investigation into the transformation of work, January 2007.

Thomson, P. and Graham, J. (2005) *A Woman's Place is in the Boardroom*. Palgrave Macmillan.

Tosolini, A. (2005) Speech at the WIN (Women's International Networking) Conference in Geneva.

Tucker, S. (2007) "Awkward 'gender moments' relived", *Financial Times*, 22 January.

UNDP (2006) launch of the Arab Human Development Report 2005: Toward the rise of women in the Arab world, 6 December.

Unilever (2007) "Beauty has no age limit", www.unilever.com/ourbrands/beautyandstyle/articles.

US Department of Education (2005) National Center for Education Statistics.

Vigeo, www.vigeo.org.

Vincent-Lancrin, S. (2008) "The Reversal of Gender Equalities in Higher Education: An Ongoing Trend" in *Higher Education To 2030 – Volume 1: Demography*, OECD.

Waldmeir, P. (2007) "US employers fear broad scope of class action suits", *Financial Times*, 8 February.

Warner, F. (2006) *The Power of the Purse*, Pearson Prentice Hall.

Warner, J. (2005) *Perfect Madness, Motherhood in the Age of Anxiety*, Penguin.

Widell Christiansen, M. (2004) Project Manager, Design (Volvo Cars), speaking at WIN Conference.

WIN Conference (1999) Milan, October.

Wirth, L. (2002) ILO, "Breaking Through the Glass Ceiling: Women in Management", Luxembourg conference.

Wittenberg-Cox, A. (2009) "Hot topic in Asia too", 20-first.com.

Wittenberg-Cox, A. (2009) "Transformational change driven from the top", 20-first.com.

Women's Forum (2006) Deauville, France, October, www.WomensForum.com.

Women and Work Commission (2006) "Shaping a fairer future", February.

World Bank (2007) "Economic Status of Women", web.worldbank.org/WBSITE/EXTERNAL/NEWS, 22 February.

World Bank http://web.worldbank.org/wbsite/external/topics/extgender.

World Economic Forum (2005) The Gender Gap Report.

INDEX

24/7 cultures 212, 283
80/20 rule 224

abortions 224
Accenture 33
accountability issues,
    promoting women 76
accountancy firms 57
ad agencies 51–2, 68, 143
adaptability needs, cultural
    issues 204
age factors, women 47, 56–7,
    83–5, 93–5, 111, 119, 143,
    197, 257, 259, 296–7,
    308–9
Age Masters 297, 300
ageing populations 4, 27, 38,
    193, 224, 301
  see also demographics
agents of change 277
  see also change
AIB Group 249
Alcatel 102, 211

Alesina, Alberto 290
Alexander, Helen 274
alienating cultures 62–5
Alliot-Marie, Michèle 136, 208
alpha males 258
alternative careers,
    motivations 54
alternative views, power
    issues 270
Amazone Euro Fund 41
ambition phase, career-life
    styles 254–67
Amemiya, Hiroko 222
American Express 292
Amnesty International Business
    Group 312
Andrews, Jim 147, 185
Andrietti, Bernadette 261
Anglo American 128, 210,
    271
annual reports 75
Antoine, Cara 122
Apple 104

Arab world
  Islamic financing 266
  working women 213, 216,
    250
Archer Daniels Midland 128
Areva 238
Armstrong, Louis 56
Arnold, Colleen 250
ascendancy issues, women
    1–2, 30–3, 312–26
Asia 14, 17, 23, 41, 66, 74, 81,
    175, 218, 223–6, 244, 284,
    325
  see also individual countries
  country comparisons 197
Aspire 243, 247
Assa Abloy 296
assertiveness training 67, 115
Association of Executive
    Search Consultants 291
AstraZeneca 312
Atomic Energy Authority 271
attitudes of managers 129
attractive workplaces 54
audits 129, 156
Auer, Peter 265
Aurora 247
Australia 262–3
Austria 218, 238
authenticity 101, 243–4
awakening benefits, leadership
    teams 150–1

awareness-building workshops
  bilingualism building
    blocks 141, 170
Axiom Legal 292

Babcock, Linda 245
babyboom generation 300
Bachelet, Michelle 216
Bain & Co. 189–90, 268
Bakewell, Joan 132
Bakker, Peter 70
Bando, Mariko 220
Bangladesh 318
Bank of Scotland 102
banking industry 11–12, 84–7,
    89, 317–9
Barclays Wealth 85
Barletta, Marti 80
barriers, women 101, 126
Barroso, José Manuel 313
BBC 207
Belgium 218, 226
benchmarking exercises,
    UK 233
"best" biases, diversity
    issues 121
Best Buy 90
BHP 238
biases 52, 122, 142, 144, 241,
    279
"bilingualism" see "gender-
    bilingual" concepts

birth rates 2, 27–30, 193, 195,
      241, 219, 302
   see also demographics
BlackBerry 293
Blair, Cherie 75
blogs 314
"blue ocean" 20, 95
boards of directors 14, 17, 40
   see also executive
      committees; top jobs
   audit of attitudes 129
   better boards 70
   business issues 17, 22, 61,
      151, 156, 163, 165, 325
   dynamics 70
   legislation considerations
      73
   male-dominated preserves
      44, 89, 100, 104, 119,
      167, 185, 187, 299
   statistics 29, 44, 50, 52, 102,
      158, 202, 217
   tokenism 73
Booz Allen Australia 262
Boston Consulting Group 79
BP 11, 105, 145, 266
Brabeck-Letmathe, Peter 49–50,
      180
brainpower
   "grey" brainpower 296, 302
Brazil 19, 134
breadwinning roles 17

breastfeeding rights 216
Bricorama 104
Brizendine, Louann 114
Brown, Dean J. Frank 46
Brundtland, Gro Harlem 211
BT 306–7
budgets 22, 86, 140, 151,
      178–9, 229, 286
   concepts 123, 253, 270,
      278, 325
   key success factors 146,
      149
building blocks, "gender-
      bilingual" concepts 138
Burgmans, Antony 154
Burmaster, Alex 91
burn-out dangers 260
Burnell, Dame Jocelyn Bell
      115
business issues
   key success factors 146, 149
business schools 18, 45–6, 165,
      205, 212, 246–7
   see also MBA students
   critique 247–8
Business Week 45
business-case definition, key
      success factors 146, 149
business-to-business market
      80
busyness problems 245
Butler, Sarah 262–3

Caesar 270
Caleel, Thomas 47
Canada 41, 71, 74, 323
Cannon, Fiona 289
car-buying decisions 97
"career as snowflake" 253
career-life styles 254–67
    ambition phase 254–67
    "career as snowflake" 253
    concepts 123, 253, 270, 278,
        325
    culture-shock phase 255–7
    flexibility issues 144–5, 174,
        227, 243, 301, 303, 304,
        305, 308
    foreign assignments 308
    M-shaped career curves 251
    the "Me" generation 302
    phases 254, 264, 308
    self-affirmation phase 264–7
Carroll, Cynthia 210, 271
Cassani, Barbara 174, 272
Catalyst 14, 40, 122–6, 211
Center for Creative Leadership
    244
Center for Work-Life Policy 55,
    211
Centre for Women in Business
    (LBS/Lehman Brothers)
    46–7
CEOs 6, 118, 134, 159, 177,
    186, 190–1, 307, 320, 324

see also leadership teams;
    top jobs
change 1–2, 5, 7–9, 11–12, 15,
    18–19, 22, 25, 27, 31,
    45–7, 50–1, 62, 64, 70–1,
    73, 90–1, 93–4, 103, 105,
    119, 127–8, 130, 132, 137,
    140, 142, 151–2, 154, 156,
    160–2, 166, 168–70, 173,
    176, 178–9, 181, 183,
    185–6, 189–90, 192, 203–4,
    209–10, 216, 220–1, 229,
    233, 261, 263–4, 270–1,
    276–7, 284, 297, 299, 302,
    305–6, 308, 311, 313–17,
    321, 323–6
    agents of change 8, 277
    cognitive hurdle 151
    key success factors 146, 149
    leadership teams 20, 75,
        127, 140
    noise-making issues 151,
        169
    resistance issues 131
    work patterns 308
    workshops 24, 60, 139, 141,
        179, 181, 273, 276
Chase, Rodney 266
Cheung, Fanny 223
Chicago Tribunal 291
child tax credits, UK 231
childbearing see motherhood

childcare subsidies 227, 229, 290
Chile 316
China 1, 19, 27, 79, 177, 199, 223–6, 300
  ageing population 27, 38, 193, 224, 301
  country comparisons 70, 156
  infanticide scandal 224
  motherhood 202, 207, 211, 224, 232, 257, 314
  top jobs 4, 11, 144
  women 1–33, 35–77, 79–107, 110–28, 130–56, 158–60, 162–6, 168–74, 176–202, 204–74, 276–82, 284, 286, 288, 290, 292–4, 296, 298–302, 304, 306–9, 312–26
Churchill, Winston 311, 326
Churchman, Sarah 60, 304
Cisco 292
Citigroup 86
Citroën 97–8
City of London 46
Civil Service 111, 220
Clark, Pilita 228
"client-driven" cultures 57
Clinton, Bill 211, 317
Clinton, Hillary 313
coaching 20, 139, 141–3
"codes", politics 141

cognitive hurdle, change 151
commitment factors 62
communications
  external communications 27, 145, 172
  feedback issues 256
  "gender-bilingual" concepts 17–21, 133, 146, 180, 321
  informal conversations 248–9
  mixed messages 151, 173
  networking 20, 64, 66–7, 69, 86, 124, 139, 141–2, 153, 155, 164, 178, 181, 205, 232, 242, 246, 255, 258–61, 264, 267–8, 278–80, 285, 291, 294, 303–4, 309
  strategies 6, 9, 80, 96, 127, 139, 170, 182, 321, 331, 333
  styles 18, 63, 113–14, 136–8, 141, 146, 207, 237, 240, 247, 278–9, 285, 305
  vocabulary differences 51, 135
former communist states of eastern Europe 29
companies
  see also boards . . .
  benchmarking exercises 233

corporate governance 41–2,
71
cultural issues 204
disorganization benefits
293–6
dual-career partnerships 260
flexible working 144, 175,
213, 231, 263, 283
future prospects 316
"gender-bilingual" concepts
321
long-term employment
relationships 265
meritocracies 24, 125, 147
new approach to gender
119, 129
opportunities for
companies 321
performance issues 308
private/public sector
considerations 29–30,
42–4, 57, 73, 197,
208–210, 227–34
restructuring trends 245
sector trailblazers 118–9
short-termism 12, 320
start-ups 80, 119, 178, 293
strategic issues 180
successful implementation
22, 149, 151, 153, 155,
157, 159, 161, 163, 165,
167, 169, 171, 173, 175,
177, 179, 181, 183, 185,
187, 189, 191
top jobs 4, 11, 144
traditional approaches 109,
147, 322
competitive advantages 8, 15,
32, 97, 118, 144, 149, 188,
283
complementary skills 32
conclusions 146, 180, 311, 313,
315, 317, 319, 321, 323, 325
confidence 2, 20, 39, 137, 142,
238, 248–9, 264, 307, 317,
323
construction sector 5, 44
consultancy firms 284–7
consumer research 15–16, 80,
107
consumers
see also customer services;
markets
electronics industry 89–90
segmentation issues 91–107
statistics 29, 44, 50, 52, 102,
158, 202, 217
women 1–33, 35–77, 79–107,
110–28, 130–56, 158–60,
162–6, 168–74, 176–202,
204–74, 276–82, 284,
286, 288, 290, 292–4,
296, 298–302, 304,
306–9, 312–26

Cook, Mike 178
corporate governance 41–2,
71
corruption, power issues 270–1
Council of Women World
Leaders 315–16
country comparisons 197, 285
see also cultural issues;
individual countries
Asia 14, 17, 23, 30, 41, 66,
74, 81, 175, 218, 223–6,
244, 284, 325
former communist states of
eastern Europe 29
fertility rates 38, 194–5, 197,
202, 219
France 27, 55, 71, 74, 79,
104, 134, 136, 153,
155, 189, 198, 202–3,
205–11, 214–15, 218,
226, 253, 261–2, 267,
313, 315–17
Germany 63, 79, 198–9,
202–8, 215, 217–18, 220,
226
job tenure 265
maternity leave 65, 162, 198,
207, 211, 213, 217, 231,
262
private/public sector
considerations 198, 199,
203–5

UK 5, 7, 13, 27, 30, 41–4,
48, 56–8, 60, 63, 73, 79,
85–91, 94, 102, 110–11,
135, 144, 155, 175, 205,
208, 210, 218, 225–6,
231, 233, 247, 271–4,
283, 288, 293, 301
US 3, 5, 7, 14–15, 24, 27–30,
38–40, 44, 48, 54, 57,
63, 66, 69, 74, 79–80,
83–6, 88, 97, 110–12,
118, 121, 123, 125, 128,
134, 195, 197–9, 207,
211–16, 221–2, 226
courage 6, 153, 235, 319, 326
Cox, Vivienne 266
Cranfield 41, 71–2, 128, 178,
232, 247, 276
creative directors, ad agencies
50
cultural issues 204
adaptability needs 32, 305
alienating cultures 62
audits 52, 71, 107, 129, 143,
147, 156, 157, 181
"client-driven" cultures 57
concepts 16, 29, 103, 120,
123, 136, 145, 219, 244,
253, 270, 278, 282, 325
country comparisons 70, 156
financial services industry
84, 177

future prospects 316

new approach to gender 119, 129

quotas 49, 66, 73–5, 159, 228

culture-shock phase, career-life styles 255, 256–7

Cunningham, Jane 81

customer services

see also consumers

biases 52, 121–3, 129, 142, 144, 241, 279

Czech Republic 217–18

Czerniawska, Fiona 286

daiba-shitii (diversity) 222

Daily Telegraph 11, 220

Daly, Kevin 38, 81, 229

Daniels, Eric 135

Datamonitor 85–6

Davos conference 3

de Beauvoir, Simone 31

de Margerie, Christophe 70, 275

DeBeers 95

Deloitte 60, 165–6, 178–9

demographics 7, 27–9, 32, 76, 214, 217, 224, 229, 281, 296, 299, 309

see also ageing populations; birth rates

Demos 293–296

Denmark 195, 198

derivatives markets 85

Dervis, Kemal 200

Deutsche Bank 172–3

DIAFORA 336

Diageo 284–5

differences

genetic differences 137–8, 232–3, 235–7, 258–9, 279–80

valuing differences 17–22

DiPiazza, Samuel, Jr 35, 123

disabilities 121

discrimination 36, 62, 110–2, 123, 143, 159, 220, 238, 248, 278–9

see also bias . . .

lawsuits 62, 110–2, 118, 259

positive discrimination 123, 159, 278

disorganization benefits 293–6

diversity issues 17–27

audits 129, 156

"best" biases 121–6

concepts 123, 253, 270, 278, 325

critique 116, 179

Japan 3, 16, 25–6, 29, 38, 82, 84, 101–2, 195, 197–199, 218–24, 226–7

minorities 21, 23, 118–20, 173

valuing differences 17–22

do-it-yourself 104
Dove 16, 94
Dow Jones Sustainability
    Index 307
Dowd, Maureen 273
Drucker, Peter 281
dual-career partnerships,
    companies 260

EADS *see* European Aeronautic
    Defence and Space
    Company
eBay 271
"Echo Boom" *see* "Me"
    generation
economic growth crucial
    areas 43
  skills shortages 36, 43, 229
  women 288
The Economist 1, 37, 29, 67,
    85, 120, 194, 208, 224,
    274, 290
Eden McCallum 285–7
education
  business schools 18, 45–6,
    165, 205, 212, 246–7
  gender comparisons 197
  income correlation 79
  the "Me" generation 302–5
  statistics 29, 44, 50, 52, 102,
    158, 202, 217
  underperforming boys 39

university graduates 4, 7, 38,
    119
egalitarianism 274
electronics industry 89–90,
    102, 104
Elle 102
emerging markets 19
emotional intelligence 73, 117,
    135
employment *see* workforce
empowerment 200, 339
Enda Inter-Arabe 318
engineering sector 44
entrepreneurs 54, 80, 267–9
environmental sustainability 33
Equal Opportunities
    Commission (EOC) 57
equal opportunities
    legislation 18, 42
Equal Pay Act 1963 110
ethnic groups 93, 118, 120,
    173
EuroDisney 275
Europe 3–5, 7, 14, 17, 28, 30,
    38, 41, 43, 51, 63, 66, 74,
    81, 99, 109, 120–122, 125,
    129, 137, 189, 195–6, 209,
    211, 214–5, 218, 226, 231,
    240, 246, 250, 252, 256,
    265–6, 313–4, 316–7, 330,
    336
  see also individual countries

ageing populations 27, 38, 193

former communist states of eastern Europe 29

interventionist stance 214, 227–34, 299–300

job tenure 265

European Aeronautic Defence and Space Company (EADS) 169

European Commission 4, 43, 202, 205–6, 218, 313, 330

events 20, 60, 86, 139, 233, 297

executive committees 10, 17, 66, 68, 74, 336

see also boards of directors

audit of attitudes 129, 147, 171

business case 22, 41, 61, 140–1, 150, 156, 161–2, 169, 184, 337

business issues 6, 17, 22, 61, 151, 156, 163, 165, 325

expert positions 69, 240

external change consultants 162

external communications 27, 145

see also communications

extranets 292

Facebook 303

Farrell, Warren 246, 250

Fast Company 292

fathers 103, 203, 216, 227–8, 260, 287–9

see also men

Fathers Direct 289

Faust, Drew Gilpin 271

feedback issues 64, 90, 117, 241, 256

The Female 31, 42, 73, 114

female finances 84–91

see also income; women

Female FTSE Report 2006 71

feminists 211

fertility rates 38, 194, 197

see also motherhood

finance jobs 55

financial services industry 84, 177

Financial Times 39, 47, 63, 73, 91, 112, 134, 228, 234, 238, 317, 319, 323

Finch-Lees, Tess 173

Finland 195, 209, 299

Fiorina, Carly 271

first-mover advantages, women's markets 16

Fisher, Helen 31

FitzGerald, Niall 63, 134, 154

"fix-the-women" approaches 20

flexible working 144, 175, 231, 263, 283
  see also part-time workers
focus groups 107, 154
Ford 138
foreign assignments, workforce 308
Fortune 500 14, 40, 124
France 27, 55, 74, 79, 104, 134, 136, 155, 189, 198, 202–3, 205–11, 214–5, 218, 226, 253, 261–2, 267, 313, 315–6
  country comparisons 197, 285
fertility rates 38, 194, 197
  graduates 4, 7, 38, 57–8, 79, 119, 158, 205, 304
  social norms 114
  US 114–5
  working mothers 162, 207, 221
France Télécom 136, 267
freelance workers 285
Freeland, Chrystia 29, 323
Friedan, Betty 31
FTSE 100 42, 128, 153, 155, 210, 231
Furrer-Lech, Catherine 239, 266, 267, 275
future prospects, global business 311–2

Gartenberg, Dave 305
Gartner 89
GDP 3, 5, 88, 198, 220
  see also economic growth
Gehry, Frank 253
Gender Action Plan, World Bank 3
"gender asbestos" 53, 340
gender equality
  economic growth 1, 13, 27, 33, 43, 193, 200, 230
  equal opportunities legislation 18, 42
gender initiatives
  budgets 86, 286
  key success factors 146, 149
  launches 178–92
  male fast-trackers 167
"gender-bilingual" concepts 17, 19, 52, 105, 133, 146, 180, 321
  bias-banning building block 138, 147, 248, 253
  building blocks 138, 147, 248, 253
  empowerment building block 138, 147, 248, 253
  key success factors 146, 149
  management bilingualism 135, 140

metaphors 133, 135, 136, 252

personalised conversations 133, 309

top-management commitment 15, 26, 59, 131, 140, 144, 177, 182, 186, 188, 189, 207, 261

vocabulary differences 51, 110, 127, 135, 136, 252, 326

General Motors 83

Generation X 261, 263

Generation Y see "Me" generation

Genesis Park 303

genetic differences 18, 19, 96, 113–5, 118, 133, 135, 138, 141, 144, 186, 187, 226, 229, 237, 248, 250–2, 278–80

Germany 63, 79, 198, 199, 202–8, 215, 217, 218, 220, 226, 313, 315, 330, 333

country comparisons 197, 285

imperfections 210

Japan 3, 16, 25, 26, 29, 38, 82, 84, 101, 102, 195, 197–9, 218–24, 226, 265, 267, 330, 337

working mothers 162, 207, 221, 330

Ghosn, Carlos 26, 133, 183

Gilbert, Julie 90

Gladwell, Malcolm 150

"glass ceilings" 31, 110, 325

Global Gender Gap Report (World Economic Forum) 3, 199

globalisation effects 168, 245, 281

Go 174, 272

Goldman Sachs 3, 16, 29, 38, 81, 82, 83, 101, 194, 195, 197, 218–21, 229, 292

Google 292

Gould, Andrew 185

Graham, Jacey 70, 71, 128, 153

Grameen Bank 318

Grandes Ecoles au Feminin 56, 213, 214

Grant Thornton 225

Greece 195, 226

Green, Josephine 316

Greenleaf, Robert 237, 270

"grey" brainpower 37, 38, 296, 302

see also age factors

growth, guarantors 3

Grussing, Kate 64, 65

guarantors, growth 3

Guettel, Alec 292

Halifax 102
Halonen, Tarja 299
Hamida, Essma Ben 318
hands-on experience,
    leadership teams 20, 75,
    127, 140
Harbing, Lars-Peter 109
Harris, Mark 293
Harvard Business Review 55,
    60, 117, 150, 252
Harvard Business School 57,
    212, 246
Harvard Law School 135
healthcare 3, 36, 43, 88
hedge funds 85, 101
Heffernan, Margaret 269
Helgesen, Sally 31
Henderson, Wayne 287, 290
Henley, Sue 137
Hewish, Antony 115
Hewlett Packard (HP) 122
Hewlett, Sylvia Ann 211, 227,
    252
Heymann, Jody 216
hierarchical structures, power
    issues 240, 294
high-potential identification,
    talent 76, 143, 154, 169,
    187, 222, 286, 300, 302,
    307
historical background 8, 10,
    27, 92, 100, 250, 316

Hogan, Austin 248
Holdings, Resona 100, 101
holistic approaches 87, 105,
    177
Holland, Joshua 213
Home Depot 145
homeworking 29, 54, 56, 79,
    93, 95, 98, 202–4, 222,
    224, 288, 323
Hong Kong 223, 225
hospitality workers 43
household chores 91, 201, 214,
    219, 221, 323
HP *see* Hewlett Packard
HR directors 163, 243
HSBC 251, 301
Hungary 7, 218

Ibarra, Herminia 46, 54
IBM 119, 138, 210, 211, 250,
    300
Iceland 195, 209
Ichino, Andrea 290
IDC 205
ideas-stealing irritations 63
IMD 46, 247
immigration levels 221, 299
"impression management" 232,
    276
    see also self-marketing skills
in-betweens segment, markets
    91–3

income 5, 30, 59, 79, 80, 82,
    83, 92, 175, 203, 214,
    219–21, 229, 231, 285,
    290, 323
  education correlation 1, 3, 5,
    7, 10, 38, 39, 42, 43, 47,
    57, 79, 80, 105, 146,
    164, 208, 255
  female finances 84, 87
  statistics 29, 44, 50, 52, 102,
    158, 202, 217
The Independent 132
independent financial
    advisers 86, 87, 89
India 1, 19, 23, 27, 175, 199,
    223
infanticide scandal, China 224
informal conversations 248,
    249
  see also communications
information technology (IT)
    44, 142, 289
  see also Internet
INSEAD 46, 117, 247
integrity, power 235
Intel 211, 261, 262
International Herald Tribune
    28, 222
International Labour
    Organisation 215, 228, 265
Internet 1, 33, 80, 90, 91, 201,
    275, 316

  see also web
advertising 16, 50, 89, 90,
    91, 93–5, 99, 102, 104,
    105
  statistics 29, 44, 50, 52, 102,
    158, 202, 217
interventionist policies,
    politics 4, 64, 136, 137,
    141, 236, 237, 240, 242,
    244, 312
investment banks 3, 64, 81, 86,
    194, 221, 239, 254
investments 85, 265
IPSOS 55, 214, 331
Ireland 202, 249
Italy 7, 29, 38, 100, 195, 198,
    199, 226

Jackson, Margaret 238
Japan 3, 16, 25, 26, 29, 38,
    82, 84, 101, 102, 195,
    197–9, 218–24, 226, 265,
    267, 330
  country comparisons 197,
    285
  diversity issues (daiba-shitii)
    222
  fertility rate 38, 194, 197,
    202, 219
  Germany 63, 79, 198, 199,
    202–8, 215, 217, 218,
    220, 226, 313, 315

imperfections 200–5
job tenure 265
job tenure, statistics 265
Johnson & Johnson 103, 109, 210
JP Morgan 223
Judge, Barbara Thomas 271
Judge Business School at Cambridge 13, 45

Kanter, Rosabeth Moss 270
Karlberg, Ulf 312
Kellogg's 106
key influencers 163, 171
key success factors
  budgets 86, 286
  business issues 6, 17, 22, 61, 151, 156, 163, 165, 325
  business-case definition 150, 155–9
  change/noise considerations 177
  concepts 123, 253, 270, 278, 325
  gender initiatives 20, 22, 126, 127, 139, 140, 150, 157, 167, 171, 173, 178, 179, 322
  leadership teams 20, 75, 127, 140
  mixed messages 51, 63, 136, 150, 151, 172, 173

resistance issues 13, 115, 131, 132, 140, 151, 159, 168, 179, 300, 306, 322
Kim, Chan 20, 95, 150, 151, 163, 166
Kissinger, Henry 313, 314
knowledge workers 6, 261, 321
Korea 177, 199, 219, 226
Kowaleski, Tom 83

labels 114
labour market see workforce
Lagarde, Christine 208, 313
Lang, Ilene 123–4
language
  see also "gender-bilingual" concepts
  metaphors 133, 135, 136, 252
Laschever, Sara 239, 246
lateral thinking 70
lattice structures 295
Latvia 195, 217, 218
Lauvergeon, Anne 238
LBS see London Business School
Le Monde 71, 327, 331
Leadership Forum 63, 241, 331, 336
leadership styles 18, 113, 114, 141, 237

leadership teams 20, 75, 127, 140
  see also boards . . .; top jobs
  audit of attitudes 129, 147, 171
  awakening benefits 36, 92, 303
  change 1, 2, 5, 8, 9, 11, 12, 15, 18, 19, 22, 25, 27, 31, 45–7, 50, 51, 62, 64, 70, 71, 73, 90, 94, 105, 119, 127, 128, 130, 132, 140, 151, 154, 156, 160–2, 166, 168, 170, 173, 178, 179, 181, 183, 186, 190, 204, 209, 210, 216, 220, 221, 229, 263, 264, 270, 271, 277, 302, 305, 308, 311, 314–7, 323–5, 332, 336
  "gender-bilingual" concepts 17, 19, 52, 105, 133, 146, 180, 321
  hands-on experience 152
  key success factors 146, 149
  legislation considerations 18–9, 32, 36, 110–3, 216, 226, 231
  role reversals 153
  statistics 29, 44, 50, 52, 102, 158, 202, 217
legal profession 291

legislation considerations
  discrimination lawsuits 110
  equal opportunities legislation 18, 42
  historical background 110–3
  promotion issues 48
Lehman Brothers 47
Leroy Merlin 145
Levet, Marie-Christine 275
life expectancies 83–4, 93
  see also ageing populations
listening skills 71, 137, 168, 186, 326
Liswood, Laura 315
literature 31, 208
Lithuania 206, 218
Lloyds TSB 72, 135, 289
Lombard, Didier 136
Lombard, Marie-Christine 70
London Business School (LBS) 45–7
long-term employment relationships, companies 265
L'Oréal 43, 100
loyalties 266, 282, 304, 315
Luce, Carolyn Buck 252
Luxembourg 338

M-shaped career curves 251
Macapagal-Arroyo, Gloria 218

male-dominated preserves 44,
48–9, 66–73, 119–23,
129–33, 161–3, 232–4,
258–9
see also men
management bilingualism,
"gender-bilingual"
concepts 146
Marakon Associates 284
Marchal, Olivier 189, 325–6
marginalise marketing
approach 98
market research, biases 145
market shares 83, 298
marketing approaches 103
biases 122, 142, 144, 241,
279
marginalise marketing
approach 98
people-management
issues 281
specialise marketing
approach 96, 103
tips 52, 62, 76, 106, 279
types 57, 279
markets 13, 25, 59, 93, 96,
138, 168, 175–7, 182, 206,
284, 334
see also consumers
concepts 123, 253, 270, 278,
325
electronics industry 90

in-betweens segment 91–2
mature-women segment 93
segmentation issues 91–107
services 73, 80, 82–4, 86–7,
89
tips 52, 62, 76, 106, 279
types 57, 279
young-women segment 91–2
Marks & Spencer 94
Martin Marietta Corporation
110
maternity leave 65, 162, 198,
201, 211, 213, 217, 231,
262
matriarchal society 79, 218
mature-women segment,
markets 93
Mauborgne, Renée 150
Maznevski, Martha 46
MBA students 46–7
see also business schools
Mbaye, Cheikh Tidiane 319
McAughtry, Lauren 86
McCracken, Douglas 60, 165,
178
McLuhan, Marshall 167
McKinsey 14, 36, 41, 116, 174,
224, 285, 328–9, 335–6
the "Me" generation 302
the media 270–2, 300, 313
medical schools 45, 47
Meir, Golda 315

men
  fatherhood 289
  gender comparisons 197
  genetic differences 137–8,
      232–3, 235–7, 258–9,
      279–80
  household chores 219
  male-dominated preserves
      44, 89, 100, 104, 119,
      167, 185, 187, 299
  micro-credits 317
  paternity leave 216, 227,
      288
mentoring 141–2, 153–5, 231,
    297
meritocracies 24, 125, 147
Merkel, Angela 4, 17, 204, 217,
    313
Merrill Lynch 137
metaphors, "gender-bilingual"
    concepts 133
MetLife Mature Market
    Institute 254
Mexico 84
micro-credits 317
Microsoft 119
middle-management positions,
    women 44, 60, 135, 177,
    242
military metaphors 136
"millennials" 302–4
Miller, Paul 295

Mini 97–8
minorities, diversity issues 118,
    120
mixed messages, key success
    factors 146, 149
mobile phone market 102
mobility factors, workforce
    174, 176
Moïsi, Dominique 317
Morgan Stanley 111
motherhood 202, 207, 211,
    224, 232, 257, 314, 338
  see also fertility rates;
      women
  childcare subsidies 227, 229,
      290
  country comparisons 197
  maternity leave 65, 162, 198,
      207, 211, 213, 217, 231,
      262
  pregnancies 162, 252
  priorities 244, 274, 294, 298,
      303, 308, 323
  schools 247
motivations
  alternative careers 54
  top motivators 279
Motorola 102
Mulcahy, Anne 235, 271
Munn, Meg 43, 232
Murray, Donald 291
MySpace 303

NAFE *see* National Association of Female Executives

National Association of Female Executives (NAFE) 69

Nauiokas, Amy 85

Nestlé 24, 49–50

Netherlands 7, 205, 218, 226

networking 20, 86, 155, 205, 242, 277–8, 303–4, 333, 338

new approach to gender, cultural issues 119, 129

new models of work 284
  see also work . . .

New York Times 5, 112, 327

Newsweek 207

Nielsen/NetRatings 90

Nike 106

Nissan 25–6, 133, 183

Nobel Prize awards 115

noise-making issues, change 151, 169

Norway 66, 73, 75, 195, 199, 228, 233

Nyasulu, Hixonia 154

Obama, Barack 215, 315–6

OECD *see* Organisation for Economic Cooperation and Development

"Off-Ramps and On-Ramps" 55, 227, 252

Oie, Kjell Erik 195

Olving, Lena 275

operational roles 42, 68–9, 167–8, 185

opportunities for companies 321

opportunity cost 8–9

Opportunity Now campaign, UK 231

"opposite-sex-as-opponent" 31

Organisation for Economic Cooperation and Development (OECD) 3

"organizational excellence" 41

outsourced training 294

overview 96

Oxfam 319

Palomar-Fresnedi, Rhodora 154, 218, 236

parenthood
  see also motherhood
  men 214–15, 218–19, 222–4, 227–9, 232, 234, 236–41, 246, 248–51, 253, 258–60, 263, 265–6

part-time workers 5, 43, 205, 218, 220, 226, 231, 262–4
  see also flexible working

paternity leave 216
  see also fathers

patient managers, audit of
    attitudes 129–30
pay 4, 23, 37, 43, 65, 70, 98,
    105, 110–12, 115, 143,
    145, 153, 178, 195, 203,
    215, 217, 222, 224, 226–7,
    231, 283–5, 304, 323, 327,
    331
  audits 143
  biases 143
  executive remuneration
    concerns 320
Pearson 210
Pensions 4, 38, 197, 299,
    300–1
  see also retirement
Pepsico 128, 275, 320
perceptions, about women
    100, 225, 236, 252, 313,
    329
performance issues
  biases 142, 144
  companies 1–2, 6–9, 11,
    13–20, 22, 25, 27,
    29–32, 36–44, 47–52,
    54–5, 61–2, 64–77, 80,
    91, 94–8, 100, 106,
    109–10, 113–16, 119–20,
    123, 125–9, 137, 139,
    142–6, 150, 153–7,
    163–4, 166, 168, 171–5,

178, 180, 183, 186, 197,
    208–10, 214, 222, 223,
    225–7, 231, 233–5, 237,
    240–1, 246–7, 250–2,
    254, 256–7, 260–1,
    264–5, 269, 277–8, 280,
    282–4, 286, 288–290,
    292–3, 295–6, 298–301,
    303, 306, 309, 311, 317,
    320–1, 323, 324, 326
  evaluations 76, 144, 256,
    277, 279
  gender comparisons 144
  output/input measures 305
  teleworking 144
personalised conversations,
    "gender-bilingual"
    concepts 17, 19, 52, 105,
    133, 146, 180, 321
Peters, Tom 80
Peyrache, Marie-Claude 267
Pfizer 320
Philippines 177, 199, 218,
    225–6
Philips Design 316
Phillips, Ida 110
photos, annual reports 75
pink products 90
plodding managers, audit of
    attitudes 131–3
plumbing sector 44

Poland 217, 276
politics
  80/20 rule 244
  "codes" 141
  discomforts 237
  interventionist policies 75,
    214, 236
  private/public sector
    considerations 27, 30,
    43–4, 57, 73, 75, 208–11,
    214, 225–7, 229–31
  taxation policies 290, 331
  women 6, 29, 38, 54, 121,
    194, 197–8, 200, 208,
    211, 218, 228–9, 257,
    260, 290
Portugal 226
positive discrimination 123,
  159, 278
Poutiainen, Heikki 296–7
poverty 200, 311, 317–19
power issues 15, 18–21, 31,
  40, 44, 48, 69, 70, 79, 81,
  89–90, 95, 101, 128, 137,
  156, 182, 208–9, 212,
  222–3, 234–8, 240–1, 253,
  257, 266, 269–70, 273–5,
  278–9, 285, 312–13, 323–4,
  326, 331–2, 338
  alternative views 270–1
  corruption 273

discomforts 162, 237, 271
  hierarchical structures 294
  the media 270–2
"preferable lifestyle" offerings
  60
pregnancies 162, 250
Price, Belinda 111
Price, Fiona 87
PricewaterhouseCoopers
  (PwC) 26, 35, 60, 123,
  303, 336
priorities, motherhood 202,
  207, 211, 224, 232, 257,
  314, 338
prioritise marketing
  approach 103–7
private banks 84–6
private equity firms 85
private limited companies
  6–9
  see also companies
private sector, public sector
  30, 226–7, 230
processes, bilingualism
  building blocks 135,
  138–46
Procter & Gamble 210, 276
product development, biases
  145
professional services firms
  59–60, 158, 302

profit-and-loss responsibilities
69, 258

progressive managers, audit of
attitudes 130, 159–61

promotion issues
concepts 9, 27, 48, 59, 64,
66, 69, 111, 142–4, 170,
176, 221, 240–1, 248,
250, 253, 258–9, 266,
274, 277, 280
legislation considerations 18,
36, 42, 73, 110, 183,
203, 211, 226
operational roles 42, 68–9,
121, 167–8, 185
sector trailblazers 125
statistics 29, 44, 50, 52, 102,
158, 207, 217
tips 76

"pseudo-men" labels 114

psychology of women 242, 278

public limited companies 15,
73
see also companies

public sector, private
sector 30, 226–7, 230

pulsars 115

purchasing power 15, 31, 81,
90, 156
see also consumers

PwC see
PricewaterhouseCoopers

Qantas 238

quotas 49, 66, 73–5, 159, 228

rating agencies 68

recruitment issues 9, 22, 26,
48, 50–3, 62, 136, 143,
158–9, 172, 221, 279, 283
adverts 50–1
biases 139, 142–5
concepts 9, 22, 26, 48, 50–3,
62, 136, 143, 158–9,
172, 221, 279, 283
female applicants 50–2,
86–9, 122, 171–3, 308–9,
321–2
financial services industry
84, 177
tips 52

regulations 2

religion 118

remuneration see pay . . .

Renault 26, 133, 183

resignations 188

resistance issues 13, 115,
131–2, 140, 151, 159, 168,
179, 300, 306, 322

Resources Global Professionals
291

restructuring trends, companies
265, 281, 284

retention issues 26, 48, 57,
60–2, 178, 283

"client-driven" cultures 57–60
concepts 26, 48, 57, 60–2,
    178, 283
"grey" brainpower 296–302
structural factors 53
tips 62
retirement 50, 83, 93, 125, 229,
    251, 253–4, 282, 296–8,
    300–1, 332, 335
see also pensions
returns on equity 14, 40–1
Reuters 134, 292
reverse mentoring 141, 154
Roberts, Philippa 81
role reversals, leadership teams
    153–4
Roman Catholics 202
Romania 217–18
Royal Institution of Chartered
    Surveyors 56
Royal, Ségolène 208, 313–16
Russia 19, 199
Russo, Pat 210
Rwanda 48
Rychtaríková, Jitka 217
Ryle, Martin 115

Saatchi & Saatchi 89
"sameness" pressures 113–14
Sapphire Partners 64–5
Sarkozy, Nicolas 136, 206, 208,
    313–4

Scandinavia 38, 73, 79, 143,
    227–8
Scardino, Marjorie 210
Schlumberger 166–8, 184–6,
    188
schools
    see also education
    motherhood 232
    underperforming boys 39
scientific research and
    development 43
sector trailblazers 125
    see also individual industries
segmentation issues, markets
    105, 159
self-affirmation phase,
    career-life styles 264
self-confidence 39, 238, 248,
    317
self-marketing skills 276
    see also "impression
        management"
Senegal 319
Senge, Peter 270
services, markets 82–3
sex 6, 31, 36–7, 91, 110–12,
    118, 191–2, 238, 271,
    319
Sex Discrimination Act 110
sexism 94
Sheilas' Wheels 102
short-termism, companies 320

shut-your-eyes marketing
approach 96–7
Siemens 102
Silverstein, Michael J. 79
Skidmore, Paul 295
skills
complementary skills 32
"grey" brainpower 296, 302
listening skills 71, 186
the "Me" generation 302
natural skills 130, 160, 186,
234, 259
self-marketing skills 276
shortages 2, 7, 26, 36–7,
43–4, 61, 76, 205, 214,
229, 299
technology 33, 44, 89–90,
104, 249, 261–2, 283,
291, 293–4, 303, 308,
314, 316
Slovenia 217
Smeal, Tony 284–5, 287, 290
social responsibilities 311
Sonatel 319
Spain 209, 211
Special K 106
specialise marketing approach
103
Spence, Dr Betty 70, 94
Špidla, Vladimir 4, 214
stakeholders, biases 145
start-ups 80

State Farm Insurance
Company 111
Stephenson, Carol 71
stereotypes 19, 98, 237,
255, 260
Stewart, Alysoun 225
Stewart, Martha 271
"sticky floors" 110, 224,
258, 325
Stocking, Barbara 319
strategic issues
budgets 86, 286
gender divides 7
gender initiatives 20, 22,
126–7, 139–40, 150,
157, 167, 171, 173,
178–9, 322
structural issues
hierarchical structures 240,
295, 315
lattice structures 295
restructuring trends 65, 245
retention 26, 48, 57, 60–2,
178, 283
successful implementation,
key success factors 22
succession planning 70, 76,
144, 279
surveying profession 56
Sweden 7, 29, 75, 218,
312
Switzerland 197, 239, 319

systemic bias 142
see also bias . . .
systems, bilingualism
    building blocks 138

T-Online 275
talent 4, 7, 9–11, 15, 35–7, 42,
    44–5, 47–8, 52, 76, 95,
    101, 106, 120, 125, 129,
    146, 156, 168, 174, 181–3,
    191, 206, 209–10, 214,
    233, 241, 281–2, 286, 300,
    302, 307, 321
see also skill . . .
concepts 123, 253, 270,
    278, 325
"grey" brainpower 296, 302
high-potential identification
    143
the "Me" generation 302
natural skills 32
trends 281, 283–4, 304, 309,
    316
under-used talent 42
"wars" 31, 36, 261
women 4, 7, 9, 11, 15,
    35–7, 42, 44–5, 47–8,
    52, 76, 95, 101, 106,
    120, 125, 146, 156, 168,
    174, 181–3, 191, 206,
    209–10, 214, 233, 241,
    281–2, 302, 307, 321

Tannen, Deborah 114, 135,
    240, 274
taxation policies 290
technology 33, 44, 89–90, 104,
    249, 261–2, 283, 291, 293–4,
    303, 308, 314, 316, 321
    see also Internet
teleworking 144
Tézé-Limal, Sandrine 268
Thailand 117, 225
Thatcher, Margaret 315
Thomson, Peninah 70–1, 153
three Ws, concepts 33, 316
Time 313
"Tipping Point Leadership" 150
TNT 70
tokenism 73
Tokyo Electric Power 222
top jobs
    see also boards . . .;
        leadership teams
    former communist states of
        eastern Europe 29
    legislation considerations
        110, 203, 211
    the media 28, 46, 68, 172,
        180, 270–2, 300, 313
    promotion issues 9, 27, 48,
        59, 64, 66, 69, 111,
        143–4, 170, 176, 221,
        241, 253, 258–9, 266,
        277, 280

statistics 29, 44, 50, 52, 102,
158, 202, 217
women 4, 11, 146
top-management commitment
see also leadership teams
"gender-bilingual" concepts
17, 19, 52, 105, 133,
146, 180, 321
Tosolini, Alex 276
Total 14, 40, 45, 59, 83, 91,
261
total shareholder returns 14
traditional approaches,
companies 109, 322
training 20, 26, 52–3, 67, 105,
115, 139, 141–2, 144, 146,
179, 184, 204, 206, 245–7,
256, 298
see also education
assertiveness training 21, 67,
115
business schools 18,
45–6, 165, 205, 212,
246–7
importance 243, 276, 280,
317, 324
outsourced training 246
transport industry 132
travel costs 305
trends, talent 281–310
trust 50, 249
Tunisia 318

Turkey 84
turnover analyses
see also retention . . .
workforce 54–5, 57, 61, 111,
124–5, 174, 193, 197,
204, 210, 213, 219–20,
223, 284, 290, 297–9,
305, 322
Twiggy 94
Tyson, Laura 45

UBS 239, 266–7, 275
UK 5, 7, 27, 30, 41–4, 48,
56–8, 63, 85–91, 94, 102,
110–11, 135, 144, 155,
175, 205, 208, 210, 218,
225, 231–3, 243, 247, 273,
288, 293, 301, 305, 321,
324
ageing population 27, 38,
193, 244, 301
benchmarking exercises
233
child tax credits 231
consumers 15, 31, 80, 82–3,
90, 184
country comparisons 197
extended school hours
232
Foreign Office 260
FTSE 42, 71–3, 128, 153,
155, 210, 231

independent financial
    advisers 87
Internet 33, 80, 90–1, 201,
    275, 316
legislation 18, 36, 42, 110,
    203, 211, 226
Opportunity Now campaign
    231
pay gaps 4, 43, 226
politics 4, 64, 136–7, 141,
    236–7, 240, 242, 244,
    312
public/private sector
    initiatives 27, 214, 226,
    230–1
teleworking 144
wealthy women 86
under-used talent 42
understanding women 16
    UNDP see United Nations
        Development
        Programme (UNDP)
UNESCO 43
Unilever 16, 63, 94, 134,
    154–5, 219, 236
United Nations Development
    Programme (UNDP) 200
university graduates
    see also education
    women 4, 7, 38, 119
US 3, 5, 7, 14–15, 24, 27–30,
    38–40, 44, 48, 54, 57, 63,
    66, 69, 76, 79–80, 83,
    84–6, 88, 97, 110–12, 118,
    121, 123, 125, 128, 134,
    197–9, 207, 211–16, 221–2,
    252, 254, 265, 268–9, 283,
    292, 294, 313, 315–17,
    321
consumers 15, 80, 83
country comparisons 197
discrimination lawsuits 110
elections (2008) 215, 217,
    233, 306, 316
feminists 211
fertility rates/employment
    correlation 38, 194, 197,
    202, 219
France 27, 55, 71, 74, 79,
    104, 134, 136, 153, 155,
    189, 198, 202–3, 205–11,
    214–15, 218, 253, 261–2,
    267, 313, 315–17
imperfections 210
legislation 18, 36, 42, 110,
    203, 211
life expectancies 83–4, 93
maternity leave 65, 162, 207,
    211, 213, 217, 231,
    262
slow progress 68, 75, 123
workaholic cultures 212
working mothers 162, 207,
    221, 227

valuing differences,
concepts 16–7, 123, 253,
270, 278
victimhood 118
videoconferencing 293
Vigeo 68
Vinnicombe, Susan 223
Virgin Mobile 292
vision 135
vocabulary differences,
communications 139, 145,
306, 326
voluntary networks, key
success factors 146, 149,
178
Volvo 16, 103, 145, 275

Wal-Mart 112
Wall Street 111–112
Wall Street Journal 94
Wallace, Vanessa 262
Wallace, Wanda 63, 241
Warner, Fara 94
Warner, Judith 207, 212
"wars"
metaphors 133, 135, 136,
252
talent 35–7, 39, 57, 59, 188,
286, 305, 307
Washington Post 315
wealth 85–6, 88, 320
see also income

weather, three Ws 33, 316
web
see also Internet
three Ws 33, 316
Weir, Helen 31, 274
Wellington, Sheila 211
Wente, Margaret 273
Wharton 47
Wheaton, Alison 155
Whitman, Meg 271
Wittenberg-Cox, Avivah 153
WL Gore & Associates 294
"Women 30" basket 81–2
women
age factors 47, 56–7, 83–5,
93–5, 111, 119, 143,
197, 257, 259, 296–7,
308–9
alienating cultures 62, 161,
232
Arab world 200
ascendancy issues 200
barriers 4, 92, 101, 110, 124,
126, 129, 192, 239, 259,
289, 330
brainpower 37–8, 296, 302
burn-out dangers 260
business issues 6, 17, 22,
151, 156, 163, 165,
325
business schools 12–3, 18,
45–7, 246–8

career-life styles 54, 142–3, 187, 189, 260–1, 278–80, 308

former communist states of eastern Europe 29, 215

conclusions 311–25

consumers 15, 31, 80, 82–3, 90, 184

country comparisons 27, 197–8, 202, 205, 251, 267, 314, 316, 318

economic growth 1, 13, 27, 33, 43, 193, 200, 230

entrepreneurs 54, 80, 267–9, 332

fertility rates/employment correlation 194, 197

future prospects 33, 316

"gender-bilingual" concepts 17, 19, 52, 105, 133, 146, 180, 321

genetic differences 137–8, 232–3, 235–7, 258–9, 279–80

income 97–83, 219–20

leadership styles 114, 141

loyalties 266, 282

the media 370–2

micro-credits 317

middle-management positions 44, 60, 135, 138, 242

motivations 59, 85, 146, 164, 278, 290

perceptions about women 100, 225, 236

politics 4, 64, 136–7, 141, 236–7, 240, 242, 244, 312, 328–9, 336

promotion issues 48, 59, 64, 66–7, 69, 111, 142–4, 240–2, 246, 248, 250, 253, 259, 266, 274, 277, 280

"pseudo-men" labels 114

psychology of women 242, 278

recruitment issues 9, 22, 26, 48, 50–3, 62, 136, 143, 158–9, 172, 279, 283

retention issues 26, 48, 57, 60–2, 178, 283

retirement 50, 83, 93, 125, 229, 251, 253–4, 282, 296–8

strategic side 7

talent 6–9, 11, 15, 29, 35–7, 39, 41–5, 77, 120, 125, 127, 129, 138, 146, 150, 188–9, 228, 283–99, 321–32

three Ws 33, 316

top jobs 4, 11, 144

training 52–3, 67, 115, 139,
141–2, 245–6, 256
under-used talent 42–4
understanding 234, 246, 252,
282
university graduates 4, 7, 38,
119
valuing differences 17–22
vocabulary differences
135–136, 252, 326
workforce 2, 5–7
working mothers 162, 207,
221, 330
"women-friendly" approaches
281, 321
womenomics 1–30, 110, 220,
331
"women's Davos" see Women's
Forum for the Economy
and Society
Women's Forum for the
Economy and Society
74–5, 133, 190, 327–8,
330–1
"women's issues" 118
work-life balance 19, 173–4,
227, 284, 287, 304, 308
workaholic cultures 212
worker bees, psychology of
women 242
workforce 2, 5–6, 15, 18, 44,
54–5, 57, 61, 111, 125,

174, 193, 210, 213, 219–20,
223, 284, 290, 297–30,
322, 328, 334
Arab world 200
attractive workplaces 54,
300, 302, 309
burn-out dangers 260
career-life styles 54, 142–3,
187, 189, 260–1, 278–80,
308
changing work patterns 330,
332, 337–8
former communist states of
eastern Europe 29, 215
country comparisons 27,
197–8, 202, 205, 251,
267, 314, 316, 318
empowerment 200, 339
fathers 227–8, 287–9
fertility rates 194, 197
foreign assignments 308
freelance workers 285
"grey" brainpower 296,
302
immigration levels 29, 42,
299
knowledge workers 6, 261,
321
long-term employment
relationships 265
the "Me" generation 302
mobility factors 37

new models of work 284,
286
pay 43, 65, 70, 98, 105,
110–2, 115, 143, 145,
153, 178, 195, 203, 227,
231, 283, 285, 323, 327
promotion issues 48, 59, 64,
66–7, 69, 111, 142–4,
240–2, 246, 248, 250,
253, 259, 266, 274,
277, 280
recruitment issues 9, 22, 26,
48, 50–3, 62, 136, 143,
158–9, 172, 279, 283
resignations 188
retention issues 26, 48, 57,
60–2, 178, 283
skill shortages 2, 76, 299
statistics 29, 44, 50, 52, 102,
158, 202, 217, 329, 338
technology 44, 88–90, 104,
249, 261–262, 276, 283,
291, 293–4, 303, 308,
321
teleworking 144

top jobs 4, 11, 144
turnover analyses 54, 286,
292, 298, 306
workforces, retirement 38, 93,
297
working lives, duration 253,
282
working mothers 162, 207,
221, 227, 330
workshops, change 179
World Bank 3, 200
World Economic Forum 3,
193, 197, 199, 224
World Health Organisation 211

Xerox 128, 210, 235, 271, 320

Yaccato, Joanne Thomas 152
young-women segment,
markets 92, 103
YouTube 303
Yunus, Muhammad 318

Zapatero, José Luis
Rodriguez 209, 226

Printed and bound by CPI Group (UK) Ltd, Croydon, CR0 4YY
15/10/2021

03087422-0001